"For thirty years I have benefited from Wayne Mack's m[...] *time* has the qualities one finds throughout his work: it is [...] tical. What more could you want? It roots marriage in Christ and the gospel, and in separate sections devoted to men and women it identifies the callings God has clearly given them in Scripture. This book bears reading and rereading by couples together!"

—TEDD TRIPP
PASTOR, AUTHOR, CONFERENCE SPEAKER

"The Macks have done it again! In *Sweethearts for a Lifetime*, they offer virtually everything a believing couple would need to know and apply in order to walk together as man and wife. Not content with those who presume that God's Word is nothing but ancient rhetoric, they skillfully speak of how the Bible's timeless message applies in the twenty-first century. Their new book not only challenges Christian marriages that have grown stale and lifeless, but also provides keen advice for strengthening and maturing marriages that are already healthy and prospering. In whatever state you see your own marriage, I am confident you will find here the principles and practices you've searched for as you seek to reflect Jesus Christ's relationship to His bride— the church."

—LANCE QUINN
PASTOR-TEACHER, THE BIBLE CHURCH OF LITTLE ROCK;
PRESIDENT OF THE NATIONAL ASSOCIATION OF NOUTHETIC COUNSELORS (NANC)

"It is always with confidence and joy that I recommend Dr. Mack's books. He is so thorough and so thoroughly biblical. When you read them, you know that you've just spent valuable time with our Lord and His powerful Word."

—ELYSE FITZPATRICK
AUTHOR, WOMEN'S CONFERENCE SPEAKER;
COUNSELOR AT INSTITUTE FOR BIBLICAL COUNSELING AND DISCIPLESHIP

"In his usual thorough, thought-provoking style Dr. Mack examines various marital issues through a biblical lens and presents biblical solutions to move believers to victory and growth in their marriages. To help believers make the truths about marriage a reality in their lives, each chapter concludes with practical applications. This is a very practical book for all married or soon-to-be-married believers, and for biblical counselors and the people they counsel."

—ROBERT SMITH, M.D.
AUTHOR; ACADEMY STATUS IN AND BOARD MEMBER OF NANC

"*Sweethearts for a Lifetime* is a thoroughly biblical and eminently practical resource for couples, as well as the counselors seeking to help them. Each chapter reads like a conversation with a godly friend and includes aids for applying Scripture to real life. In her section, Carol Mack comes alongside women, helping them to understand and appreciate the profound role God has given them in marriage. This is a great companion to Dr. Mack's other books, *Strengthening Your Marriage* and *Your Family God's Way*."

—KEVIN M. BACKUS
SENIOR PASTOR, BIBLE PRESBYTERIAN CHURCH OF GRAND ISLAND;
FELLOW AND MEMBER OF THE BOARD OF NANC

"What would you look for in a Christian book that merits a five-star rating? It would have to be doctrinally sound, spiritually enriching, intellectually enlightening, and practically helpful. That is how I would categorize *Sweethearts for a Lifetime*, and that is why I enthusiastically commend it. Christian marriages are meant to get better over time. It is for want of knowing and applying the truths Wayne Mack has spelled out so well in this book that many marriages do not improve. In 1 Peter 3:7 husbands are commanded to live with their wives in an understanding way. I do not know of a better book to equip and enable a husband to make the most of his marriage and to be an instrument of happiness and holiness in partnership with his wife. Get this book and read it through at least twice!"

—MARTIN HOLDT
PASTOR, CONSTANTIA PARK BAPTIST CHURCH;
RADIO MINISTER, WORLDWIDE CONFERENCE CONVENER, SPEAKER

SWEETHEARTS FOR A LIFETIME

Making the Most of Your Marriage

SWEETHEARTS FOR A LIFETIME

Making the Most of Your Marriage

WAYNE A. MACK
AND
CAROL MACK

P&R PUBLISHING
P.O. BOX 817 • PHILLIPSBURG • NEW JERSEY 08865-0817

Page design by Kirk DouPonce, Dog Eared Design
Typesetting by Lakeside Design Plus
Ring image © Stockdisc/Stockdisc Classic/Getty Images

Printed in the United States of America

Library of Congress Control Number: 2006934077

ISBN-13: 978-1-59638-032-5

With deep appreciation we dedicate this book to Hanrais and Jacolien Brink with whom we lived for the first two and a half months after coming to South Africa for ministry. We do this because we saw many of the *Sweethearts for a Lifetime* principles discussed in this book portrayed in their relationship. From what we observed at close range and over a period of time we could recommend them to others as a couple whose relationship is worthy of being emulated.

CONTENTS

FOREWORD

I predict that you will say four things about this book after you have read it. Like me, you will conclude that it is not only (1) very much needed, but also (2) biblical, (3) clear, and (4) very practical.

The book is needed for people like me: Christians married for decades and still committed to their spouses but who tend to take them for granted, neglecting to nurture the relationship properly. It is also needed for couples who are "sticking it out" in marriages that long ago ceased to be warm and loving. Here they will find understanding about what went wrong and get back on the path of being sweethearts. Newlyweds will find this a clear guide to building and sustaining a solid, happy marriage.

The Macks are known as careful students of the Scriptures. Those unfamiliar with Wayne's previous writings will note the abundant use of God's Word on every topic and almost every page. The application projects at the end of each chapter provide numerous biblical references for further study. The authors write from the firm foundation of God's revelation about marriage rather than from the changing fads of man's theories. Readers of previous works will appreciate the historical, grammatical, and contextual interpretation of the Bible in this volume as well.

Clarity is needed because we live in a day of great confusion, frustration, failure, and outright rejection of the institution of marriage.

Many people I counsel admit that they do not know anyone who has a happy marriage. One person told me that he had no idea how to make a marriage work and did not want to become another statistic, so he was not going to get married. This book provides clear, understandable explanations of what the Bible teaches and how it should relate to our lives. The topics are addressed in a logical fashion, and chapters have an evident outline that makes answers available to anybody genuinely looking for them.

Wayne, Carol, and Josh Mack are all biblical counselors. That is very evident in the many practical tools they provide to help readers apply God's Word to their lives. There are several self-assessment inventories to help both individuals and couples discover areas where growth is needed. Most chapters have discussion questions to further aid understanding and application. Counselors will see encouraging progress in counselees as they are instructed not only to read the chapters but also to complete the application projects.

I urge you to read and apply to your own marriage what you learn from this book. I know you will enjoy the results! But don't be selfish— share it with others. I intend to use this book as a frequent homework assignment in my own counseling ministry.

Randy Patten
Executive Director,
National Association
of Nouthetic Counselors
(NANC)

INTRODUCTION

As a person married more than forty-nine years, a pastor, a college professor, and a biblical counselor who has been involved in ministry since 1957, I have personally observed marriages in all sorts of conditions—some very good, some good, some not so good, some downright horrible, and some on the verge of total disintegration. I have seen marriages that started out well and continued well and even improved over a period of time; others that started well and then declined; and others that didn't start well and never improved—if anything, they grew worse. Of very few marriages can it be said that the people remain real sweethearts throughout their entire lives. And even for those of whom it can rightly be said, there is always a need for maintenance, checkups, evaluations, and constant vigilance. For the others, the need for godly, biblically directed assistance is of still greater importance.

Carol and I have written this book to provide the resources for enriching and enhancing the marriages of people who find themselves in any of the aforementioned situations. We've written it to enhance and enrich marriages with biblically derived insights and practically designed exercises. We have kept the chapters relatively short so that a husband and wife may read the material and do the application and discussion exercises together as a daily devotional time. The intention is that they read one chapter a day and do all or at least some of the application and discussion exercises, move on to the next chapter, and repeat this procedure day after day until they have completed the entire book. I am convinced that if couples will work through this book and apply the truths found here, the book's intended purpose will be fulfilled.

The book is divided into three main sections: Part 1 discusses the six *P*s of a good marriage relationship. Part 2 focuses on how a husband can be a fulfilled and fulfilling mate to his wife. Part 3, written by my wife, Carol, expands on how a wife can be a fulfilled and fulfilling partner to her husband. I am convinced that people who are believers and who will conscientiously study and apply the truths will, by God's grace, sustain or recover the sweetheart aspect of their marriages. I believe this, not because I am so smart or so clever, but because the perspectives and applications that you will be reflecting on throughout this volume are derived from the book (the Bible) whose ultimate Author is the all-wise and all-knowing God who planned the marriage relationship and knows exactly what will make it the blessing and joy He intended it to be.

In the writing of this book, I received much help from a number of people. First, as has been the case with a number of other books I have written, Janet Dudek assisted with her excellent editorial suggestions about wording, phrasing, and condensing. My wife did her usual thing in terms of proofreading, and in this instance she did even more than that—she is the author of Part 3 on the fulfilled and fulfilling wife. And special thanks are due to our son Joshua Mack for his work on chapters twenty-three and twenty-seven. Joseph Hess devoted a considerable amount of time to carefully reading the material and making editorial suggestions. To Al Fisher and the other good folk at P&R Publishing I also want to express my gratitude for endorsing the idea and format of this book and for encouraging me to put the material into print and make it a part of the Strength for Life series that they have developed for my materials. Thanks to all of you for the privilege of being laborers together with you for Christ and His people. Especially, thanks go to our great God, for putting me into the ministry and giving me something to write and preach about. To God be the glory.

—Wayne Mack

Part 1

HOW TO KEEP
A GOOD
MARRIAGE
GOING

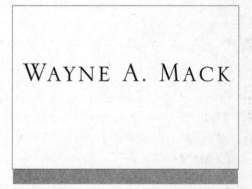

WAYNE A. MACK

1

COMMITTING TO GOD'S PURPOSES FOR MARRIAGE

In 1975, on the day that would have been her thirty-sixth wedding anniversary, Ann Landers wrote a very unusual column, admitting to her readers that the queen of newspaper advice columnists simply had no answer for why her own marriage had fallen apart. After thirty-six years she and her husband had decided to call it quits and get a divorce. At the end of the column she admitted that she simply had no explanation. The answer lady had drawn a blank.

While Ann Landers may not have had an answer, I believe that I do. I believe that what happened in her marriage is the very same thing that happens in countless other marriages every day. I also believe that it does not have to happen, for one very good reason: God—the Author of marriage—has given us a marriage blueprint that is foolproof. And if we are willing to follow His plan, we may be sure that we will never have to wonder why something that started out so good ended up so bad. The truth is that with God's help, husbands and wives can remain sweethearts for a lifetime.

As I became involved in planning and writing this book, I decided, for what I think will be obvious reasons, to call it *The Sweetheart Book*.

Yet for what I think will also be obvious reasons, I also thought about calling it *The Excellent Marriage Book* because in it we will be explaining, illustrating, and applying the directives and principles that God, the originator and designer of marriage, has to teach us about how to have, and continue to have, a maximum marriage. In scholastic terminology, I want to help people to have an "A" rather than a "B," "C," or "D" kind of marriage. In this book, I am going to focus on what it means and what it takes to have an "A" kind of marriage because I believe that an "A" kind of marriage not only is possible for God's people, but is His will for them.

Marriage, as I indicated, was God's idea. It was God who created the first man and woman and introduced them to each other. God gave them their premarital counseling and administered their marriage vows. In order to understand what marriage is all about, then, we need to look at what God has said about it in His Word. And God planned that marriage would be good for us; that it would enhance rather than exasperate us; that it would enrich our lives rather than impoverish.

COVENANT MARRIAGE

In Genesis 2:24, God declared that His blueprint for marriage involved a very special kind of commitment: "For this cause a man shall leave his father and his mother, and shall cleave to his wife; and they shall become one flesh." The words translated "shall cleave to" involve the idea of making a covenant. Malachi 2:14 states this idea clearly: "The LORD has been a witness between you and the wife of your youth . . . She is your companion and your wife by covenant." Proverbs 2:17 states the same concept.

In the Bible, a covenant is a formal, solemn, binding, and irrevocable arrangement involving promises and obligations. It commits two or more people to perform certain actions. God's covenant with us as His people is a good example. In Hebrews 8:10–12 the writer quotes Jeremiah 31:33–34, in which the Lord says, "For this is the covenant that I will make with the house of Israel after those days . . . I will be their God, and they shall be My people . . . and I will remember their sins no more." God has committed Himself to the forgiveness of His people's sin through their faith in Jesus Christ. From the promises that He has made in His Word and what we know about His character, we can be absolutely sure that His commitment will never be annulled or voided in any way.

By calling marriage a covenant, God has called us to this same level of commitment to our partners in marriage. The husband and wife are likewise making a formal, solemn, binding, and irrevocable agreement to each other to fulfill certain obligations and perform certain actions toward each other. R. C. Sproul explains:

At this point, I would like to make a rather bold assertion. In every single marriage that ends in disaster, some stupid decisions were made with respect to God's regulations. If God's regulations were followed scrupulously, there would not only be no divorce, *there would be no unhappy marriages.* To violate the regulations of God is not only an exercise in disobedience, but an exercise in foolishness as well. If you want a happy marriage, the most intelligent thing you can do is to submit to God's regulations. They are designed to promote and protect your full happiness. God carefully planned them. But before the regulations of God can work for our happiness, we have to know what they are. Again, study is required that we may not only know the wisdom of God, but that we may master it. (In my college classes, the difference between an "A" and a "B" was the difference between knowledge and mastery of the material. [Who wants to be satisfied with a "B" or a "C" or a "D" kind of marriage?] Who wants to be satisfied with anything less than an "A" marriage?)

Confidence in the wisdom of God is closely related to our obedience to Him. A great delusion is contained in the thought, "If I keep His commandments, I will not be happy." Herein is the fundamental human delusion. There may, of course, be pleasure in disobedience, but there can never be happiness. And happiness in the Biblical sense is more than a warm puppy. When I experience a conflict of interest or conflict of desires between what I want and what God requires, then I know the moral crisis is sin. When I choose my own desire and insult the integrity of God's wisdom, I, at the same time, reveal myself to be a fool.[1]

Most, if not all, problems in marriages arise because people either do not know God's blueprint for marriage or are not willing to follow it. Unhappy marriages and divorces cannot result when people know and follow God's perfect design.

A PROBLEM WITH COMMITMENT

A farmer went to an attorney to get help in acquiring a divorce. The lawyer said to him, "Do you have any grounds?" The farmer replied, "Yup, I've got about three hundred acres." The lawyer said, "You're not understanding me. Do you have any case?" The farmer said, "No, I don't have a Case, but I do have a John Deere, and that's what I farm my three hundred acres with." The lawyer tried again: "No, no, no. You're still not understanding me. Do you have a grudge?" To which the farmer replied, "Yup, that's where I keep my John Deere." "You're still not understanding me," said the lawyer. "Do you beat your wife up?" The farmer answered, "Nope, she gets up at five o'clock just like I do." Finally, the frustrated lawyer said, "Sir, I'm trying to find out if you have any reason for getting a divorce." "Well," said the farmer. "You see, we have this communication problem."

This farmer and his wife did have a communication problem, but the real reason for difficulty in their and any other marriage with serious problems is a problem with *commitment*. When a marriage crumbles and ends in divorce, it is because both partners were not fully committed to God's blueprint for marriage and were not living it out in their relationship.

More often, people tend to structure their marriages according to their own ideas or according to the world's current ideas of what marriage should be about. Psalm 1 warns us against this kind of thinking:

> How blessed is the man who does not walk in the counsel of the
>   wicked,
> Nor stand in the path of sinners,
> Nor sit in the seat of scoffers!

But his delight is in the law of the LORD,
And in His law he meditates day and night.
And he will be like a tree firmly planted by streams of water,
Which yields its fruit in its season,
And its leaf does not wither;
And in whatever he does, he prospers. (Ps. 1:1–3)

The words of this psalm apply to every area of life, including marriage. If we choose to listen to ungodly people and follow the example of sinners, we will experience great difficulty. On the other hand, if we remain faithful to the Word of God, we will experience great blessing in all things.

APPLICATION
AND DISCUSSION

1. What does R. C. Sproul indicate makes the difference between having a really good marriage and having a bad marriage?

2. In what biblical text do we find God's blueprint for marriage?

3. Why do we call this text God's blueprint for marriage?

4. Why is following God's blueprint an essential aspect of having a good marriage? Why is following the instructions of this text a wise thing to do?

5. Besides the fact that having an "A" kind of marriage requires following God's blueprint, what other basic requirement does this chapter indicate is an absolute necessity for spouses' remaining sweethearts for a lifetime?

6. Do you agree? Why or why not?

7. What is the general definition of the word commitment?

8. What does commitment in marriage mean? How would you respond if someone were to say to you, "I hear that God's kind of marriage requires commitment. Please help me to understand what

that means. Explain what it means for a husband to be committed to his wife and a wife to her husband"?

9. What is the significance of the fact that the Bible describes marriage in terms of a covenant? What does it mean to make a covenant?

10. Why is it that some people aren't willing to commit themselves to God's blueprint for marriage?

11. Evaluate the grade level of your marriage. Would you say that you have an "A," "B," "C," "D," or "F" kind of marriage?

12. List and discuss your reasons for grading your marriage as you did.

13. In which direction is your marriage going? Is it getting better and better or worse and worse?

14. List and discuss your specific reasons for the answer you gave to the previous question.

2

LET'S BE FRIENDS

Assuming that all of us have at least some room for improvement in our marriages and some areas in which we have listened to the world rather than God in structuring our marriage relationships, what do we need to do to actively work toward that "A" kind of marriage that God intends for us? To do this, we must understand and be committed to the six keys (or *P*s) of God's blueprint for marriage: the *purposes* of God for the marriage relationship, the *priority* of the marriage relationship, the *purity* of the marriage relationship, the *perspiration* required to maintain the marriage relationship, the *permanence* of the marriage relationship, and the *preeminence* of Christ in the marriage relationship. In the rest of this book, we will take a careful look at the six *P*s of an "A" kind of marriage.

THE PURPOSE OF COMPANIONSHIP

For us to enjoy an "A" kind of marriage, we must understand and be committed to the first *P*: God's *purposes* for marriage. Genesis 2:18 reveals one of these purposes: "Then the LORD God said, 'It is not good for the man to be alone; I will make him a helper suitable for him.' " God intended that the marriage relationship provide companionship for His people. Proverbs 2:17 calls the husband "the companion of her youth," and Malachi 2:14 likewise refers to the wife as the husband's companion.

This purpose is also seen in God's command in Deuteronomy 24:5 for new husbands to be exempt for one year from military service or any other duty that would take them away from the home for an extended period: "When a man takes a new wife, he shall not go out with the army nor be charged with any duty; he shall be free at home one year and shall give happiness to his wife whom he has taken." God intended for the man to spend his first year of marriage not in making a name for himself in battle or business but in rejoicing in the wife of his youth. His primary responsibility at this crucial time was to get to know his wife, make her happy, and begin to develop a deep friendship that would very likely continue throughout the rest of their lives together.

Many other verses in Scripture refer to this idea of companionship between the husband and wife. According to 1 Peter 3:7, "You husbands in the same way, live with your wives in an understanding way . . ." Peter also commanded wives to be devoted to their husbands (3:1). In 1 Corinthians 9:5, Paul stated that although he had the right to take a wife with him in his ministry, he had denied himself that privilege so that he could devote himself wholly to his work. He knew that his missionary life would not allow him to fulfill the responsibility of being a devoted companion to another person.

In the forty-some years that I have been involved in the ministry of counseling, I have discovered that many couples live together but are not really friends. In fact, I would go so far as to say that many of them have no idea what friendship with a spouse entails. And so I have put together what I call the Intimacy Inventory. I encourage you and your spouse to sit down together and work through this inventory to get a better idea of the level of true friendship in your marriage relationship. This inventory will also provide a guideline for you regarding the things you ought to be doing to fulfill God's purpose for your marriage in the area of companionship. Use what you discover as a catalyst for improving any companionship aspects in which you are deficient. Make plans for change. Don't settle for anything less than an "A." Later, in chapter 37, we will discuss the issue of companionship and friendship in greater depth. Most of what is said will be addressed to the wife, but almost all of what is written about what it means to be a friend can also be applied to the husband.

DEEP FRIENDSHIP/INTIMACY INVENTORY

Genesis 2:18, Proverbs 2:17, and Malachi 2:14 indicate that one of God's purposes for the marriage relationship is a deep and lasting companionship/intimacy. In fact, when two people marry, part of the commitment they make to each other is that each will be the other's best and closest companion or friend. Because this is true, it is important for married people to know what true friendship/intimacy involves. The following inventory was designed to provide guidelines for becoming best friends and as an evaluative tool for diagnosing ways in which your friendship/intimacy needs to be and can be improved.

Instructions: Read through the statements and think carefully about your relationship with your spouse. After each statement you will find scriptural references on which the statement is based, which you might want to look up. Then evaluate the depth of your friendship according to the following rating scale:

4 = usually; 3 = often; 2 = sometimes; 1 = seldom; 0 = never

Put the appropriate number for yourself on the first blank and put the number that you think would be appropriate for your mate on the second blank.

The following questions illustrate what a deep and growing friendship in marriage involves:

SELF MATE

____ ____ 1. Are you really devoted to your mate; do you have a high degree of commitment to your mate? (Gen. 2:24; Matt. 19:5–6)

_____ _____   2. Do you have a growing and deepening biblical love for the other person? (1 Thess. 3:12; 4:9–10)

_____ _____   3. Do you accept the other person without being judgmental or condemnatory? (Rom. 14:1, 13; 15:7)

_____ _____   4. Do you have a sincere desire to meet the needs of the other person and a willingness to put the other person's needs ahead of your own? (Phil. 2:3–4)

_____ _____   5. Are you willing to be forbearing with your mate, patiently allowing your mate to make mistakes without becoming angry or allowing these mistakes to damage your relationship? (1 Cor. 13:4–7; Eph. 4:3; Col. 3:13)

_____ _____   6. Do you practice hospitality with your mate; are you warm and enthusiastic and friendly toward your mate? (Rom. 12:13; 1 Peter 4:8–9)

_____ _____   7. Do you allow the other person to be himself/herself in your presence; do you refrain from putting so much pressure on your mate that your mate feels condemnation and rejection? (Rom. 15:6–7)

_____ _____   8. Do you do whatever you can legitimately do to avoid tension and conflict in your relationship? (Rom. 12:16, 18; 14:19; Phil. 2:1–2; 4:2)

_____ _____   9. Do you essentially possess the same moral values, the same reverence for God, and the same basic desire to live for Christ? (1 Cor. 1:10–11)

_____ _____   10. Are you fully honest with your mate, being trustworthy, truthful, and dependable? (Eph. 4:25; Col. 3:9)

_____ _____   11. Do you quickly seek reconciliation whenever you have hurt the other person? (Matt. 5:21–26; James 5:16)

_____ _____   12. If you have sinned against your spouse, do you quickly ask for forgiveness? (Matt. 5:21–26; James 5:16)

____ ____ 13. Do you actively try to build up your mate spiritually? (Eph. 4:29; 1 Thess. 5:11)

____ ____ 14. Do you seek to be reconciled to your mate when he or she has sinned against you? (Matt. 18:15; Luke 17:3)

____ ____ 15. Do you gently, kindly, and lovingly rebuke your mate when there is a pattern of sin in his or her life? (Prov. 27:5–6, 9; Gal. 6:1–2)

____ ____ 16. Do you make it a habit of meeting as many of his or her personal needs and desires as you can? (Luke 10:25–37; John 13:14–15; Gal. 5:13; 1 John 3:17–18)

____ ____ 17. Do you understand and feel the hardships and pain your mate experiences? (Rom. 12:15; 1 Cor. 12:25–26; 1 Peter 3:8)

____ ____ 18. Do you provide comfort for your mate when he or she is experiencing sorrow; are you faithful and available when your mate is going through adversity? (Prov. 17:17; 18:24; 2 Cor. 1:3–4; 1 Thess. 4:18)

____ ____ 19. Do you defend and protect your mate when he or she is being attacked? (Prov. 17:17; 18:24; 1 John 3:16)

____ ____ 20. Do you encourage your mate to live a holy, pure, and obedient life by your example and thoughtful words? (Heb. 3:13)

____ ____ 21. Do you pray regularly for your mate? (Eph. 6:18; James 5:16)

____ ____ 22. Do you make your possessions available to your mate; do you regard whatever you have as belonging to your mate as well as to you? (Luke 10:25–37; Acts 4:36–37; Rom. 12:13)

____ ____ 23. Do you join your mate in numerous activities? (Phil. 1:5; 4:3)

____ ____ 24. Do you share your thoughts, feelings, desires, concerns, joys, fears, etc., with your mate on a deep level? (John 15:15)

____ ____ 25. Do you patiently listen to your mate, and do you really show an interest in what interests or concerns your mate? (Job 21:1–2; Prov. 18:2, 13; Phil. 2:4)

____ ____ 26. Are you willing to talk about whatever is of interest and concern to your mate? (Rom. 12:10; Phil. 2:3–4)

____ ____ 27. Do you refrain from doing anything that would encourage your mate to stumble into sinful thinking, speaking, or behaving? (Prov. 27:14; Rom. 14:13; 1 Cor. 13:7)

____ ____ 28. Do you spend large amounts of time with your mate? (Prov. 17:7; 18:24; 1 Peter 3:7)

____ ____ 29. Do you regularly express appreciation and gratitude to your mate? (I Peter 3:7; Prov. 31:10-12, 28; I Peter 3:1, 2; Prov. 12:1; Eph. 5:33)

____ ____ 30. Do you recognize and accept the differences between men and women in general and you and your mate in particular? (Gen. 1:27; 2:23; Rom. 12:3–8)

____ ____ 31. Do you put the best possible interpretation on what your mate says or does? (Matt. 7:12; 1 Cor. 13:5)

____ ____ 32. Do you show respect to your mate in private and in public? (Rom. 12:17; 2 Cor. 8:21)

____ ____ 33. Are you as concerned (or even more concerned) about your mate's physical/sexual desires as you are about your own? (1 Cor. 7:3–4; Phil. 2:3–4)

Scoring: After rating all the statements for your relationship with your spouse, add up the total score. As a general guideline, if you scored 128–160 for your relationship, you are probably experiencing a deep friendship/intimacy (companionship) and you are basically fulfilling one of God's primary purposes for marriage. Praise God for the help He has given you in this area, and continue to practice biblical guidelines for your companionship.

If you scored 96–127, your friendship/intimacy does need some improvement. Identify areas in which you need to improve, discuss these areas with your spouse, make a commitment and plans to work on these areas, seek God's help for change, and put your plans into practice.

If you scored less than 96, you need to seriously consider that your relationship is not fulfilling one of God's primary purposes for marriage. Identify areas in which you need to improve, if possible. Discuss these areas with your spouse, make a commitment and plans to work on these areas, seek God's help for change, and put your plans into practice. It may be that if you scored less than 96, you should seek the help of a godly, biblical counselor to make the changes that should be made.

List areas of companionship/intimacy in which your relationship is flourishing:

_____
_____
_____
_____
_____

List areas of companionship/intimacy in which your relationship needs improvement:

_____
_____
_____
_____
_____

RELATIONSHIP-BUILDING
ACTIVITIES

1. Express your love by developing Relationship-Building Activities. To qualify, an activity must:

Be active (not passive).
Make you aware of each other.
Provide opportunity for communication.

2. Brainstorm at least thirty Relationship-Building Activities.

3. Reduce to five or six manageable Relationship-Building Activities.

4. Schedule several for the next month. Put them on your calendar and then do them.

3

DON'T FORGET ABOUT
THE CHILDREN

God's second purpose for marriage is to have and raise children properly. This is made clear in Genesis 1:28, when God commanded Adam and Eve to "be fruitful and multiply, and fill the earth." The Lord has commanded married people, if they are physically able, to have children. While the world may give us many reasons for ignoring this part of marriage—kids are too expensive, too time-consuming, or too much trouble—the family is clearly part of God's plan for His people. As Malachi 2:15 (Amplified Bible) points out, "And did not God make you and your wife one flesh? . . . And why did God make you two one? Because He sought a godly offspring from your union."

Many other verses in Scripture talk about the blessing that God gives to His people through their children. Psalm 127:3–5 says, "Behold, children are a gift of the LORD, the fruit of the womb is a reward. Like arrows in the hand of a warrior, so are the children of one's youth. How blessed is the man whose quiver is full of them . . ." Psalm 128:1–4 promises, "How blessed is everyone who fears the LORD . . . Your wife shall be like a fruitful vine within your house, your children like olive plants around your table. Behold, for thus shall the man be blessed who fears the LORD."

RAISING GODLY CHILDREN

God wants most couples to have children, but His purpose for marriage goes beyond that. His purpose also includes raising those children properly for Him. We see this purpose in 1 Timothy 2, where Paul explained certain aspects of the husband–wife relationship. After commanding the men to be leaders and teachers in the church, Paul turned his attention to the women and said that they "will be preserved through the bearing of children if they continue in faith and love and sanctity with self-restraint" (2:15). In other words, the opportunity for women to have an impact in the world and in the church comes through having and raising godly children.

According to a familiar adage, "The hand that rocks the cradle rules the world." How true this is in the sense that a godly woman can have a tremendous impact on the lives of her children. Many a man who has had a great impact on the world would tell us that the person who influenced him most in his life was his mother. From the Bible, we know that Timothy was raised by a godly mother who taught him the Scriptures. And Samuel the prophet was the son of Hannah, a woman who pleaded with God for a child and then dedicated that child to the Lord's service for his whole life. Women have a tremendous responsibility and privilege to be a primary influence in the lives of their children.

Of course, fathers play a very important role in their children's lives as well. Scripture is clear in its teaching that both parents are responsible for raising their children in a God-ordained way. Ephesians 6:4 exhorts fathers not to provoke their children to wrath, but to "bring them up in the discipline and instruction of the Lord." Proverbs 1:8 says, "Hear, my son, your father's instruction and do not forsake your mother's teaching." Fathers and mothers are to work together in training up their children in the ways of the Lord.

I suggest that husbands and wives do some inventory in this area of marriage as well. Together, work through the Parenting Inventory found at the end of this chapter and rate how well its principles are being implemented in the home. Decide what areas of parenting need work and how they could be improved. To facilitate the fulfillment of God's purpose for your marriage in this area, I also recommend to couples that they study together chapters 7 and 8 of my book *Strengthening Your Marriage* and all of Tedd Tripp's book *Shepherding a Child's Heart.*[1] Though it may seem unrelated to the husband–wife relationship, Scripture indicates that parenting is an important part of God's blueprint for marriage. So whatever you do, don't forget about the children.

At this point, some may ask: What about couples who would like to have children, but for physical reasons can't? I have known and you probably know (or you may even be) a couple for whom this is the situation. Does that leave such people out of the child-raising endeavor? No, not at all! These couples have options for being involved together in this area. Like many other couples who face this trial, they may consider adopting children whose biological parents have decided for various reasons not to raise them. Fortunately, there are Christian agencies that are fulfilling a worthy ministry in facilitating the adoption of children into Christian homes. In addition, the couple may devote themselves without being intrusive to helping others raise their children for Christ.

As a pastor, I could tell you of couple after couple who have ministered to the children of other brothers and sisters in Christ in marvelous ways through cheerful and eager service in the nursery, in Sunday school classes, in youth activities, in Awana, in Bible study groups, in sporting events, in babysitting, etc. In our case, all of our children are now out of our home, but we can look back with gratitude on all the people who showed an interest in our children and helped us in the child-raising process. And as people who no longer have younger children, we are still involved together in raising children as we assist others who do have children in the home. The opportunities for a couple without children to be involved in helping others to raise their children for Christ are innumerable and unending. The point is that every Christian couple, as a part of God's purpose for marriage, should be committed to joining together in ministry to children.

PARENTING INVENTORY

To make the contents of this chapter very practical, evaluate yourself and your mate on each of the following questions using this rating scale:

4 = usually;   3 = often;   2 = sometimes;   1 = seldom;   0 = never

As you complete this inventory, look up the supporting Scripture verses. Also, review the questions on which you scored 2 or less and discuss plans for improving in these areas. Periodically review and evaluate your child-rearing efforts by going over and discussing this inventory.

In Your Parenting Efforts, Do You:

SELF MATE

_____ _____ 1. View having and raising your child as a great privilege as well as a responsibility? Do you agree that having your child and raising that child in a God-ordained way is one of the most important things that any person can do in life? (Ps. 127:4–5; 128:3)

_____ _____ 2. Make sure that your expectations of your child are realistic in terms of the child's age and abilities? (Matt. 18:10; 1 Cor. 13:11)

_____ _____ 3. Love your child freely and avoid relating to your child on a performance basis? (Rom. 8:39; 1 John 4:10, 19)

_____ _____ 4. Look for opportunities when you can commend your child? Express your appreciation by words, expressions, actions? Do you do this more frequently than you criticize and correct? (Phil. 1:3; 4:8; 1 Thess. 5:11)

_____ _____ 5. Give your child freedom to make decisions when serious issues are not at stake? Relate to your child in such a way that he or she is being brought to maturity rather than dependence on you? (Eph. 4:13–15; Col. 1:27–28)

_____ _____ 6. Refuse to compare your child with other children? Respect his or her individuality? (2 Cor. 12:13-14; Gal. 6:4)

_____ _____ 7. Refrain from mocking or making fun of your child? Refrain from demeaning or belittling him or her? Refrain from calling him or her names or saying demeaning things, such as "you are so dumb," "stupid," "clumsy," "no good," "impossible," "can't you ever do anything right," and "you're never going to amount to anything"? (Prov. 12:18; 16:24; Matt. 7:12; Col. 4:6)

_____ _____ 8. Refrain from scolding your child or calling attention to his or her faults in the presence of others? (Matt. 16:22–23; 18:15; 1 Cor. 16:14)

_____ _____ 9. Avoid making threats or promises that you don't keep? (Matt. 5:37; Col. 3:9; James 5:12)

_____ _____ 10. Say "no" if the occasion warrants it? When you say "no," do you mean it and stick to that "no"? (Gen. 18:19; 1 Sam. 3:13; Prov. 22:15; 29:19)

_____ _____ 11. Avoid overreacting or losing control of yourself and yelling or screaming or shouting at or hitting your child when he or she doesn't live up to your expectations or behave as you want him or her to behave? (1 Cor. 16:14; Eph. 4:26–27; 1 Tim. 5:1–2; 2 Tim. 2:24–25)

_____ _____ 12. Communicate optimism and positive expectancy to your child and avoid communicating by word or action that you have given up on him or her or that you think of him or her as a total and hopeless failure? (1 Cor. 13:7; 2 Cor. 9:1–2; Philemon. 21)

____ ____ 13. Make sure that your child knows what you expect of him or her? Do you clearly and specifically explain to your child what you want him or her to do and not to do and why and how you want him or her to do what you want done? (Ex. 20:1–17; Matt. 5:1–7:27)

____ ____ 14. Ask your child's opinion and include him or her in some of the family planning? (John 6:5–6; Rom. 1:11–12; 2 Tim. 4:11)

____ ____ 15. Admit it and ask for forgiveness when you make a mistake or sin against your child? (Matt. 5:23–24; James 5:16)

____ ____ 16. Have family conferences when you discuss family goals, projects, vacations, devotions, chores, discipline, complaints, suggestions, problems, and concerns that you or anyone else in the family might have? (Prov. 18:1–2, 13, 15; James 1:19; example of our Lord Jesus Christ when here on earth; Mark 4:10-25: Luke 10:17-20; John 14-16)

____ ____ 17. Welcome contributions, suggestions, or even respectful disagreements or criticisms from your child? (Ps. 128:3: Prov. 12:15; Titus 1:6–8; James 3:13–18)

____ ____ 18. Assess your child's areas of strengths and abilities, and encourage him or her in their development and use? (1 Cor. 1:4–7; 1 Tim. 4:14–15; 2 Tim. 1:5–6, 16; 4:5; 1 Peter 4:10)

____ ____ 19. Give your child an abundance of tender loving care? Are you liberal in your expressions of love to him or her by word and deed? (John 13:34; 1 Cor. 13:1–8; Phil. 4:1; 1 Thess. 2:19–20; 2 Thess. 1:7–8)

____ ____ 20. Give thanks to God and in a judicious way communicate to the child how you have been blessed through him or her when your child demonstrates godly character and unselfish ministry to others and when he or she manifests the fruit of the Spirit? (Eph. 1:15; Col. 1:3–4; 1 Thess. 1:3–10; 2 Tim. 1:16; Philem. 3–5)

_____ _____ 21. Exhibit more concern about your child's Christian attitudes and character than you do about his or her performance, external beauty, or achievements in scholastics, music, athletics, or anything else? (1 Sam. 16:7; Prov. 4:23; Matt. 23:25–28; Gal. 5:22–23; 1 Peter 3:4–5)

_____ _____ 22. Have a lot of fun with your child? Do you play together, laugh together, do recreational things together, and generally enjoy being with one another? (Deut. 6:7–9; Ps. 128:3; Prov. 17:22; Eccl. 3:4)

_____ _____ 23. Especially enjoy doing the things that your child likes to do? (Rom. 12:10; Eph. 5:21; Phil. 2:3–4)

_____ _____ 24. Consistently live your godly convictions before your child? Can your child learn how to be a true disciple of Christ by observing your example as well as by listening to your words? (Deut. 6:4–9; Phil. 4:9; 1 Thess. 2:10–12; 2 Tim. 1:5, 7)

_____ _____ 25. Administer discipline to your child fairly, consistently, lovingly, and promptly, and pair it with constructive instruction? (1 Sam. 3:13; Prov. 13:24; 19:18; 22:15)

_____ _____ 26. Look upon your child as a human becoming as well as a human being? Do you recognize that the task of parenting is a process, not an event—a process that takes years to accomplish—and do you act accordingly? (Prov. 22:6; Isa. 28:9–10; 1 Cor. 15:58; Gal. 6:9; Eph. 6:4)

_____ _____ 27. Realize that the most important goal of your parenting is to help your child become Christ's disciple who is becoming more and more like Jesus Christ in every aspect of his or her life? Do you act accordingly? If someone were to observe the way you relate to your child, would that person be able to tell that this is your main concern? (Matt. 28:19; Eph. 4:15; Col. 1:28)

_____ _____ 28. Recognize that it is your God-given task to help your child become prepared for life in this world and therefore useful in this world, as well as prepared for the life to come? (Deut. 6:4–9; Ps. 78:5–7; Prov. 1:1–31:31; Eph. 6:4; 2 Tim. 3:15–17)

_____ _____ 29. Strive to be aware of and sensitive to the needs, feelings, fears, struggles, and difficulties that your child experiences, and are you ready to assist, support, and encourage him or her in any way you can, even if it involves great sacrifice and self-denial? Does your child know that he or she can count on you to be there for him or her at all times? Are you a refuge and place of security for your child in the storms of life? (Prov. 14:26–27; 17:17; 18:24; 27:14; Rom. 12:15; 1 Cor. 12:26; 2 Cor. 11:29)

_____ _____ 30. Avoid the use of angry, vindictive, scorching, abusive words in your relationship with your child? Do you use wholesome and gracious words instead? (Prov. 11:9, 11; 12:16, 18; 15:1; 16:21, 23–24; Eph. 4:29, 31; Col. 4:6)

_____ _____ 31. Maintain the practice of daily Bible readings and study and prayer, making application of Scripture to your life and seeking God's help in prayer? Does your child know that you are a person who continues in prayer? (Ps. 1:1–3; Phil. 4:6; Col. 4:2–3; 1 Thess. 5:17; 2 Tim. 2:15; 1 Peter 2:2)

_____ _____ 32. Understand the what, when, and how of bringing your child up in the instruction of the Lord, as taught in Deuteronomy 6:7–9, Ephesians 6:4, and Colossians 3:21 and throughout the book of Proverbs? Do you carefully seek to use every means to fulfill that command?

_____ _____ 33. Recognize the important role that being involved in a biblical church plays in life and in God's program for evangelism of unbelievers and the edification of Christians? Are you thoroughly involved in such a church? Does your child know that you love Christ's church and that you love God's Word, serving Christ and other Christians? (Eph. 4:11–16; 1 Tim. 3:15; Heb. 10:24–25)

____ ____ 34. Make your home a center of Christian hospitality where your child will be brought into frequent contact with many Christians? (Rom. 12:13; Heb. 13:1–2)

____ ____ 35. Make it easy for your child to approach you with his or her problems, difficulties, and concerns by being a good listener? When your child needs you, do you give your child undivided attention and avoid being a mind reader or a critic? Do you make yourself available whenever you child needs you, even if you are busy? (1 Cor. 9:19–23; Philem. 4-18; James 1:19–20; 3:16–18; 1 John 3:16–18)

____ ____ 36. Recognize and act as though you are a steward of God in regard to your child—that your child is only on loan to you, that you are not the owner of your child, and that you have been commissioned to raise your child for God and according to His desires and not yours? (Ps. 127:4–6)

____ ____ 37. Realize that while God alone can save your child, bring him or her to conviction of sin, and grant repentance and faith, you are responsible to provide the environment, instruction, and discipline through which your child is probably going to come to Christ and grow in Him? Do you seek to do this by being a person who faithfully prays, seeks to practice godly speech, is an example of Christ, maintains regular family devotions, and is involved in a solidly biblical church? (Matt. 16:18; Mark 10:13–14; Rom. 3:1, 2; 10:13–17; 1 Cor. 1:18–21; Eph. 6:4; 1 Thess. 5:12–13; 1 Tim. 3:15; 2 Tim. 1:5–7; 3:14–17; Heb. 10:24–25; 13:7, 17, 24)

4

WORKERS TOGETHER

The third purpose of God for marriage is that the husband and wife be colaborers. In Genesis 1:28, God commanded both Adam and Eve to fill the earth and subdue it and rule over it. Psalm 128 speaks of the wife as a fruitful vine by the sides of the house. In other words, she also is to make a significant contribution to the household. Proverbs 31:10–27 describes the ideal wife—the excellent wife—as a worker. She is buying and selling fields, making purchases for her household, doing good works for others, making clothes and food for her husband and children, and even bringing in some income from her labors at home.

In this passage, it is important not to miss the fact that all the things that this woman does are for her husband and children. Again and again the passage states that her work is for her household. She is a busy woman, but not for her own advancement or pleasure in life. Because of this, "the heart of her husband trusts in her, and he will have no lack of gain. She does him good and not evil all the days of her life" (31:11–12).

I like the description in Acts 18 of Priscilla and Aquila. The Scripture lets us know that when Paul stayed with them, "they were working, for by trade they were tent-makers" (18:3). Though they may not have spent equal time at this task, this couple worked together as a team in the business that supported them. In Genesis 1:28, God made it clear that work was to be an important part of Adam and Eve's life together. Work was not, as some may assume, a part of the curse. Just as a husband and wife enjoy times of fun and recreation together, so also should they be committed to working together.

In many cases, it is not possible or reasonable for a husband and wife to be directly involved in each other's work. For example, for many years I served as a pastor in a local church, and then I became involved in full-time counseling and training of others to do biblical counseling. In 1992 I became chairman of the Biblical Counseling Department at The Master's College, where I administered and served as a professor of biblical counseling at the college and seminary. During my entire ministry from 1957 until the present, my wife was a vital part of everything I did in ministry. It was our ministry, not just mine. At The Master's College and Seminary, though my wife did not follow me into the classroom each day, she was still vitally involved in what I was doing as a professor. She came to campus with me often, knew the names of many of my students, and prayed over my classes with me. We had regular open houses for the students at our home, where she prepared food for them and interacted with them on a personal basis. They got to know her and she got to know them.

And the same thing was true with me in terms of the Christian-school teaching in which my wife was involved. After our children were old enough to go to school, she went back to teaching at the same schools they attended. In fact, all our children had her for a teacher at some point. When she went back to the ministry of teaching in a Christian school, it was not just her ministry; it was our ministry. I became familiar with her students and knew their names. In our devotions, we prayed for them by name, and we often discussed the various problems and challenges that she faced each day. Though neither of us was present in the other's workplace in a literal sense each day, we were still very much involved in the work being done. Throughout our lives we have always, whatever we have done, worked at it together because we believe that being colaborers is part of God's purpose for the marriage relationship.

It is important to note that in Genesis 1:27–28, the cultural mandate (as it is called) was given to the husband and wife together, not just to one apart from the other. Scripture says that God blessed Adam and

Eve as a married couple and then charged them together to be fruitful and multiply and subdue the earth. From the very beginning of human history, God made it clear that part of His blueprint for the marriage relationship was for the husband and wife to be colaborers for the glory of God and the good of others. And only when married people see it this way and function accordingly will they experience maximum fulfillment in their marriage relationship.

APPLICATION AND DISCUSSION

1. I suggest that husbands and wives sit down together and first make a list of the home or work projects that you have done together in the past. This will provide a little perspective on how often you are colaboring already.

2. Then make a list of projects in the home or elsewhere that you can do together and commit yourselves to them by scheduling them on the calendar.

3. Discuss together how much each of you knows about what the other person does during the day. Wives, how much do you know about your husband's work—his coworkers, his daily tasks, his struggles, and his goals? Husbands, how much do you know about what your wife does at work or in the home?

4. Discuss how you can be more involved in each other's work and be more of a help to each other. Find out each other's biggest challenges, greatest joys, favorite parts, and dreaded tasks. Make it a point to continue this discussion regularly so that each of you becomes truly involved in the other's work. Faithful attention to these things will help you to fulfill God's purpose of being colaborers in marriage.

5

AN OVERLOOKED ASPECT
OF GOD'S BLUEPRINT

A fourth extremely important, though often overlooked, purpose of God for the marriage relationship is a commitment to exalt and serve Christ and to build up His church in the marriage.

The Bible uses a number of meaningful and descriptive metaphors to describe the believer's relationship with Christ. It talks about Christ being the head and we the body. It speaks of Christ as the foundation of us, the building. It refers to Christ as the Master and us as His servants and Christ as the King and believers as the citizens of His kingdom. Christ referred to Himself as the vine and His followers as the branches.

One of the most descriptive metaphors, however, is found in Ephesians 5:21–32, where Christ is called the husband and believers are called His wife. In other words, the marriage relationship is a picture of our relationship to Christ as our Lord. In this passage, Paul explained some important aspects of the nature of our relationship with Christ in terms of a proper relationship between husbands and wives:

²¹And be subject to one another in the fear of Christ. ²²Wives, be subject to your own husbands, as to the Lord. ²³For the husband is the head of the wife, as Christ also is the head of the church, He Himself being the Savior of the body. ²⁴But as the church is subject to Christ, so also the wives ought to be to their husbands in everything. ²⁵Husbands, love your wives, just as Christ also loved the church and gave Himself up for her . . . ²⁸So husbands ought also to love their own wives as their own bodies. He who loves his own wife loves himself; ²⁹for no one ever hated his own flesh, but nourishes and cherishes it, just as Christ also does the church, ³⁰because we are members of His body. ³¹For this reason a man shall leave his father and mother and shall be joined to his wife, and the two shall become one flesh. ³²This mystery is great; but I am speaking with reference to Christ and the church.

Consider with me each of the verses in this passage. Verse 21 says that wives and husbands should act in a godly way toward each other out of reverence for Christ. Verse 22 says that wives should submit to their husbands as to the Lord. In other words, the way in which wives relate to and think about their husbands should reflect the way in which they think about Christ. In the same way, husbands should relate to their wives as Christ relates to the church, loving her and giving Himself for her (vv. 25–29).

In verse 30 we discover that being members of Christ's body should be the primary motivation for relating to our spouses in an unselfish manner. Verse 31 continues by teaching that our unselfishness should stem from our regard for Christ's desires. Finally, verse 32 says that God intends that the way in which Christian husbands and wives relate to each other is to be a visual demonstration of Christ's relationship with the church. In other words, Paul, in this divinely inspired passage about marriage, tells us that the goal God has in mind in marriage goes far beyond making people personally fulfilled and happy. Marriage was intended to be a means by which Jesus Christ might be honored and exalted. Marriage, as Paul describes it, is not all about us; it should be all about Him. Marriages that follow God's blueprint should cause others to think about Christ.

Think about that statement for a moment. Does your marriage cause other people to think about Christ? Do others see you and your spouse interact with each other and think about Christ's relationship with the church? These are sobering and important questions. Even your children, who see you every day at your best and worst, should be reminded of Christ and the church as they watch you interact. According to God's Word, this is what we are to strive for.

One of God's greatest purposes for marriage is that the relationship between a husband and wife exalt and serve Jesus Christ. As previously stated, marriage is not just about making each other happy, fulfilling needs, or providing security. First and foremost, a Christian marriage should exalt Christ. Husbands and wives must understand and be committed to this purpose—using their marriages as a vehicle through which Christ is honored and served and eternal work is accomplished. This means that the husband and wife, if they want to have an "A" kind of marriage, must encourage and help each other to grow in Christ and be committed to serving Him together. And in seeking to make their marriage a theater in which the glory of Christ is put on display, the husband and wife will experience the blessedness that comes from serving Christ together. In making Him the focus of their marriage, their relationship is enriched and enhanced.

One area in which husbands and wives can do this is in showing hospitality to others. A couple in our church in Pennsylvania is a wonderful example of this kind of service for Christ. When new visitors come to our church on Sunday morning, this couple is usually the first to invite them home for Sunday dinner. If someone needs a place to stay or needs help with a job, this family is eager to reach out and meet that need. Rather than looking at their time and possessions as belonging to them, this couple views all they have as a vehicle through which they can serve and bless other people in the name of Christ.

My wife and I can personally attest to this truth. We were richly blessed, as a young married couple, when an older couple opened their home to us every Sunday. These people weren't formally called to be preachers, but their marriage preached to us about Christ as we had opportunity to spend time with them. When I did an interim pastorate in England, our whole family was privileged to stay in the home of a certain couple whose marriage spoke of Christ and His church. In this home, for almost two months, we saw two people who loved each other and lived to serve Christ together. Every Sunday and on numerous other occasions, their home was open to believers and unbelievers. Through their hospitality, many unbelievers were brought to Christ and young believers were strengthened in Him. To all who came, it was evident that this husband and wife, personally and unitedly, were utterly devoted to Christ and did what they did because of what He had done for them. These are just a couple of examples, but as a Christian for more than fifty years, I have known of many other people whose marriages have spoken of Christ to believers and unbelievers alike through their hospitality.

Husbands and wives should also exalt Christ together by their church attendance and involvement in church activities. Aquila and Priscilla invited Paul into their home when he needed a place to stay, and they ministered to Apollos when he was in need of counseling. Every church has numerous opportunities for couples to serve together, whether it be in teaching Sunday school, leading youth activities, preparing meals, visiting, evangelizing, singing in the choir, or counseling and discipling others. God brings men and women together for the purpose of serving Him as a team better than each person could as an individual.

APPLICATION AND DISCUSSION

1. First, make a list of the ways in which you have served Christ and His church together in the past.

2. Then think through some activities that you could be involved in together that you are not involved in right now.

3. Discuss the ways in which your marriage exalts Christ now and the ways that it does not. Think about how you need to change as a couple and what you can do to bring about that change.

4. Go to your elders together and tell them that you desire to serve Christ better as a couple. Ask them for suggestions about what ministries you could get involved in. Or sit down with another couple in your church that is clearly doing well in this area and

discuss with them what they do and what you could be doing. My wife and I are involved in the ministry of counseling together. She sits in on sessions with me and contributes to the discussion. It's exciting for us to share this ministry and to pray together for the people with whom we are working. We go to seminars and teaching conferences together as well so that we are always serving Christ together.

5. Once when I was in Texas conducting a training seminar, one of the attending pastors told me about a family ministry project that his family had completed and was now putting into practice. He and his wife had sat down together and had written a mission statement for their family. Their mission statement read like this: "To become joyful worshipers who magnify the glory of Jesus Christ with a worshiper's heart, a disciple's mind, an encourager's tongue, a servant's hands, and a missionary's feet." They also discussed and wrote down what each of those things involved and how they would put them into practice. Then they prayed over the statement together and put it where everyone could see it. And periodically they evaluate how they are doing in fulfilling their mission statement. That's a great idea for facilitating one of God's purposes for the marriage relationship.

   After reading this chapter, you are being given this assignment because I think it is an excellent way of helping you to focus your marriage and family life on Jesus Christ. Make a mission statement for your marriage and family and then use it as a guideline and checklist for how you're doing in family ministry. Doing this will prove immensely helpful to your family relationships, and it will also increase your effectiveness in corporate service to Christ. All of these things will take time and effort, of course, but if you truly want to fulfill God's purposes for marriage, you can do no less.

6. I want to also encourage all who desire an "A" kind of marriage and family to study together my book *To Be or Not to Be a Church Member: That Is the Question.*[1] This book has many suggestions about how couples can serve Christ in the church.

7. Before you move on to the next chapters, where we will explain two more of God's purposes for marriage (oneness and completion), I urge you to take some time to prayerfully evaluate how well you and your spouse are doing in fulfilling the four purposes for marriage presented in the book thus far. Having done that, turn to the Lord, thanking Him for the help He's given you, asking Him for forgiveness for your marital sins and failure, and seeking His assistance so that you may increasingly fulfill His purposes for your marriage relationship. Memorizing and praying the following prayer would be a fitting way of responding to the challenges of this chapter:

> *O give us homes built firm upon the Savior,*
> *Where Christ is Head and Counselor and Guide;*
> *Where every child is taught His love and favor*
> *And gives his heart to Christ, the Crucified:*
> *How sweet to know that, tho' his footsteps waver,*
> *His faithful Lord is walking by his side!*
> *O give us homes with godly fathers and mothers,*
> *Who always place their hope and trust in Him;*
> *Whose tender patience turmoil never bothers,*
> *Whose calm and courage trouble cannot dim;*
> *A home where each finds joy in serving others,*
> *And love still shines, tho' days be dark and grim.*[2]

6

ONE PLUS ONE
EQUALS ONE

How can married people keep a good thing from turning into a bad thing? Or how can a married couple make a good thing an even better thing as they go through life together? Answer: they must be committed to fulfilling the purposes that God, who is the Author of marriage, had in mind when He instituted the marriage relationship. When the good thing of marriage becomes a bad thing, or when the good thing doesn't become an even better thing, you can count on it that the people involved either don't know or aren't committed to God's blueprint for the marriage relationship.

In the previous chapters, we noted four of God's purposes for marriage. In the next few chapters, we will discuss two more of God's purposes for marriage. One of those purposes is found in the last phrase of Genesis 2:24, where the Author of marriage declared, "For this reason a man shall leave his father and his mother, and be joined to his wife; and they shall become one flesh." If we want to remain sweethearts with our spouses for a lifetime, we must be committed to the purpose of comprehensive oneness in the relationship.

ONENESS: WHAT DOESN'T IT MEAN?

Misconceptions abound regarding what it means for a husband and wife to be "one." To better understand this idea of oneness, I want to start by looking at what oneness does *not* mean. First, oneness does *not* mean that husbands and wives are exactly alike. Some couples strain and stifle themselves in an effort to duplicate each other's personality, thinking that uniformity is the goal of oneness. They force themselves to like the same things, have the same opinions, share the same priorities, and have the same habits. Though they do this with the best of intentions, their "oneness" of character is no more real than Adam and Eve's covering their physical differences with clothes. This type of "oneness" makes marriage a pretense and will eventually become tedious. What is obvious on the physical level—that God made us different from each other—is true on every other level as well.

Second, oneness does *not* mean that one of the partners dominates the other so that the other shrinks into the shadows. This is not two becoming one; it is one alone. True, there is no disharmony is this kind of marriage—no arguments or differences of opinion—but neither is there harmony. The drum has overwhelmed the flute. Oneness does not mean domination.

Third, oneness does not mean that the husband and wife have a fifty-fifty marriage. Marriage is the joining of two wholes, not two halves. If each partner tries to be only a fraction of the relationship, they will soon discover that the halves do not fit perfectly together. Oneness in marriage, as God intended, requires two complete people.

ONENESS: WHAT DOES IT MEAN?

What, then, *is* oneness? Oneness is a lifelong, exclusive, comprehensive union of an entire man and an entire woman to each other. It is a type of relationship that is shared with no one else other than one's mate. It is a partnership in every area of life for as long as both partners live. In other words, there is absolutely nothing about which one spouse can say to the other, "That's none of your business." The wife has complete, unfettered access to every area of her husband's life and so also the husband to every area of his wife's life. There are no locked closets or secret hiding places.

What does this kind of union look like? We might think of it as being like an orchestra. An orchestra comprises many different instruments all playing the same piece of music. Each instrument has its own unique part to play, but all the parts blend together in such a way that they achieve perfect harmony. The husband and wife—both different and unique—come together to form a harmonious one.

Or we might compare oneness to the way in which a beautiful purple sweater is composed, when viewed up close, of tiny red and blue threads. Two very different colors, without losing their identity, blend together to make something that appears continuous and whole. Oneness does not mean that the wife cancels out or dominates the husband or that the husband cancels out or dominates the wife. Each remains an individual, and yet each is part of a beautiful, harmonious whole.

Undoubtedly, the greatest illustration of this kind of relationship is the Trinity. Scripture teaches that there is one God who exists in three persons. The Father, Son, and Holy Spirit are each unique persons of the Trinity, and yet they work and act together as one God. In marriage, two individuals work and act together as a single unit while completely retaining their individuality.

Being one flesh, as God intended for married people, means being committed to unity in every area of life. For the purpose of this study, we can break this down into at least eight broad categories. First, it means unity in the cognitive and intellectual area. Again, this does not mean that spouses must think alike. Rather, it means that husbands and wives constantly and completely share their ideas, thoughts, and opinions with each other. They tell each other what they are learning. When making a decision, each one patiently considers the other person's ideas and insights. There are no closely held thoughts—all is in the open.

This type of unity requires that both spouses make an effort to find out what the other thinks about various matters. It also requires that each person have a teachable spirit—willing to learn from and be influenced by the other person. And it requires husbands and wives to study and reflect on issues and topics together.

For example, my wife and I enjoy reading books together. We each get a copy of a book, read it at the same pace, and discuss it as we go along. This kind of activity helps us to develop oneness in the intellectual area.

Second, there should be unity in the area of emotions and feelings. In Scripture we are commanded to rejoice with those who rejoice and weep with those who weep (Rom. 12:15). When one member of the body of believers suffers, we are to suffer along with him, and when one is honored, we are to rejoice with him also (1 Cor. 12:26). If these things are to be true in the church as a whole, how much more should they be true in the marriage relationship? God wants husbands and wives to communicate their feelings to each other. He also wants us to help our mates to appropriately express and deal with their emotions. Actively entering into the joys and sorrows of our mates is oneness as God intends. Someone has picturesquely said that emotional closeness in marriage should be so deep that when one person cries, the other person tastes salt. Conversely, it means that when one person is elated and excited about something, the other person should join in that excitement.

Third, oneness includes the area of social activities and relationships. I believe that it is appropriate and beneficial for husbands and wives to develop close friendship relationships with the same people— other individuals or couples. Having common friends helps to draw spouses together; separate friends can pull two people apart. Husbands and wives should also make an effort to develop some common recreational activities. Since recreation time tends to be scarce as it is, spouses should seek to spend as much of the time they do have doing things together. This means that each person must be willing to learn to enjoy some of his or her mate's favorite hobbies and pastimes.

Fourth, husbands and wives should be one in the area of work. We talked about this idea a bit already in terms of a commitment to being colaborers. Spouses should discuss their work-related activities together and help each other as much as possible in their work. They should labor together on home projects. They should pray together about their work, empathize with each other's difficulties, and be as proud of the other's accomplishments as they are of their own.

Fifth, there must be spiritual oneness. This means that husbands and wives should be regularly praying together, reading and studying the Bible together, and discussing spiritual problems and truths. They should share common convictions and views on spiritual matters, attend and get involved in the same church, work together in some common ministries, and read Christian literature together.

The remaining oneness categories will be discussed in the next chapter.

APPLICATION AND DISCUSSION

1. I strongly suggest that after church, couples go home and discuss what they each got out of the sermon and Sunday school lessons. In our home, we spent time together every Sunday after church reviewing the Sunday school lessons and sermon as a family. We shared how we intended to change in response to the teaching that we had received. My wife and I did this with all our children when they were at home with us, and now we continue the practice with each other. Do you do this? On the way home and after you have arrived at home from the church service, do you discuss with one another the main truths that were presented, the challenges you have received, and the applications you will make? If so, continue to do so. If not, begin the practice on a regular basis. Discuss why you haven't done this up to this point and talk about how you will implement the practice in the future.

2. Oneness in spiritual matters also requires that mates share in each other's personal walk with the Lord. We ought to discuss together what we are learning in our personal devotions. Have you done this? Do you know what your mate is doing in his or her personal devotions? What method of Bible study is your spouse using? What is your mate getting out of his or her devotions? How does your mate apply what he or she is learning? As you conclude and apply this chapter, spend some time talking to each other about your own personal devotions. Make it a point to regularly share with each other what you're learning and how you're being blessed. Perhaps you could make your devo-

tional sharing time something you do when you have meals together. Doing this, as well as sharing what has happened throughout your day, would certainly make your mealtime a time of meaningful conversation.

3. We should exhort one another in our walk with Christ— rejoicing in each other's growth and blessings and encouraging each other in struggles. Hebrews 10:24–25 tells us to continually stimulate one another to love and good works as we fellowship with each other. Galatians 6:2 commands us to bear one another's burdens as an expression of our love for one another. First Thessalonians 5:11 instructs us to build up and encourage one another. These are things that all believers should be doing for one another. But if this applies to all believers, then how much more should it be true for married people. And what better opportunity could anyone ever have to implement these practices than in the marriage relationship, in which people spend more time with each other and have more exposure to what is needed by the other person than in any other relationship? Talk about how you could be more effective in fulfilling these responsibilities with each other.

Scripture also informs us that God's people are to teach and counsel one another (Col. 3:16) and help one another when they are overtaken by any trespass (Gal. 6:1). Counseling our mates through personal problems and sins, asking for and receiving forgiveness when we have sinned against our spouses, and having a readiness to grant forgiveness when sinned against should be par for the course in the marriage relationship. Again, if doing these things is our responsibility with all Christians, how can we not be impressed with the importance of doing this with our mates? In marriage, the wife is to be her husband's helper (Gen. 2:18) and the husband is to be constantly helping his wife in the process of staying spiritually clean and strong (Eph. 5:26–27).

Functioning in this way with each other is a vital part of what couples who are serious about being one flesh in the God-appointed way will do. As each spouse joins with the other in a mutual and serious commitment to oneness in spiritual matters, they can be assured that they will develop spiritual oneness in their marriage relationship. More than that, they can be assured that they are doing the very things that will help them to be sweethearts for a lifetime. Conclude your reading of this chapter by discussing how you can and will enhance the spiritual oneness of your marriage even more.

7

MORE ABOUT ONENESS

Remaining sweethearts for a lifetime will require commitment to God's purposes for the marriage relationship. Couples who know and fulfill those purposes cannot have failing marriages. Up to this point in the book, we have mentioned five of those purposes and given suggestions for developing and sustaining them. In this chapter, we continue to discuss the fifth great purpose of God—namely, that the husband and wife should become one flesh. Thus far, as we considered this purpose, we have noted what becoming one flesh does and doesn't mean and then mentioned five areas in which couples should seek to be one if they want to remain sweethearts for a lifetime. In this chapter, we pick up where we left off in chapter 6 by elaborating on several other areas of unity.

The sixth area of oneness includes the physical and sexual realms of marriage. Husbands and wives should be as concerned for their mate's physical well-being as they are for their own. This means being appropriately concerned for the other person's health and being willing to adapt to the other's physical strengths and weaknesses.

My wife had a total knee replacement in February of 2004, which meant that I had many extra responsibilities for several weeks afterward. I had to cut some things out of my regular schedule so that I could assist her with things at home that I don't normally do so that she had the rest she needed. A spouse should be eager to give assistance when his or her partner is having physical difficulties.

Oneness in the physical realm also means that a spouse must be willing to demonstrate affection to the other spouse in mutually satisfying ways. In other words, one mate has to take the time to learn about and put into practice the ways in which the other mate desires affection. At the same time, both mates must be willing to share what they desire physically as well. This means that husbands and wives must be involved in appropriately and regularly giving and receiving affection. As long as it does not violate God's Word, each must be willing to do what pleases the other in the physical realm and be available to the other physically and sexually. Spouses should decide together on the frequency of sexual relations and always put the mate's needs and concerns above their own.

Seventh, oneness includes unity in goals and aspirations. The husband and wife should discuss together and agree on what they want out of their marriage. They should have goals for their family and for their children. Financial, educational, spiritual, and other goals should be discussed and agreed upon. I believe that every couple should sit down and talk about their long-range goals, medium-range goals, and short-range goals. My wife and I are in our seventies, so our long-range goals are not as long as they used to be, but we still have them. We talk about how we are going to serve the Lord as long as He grants us life. As a couple, we strive to be united in spirit and purpose.

Finally, oneness involves standing together in the face of difficulties and trials. Proverbs 17:17 says, "A friend loves at all times, and a brother is born for adversity." There ought to be a rock-solid assurance of faithfulness in every Christian marriage. Husbands and wives should be able to count on each other for support at all times. Proverbs 31:11 says of the excellent wife: "The heart of her husband trusts in her . . ."

This means that there must not be even a hint of condemnation or belittling when adversity or failure comes. Spouses should be able to count on each other for prayer, for encouragement, for sympathy, for advice and counsel, and for help to overcome difficulties.

These are the eight things that make up true oneness in marriage. J. R. Miller described it this way:

Another important element in married life is unity of interest. There is danger that wedded lives be ripped apart because their employments are nearly always different. The husband is absorbed in business and his profession and severe daily toil. The wife has her home duties, her social life, her friends and friendships, her children and other things as well, and the two touch at no point. Unless care is taken, this separation of duties and engagements will lead to an actual separation in heart and life. To prevent this, each should keep up a constant, loving interest in whatever the other person does. The husband may listen every evening to the story of home life of the day—its incidents, its pleasures, its perplexities, its trials, the children's sayings and doings, what the neighbor said, who dropped in, the bits of news that have been heard—and may enter with zest and sympathy into everything that is told him.

Nothing that concerns the wife of his heart should be too small for even the gigantic intellect of the greatest of husbands. In personal biography, few things are more charming and fascinating than the glimpses into the homes of some of the greatest men of earth when we see them, having laid aside the cares and honors of the world, enter their own doors to romp with the children, to listen to the prattle of their children, and to talk over with loving interest all the events and incidents of the day's home history.

In like manner, every wise and true-hearted wife will desire to keep up an interest in all her husband's affairs. She'll want to know of every burden, every struggle, every plan, and every new ambition. She'll wish to learn what undertaking has succeeded and what has failed and to keep herself thoroughly familiar and in full sympathy with all his daily personal life. No marriage is complete which does not unite and blend the wedded lives at every point. This can be secured only by making every interest common to both.

They should read and study together, having the same line of thought, helping each other toward a higher mental culture. They should worship together, praying side by side, communing on the holiest themes of life and hope and together carrying to God's feet the burdens of their hearts for their children and for every precious object. Why should they not talk together of their personal pride, their peculiar temptations, their infirmities, and help each other by sympathy, by brave word, and by intercession to be victorious in living?

Thus they should live one life, as it were, not two. Every plan and hope of each should embrace the other. The moment a man begins to leave his wife out of any part of his life, or that she has plans, hopes, pleasures, friendships, or experiences from which she excludes him, there is peril in the home. They should have no secrets which they keep from each other. They should have no companions or friends, save those which they have in common. Thus their two lives should blend in one life with no thought, no desire, no feeling, no joy or sorrow, no pleasure or pain unshared.[1]

In a very practical way, this is what it means to be "one flesh."

"HOW TO DEVELOP UNITY" EXERCISE

To evaluate, assess, and improve the oneness aspect of God's blueprint for marriage, read through the following list and put a "D" in front of the activities that you are already doing; "ND" in front of the ones that you are not doing; "WD" in front of the ones that you will do. Add any other ideas you think of for common interests at the end of each category. Then make plans for increasing the activities that will improve your marital oneness, commit yourself to fulfilling those plans, and practice your plans until they become a habit pattern with you.[2]

Spiritual

____ 1. Engage in prayer, Bible-reading, and discussion.

____ 2. Pray for each other.

____ 3. Attend church and be involved.

____ 4. Share Christian service activities.

____ 5. Read and discuss Christian literature

____ 6. Participate in a Bible study group.

____ 7. Visit mission fields; entertain missionaries and Christian workers; entertain non-Christians and Christians together.

Social, Recreational

____ 1. Develop common friends.

____ 2. Plan hospitality or visiting.

____ 3. Have a fun night every week (make "fun" list, "interest" list, and "enjoy" list for partner and self).

____ 4. Have regular vacations.

____ 5. Plan a daily communication time.

____ 6. Develop family traditions.

____ 7. Involve yourselves in sports (spectator and participant), clubs, music, etc.

____ 8. Play table games.

____ 9. Develop mutual hobbies.

Productive

____ 1. Share household tasks.

____ 2. Share family projects.

____ 3. Write letters; send cards.

____ 4. Develop a family business.

____ 5. Work on budgeting, bookkeeping, or income tax together.

Children

____ 1. Have a weekly family night (make plans together).

____ 2. Develop and implement a code of conduct.

_____ 3. Have regular family conferences.

_____ 4. Support the interests and activities of your children together.

_____ 5. Read and implement chapters 7 and 8 in _Strengthening Your Marriage_[3] and chapter 3 in _Your Family God's Way_[4] together.

Sexual

_____ 1. Have regular sexual relations.

_____ 2. Write love letters to each other frequently.

_____ 3. Make a "what pleases the other person" list.

_____ 4. Have mini-honeymoons.

_____ 5. Read and implement unit 7 in _Strengthening Your Marriage_ and chapter 3 in _Your Family God's Way_.

Intellectual

_____ 1. Take courses together.

_____ 2. Read and discuss the same book.

_____ 3. Read and discuss the same newspaper, magazines, and articles.

_____ 4. Ask questions about each other's views on various topics.

Other suggestions for developing intimacy and unity through common interests

_____ 1. List ten of your mate's interests. Pick five in which you can share.

_____ 2. After you've finished this book, work through _Strengthening Your Marriage_ and _Your Family God's Way_ together.

_____ 3. Share with your mate two or three of your interests and ask him or her to join you.

_____ 4. List everything that you and your mate already share in common. Examples: Christian faith, nationality, church membership, music, Italian food, children, desire for children to become Christians or be well adjusted or be respectful, etc. Use your present commonalities as a basis for discussion and a launching pad for developing other commonalities.

_____ 5. Write down everything you know about your mate that is not derogatory. Examples: has brown hair, is 5'5" tall, enjoys sports, reads newspaper daily, likes to go to bed at 11 p.m. and get up at 7 a.m., reads Bible daily, goes to church every Sunday, wears size __ shoes (or shirt or dress or coat or hat), is a hard worker, is a neat dresser, bathes and washes hair regularly, etc. (Intimacy is developed as we get to know the other person intimately. Hence the reason for this assignment.)

____ 6. Keep a daily journal of mutual husband–wife activities. Examples: how much time you are actually together, what you actually do when you are together, where you actually go together, what your mate did that you could have done with him or her (went shopping, fixed leaky faucet, went for a walk, watched football game, went to church, etc.). Intimacy will be developed as you become interested in and share the other person's interests. See Philippians 2:3–4. Adjust your schedule so that you are free to share your mate's interests and activities.

____ 7. Make a prayer list of your mate's needs, responsibilities, problems, desires, goals, aspirations, and ambitions. Pray daily that God would help, bless, and strengthen him or her in each of them. Ask your mate how you may pray for him or her.

____ 8. Read newspaper or magazine articles or books that would interest your mate and share them with him or her. When your mate shares anything, listen carefully and express appreciation.

____ 9. Discover and list what your mate wants you to change. Ask God for help, and work on changing. This will communicate to your mate your interest in him or her (see Gal. 6:7).

8

OBSTACLES TO ONENESS

Why is it that so many couples, even Christian couples, are not experiencing the kind of oneness that J. R. Miller described in the previous chapter? I believe that one answer is that so little in our society encourages couples to make the kind of adjustments and sacrifices in their lives that are necessary for oneness in marriage. The subject is not talked about on television, printed in magazines or newspapers, or taught in classrooms. If anything, the very opposite of oneness is presented instead.

To make matters worse, many couples allow themselves to be counseled by the world. They listen to what TV psychiatrists have to say, read self-help books and magazines, and listen to the ungodly counsel of neighbors and friends. Most of this is swallowed whole, without any examination of the counsel in light of God's Word.

Couples are so busy listening to everyone else that consistent Bible study is largely neglected. After getting their fill of the world's advice, they have no inclination to search the Scripture, to read biblically based material, to faithfully sit under the solid preaching of the Scripture, or to meditate and apply Scripture to their daily lives.

They avoid spending time with godly people who will challenge and rebuke them by their lives and words. The marriages of such couples have no consistent accountability because their reference point—the world—is always changing. Pop culture, not the Bible, has become their standard.

Sadly, couples such as these fail to understand or anticipate the depth of their own selfishness. Most of us are not as concerned about our selfishness as we ought to be. Jeremiah 17:9 reminds us: "The heart is more deceitful than all else and is desperately sick; who can understand it?" Even believers need the daily help of the Holy Spirit to fulfill Paul's command, "Do nothing from selfishness or empty conceit, but with humility of mind regard one another as more important than yourselves" (Phil. 2:3). Selfishness gravely threatens the development of oneness in marriage, and unless it is constantly examined and challenged, it will surely erode the relationship.

Still further, we fail to understand and anticipate the inevitable development of disagreements and trials in marriage. It is a given that when two sinful people get together and forge a lifelong relationship, they will have difficulties and trials along the way. Because of this, we must always be on our guard against allowing these things to destroy our oneness. We must be prepared from the very beginning to handle and respond to problems in a biblical way.

When selfishness is ignored and difficulties are not anticipated and handled properly, many people seek a seemingly painless solution to their problems: extramarital affairs. Not just sexual in nature, an extramarital affair is something that occurs whenever a spouse uses anything or anyone to escape rather than deal with difficulties in the marriage. This means that an affair can come in the form of a person, a job, money or possessions, hobbies, even church activities.

For example, a Christian man might never be sexually unfaithful, but if he avoids his wife by working so much that it prevents him from spending an adequate amount of time with her or with his family, or if he spends so much time watching television, or if he disappears to the golf course or workshop, then he is being unfaithful to his wife. A Christian woman might never be involved with another man, but if she avoids her husband by pouring herself into the children, or increasingly spending time with friends, or working more at home or elsewhere, then she is being unfaithful as well. When anything (besides the Lord) becomes more important than a spouse, the other spouse is having an extramarital affair.

As a pastor and counselor, I have known of men who became very involved in church activities so that they could avoid being at home and dealing with marital problems. It was easier for them to disappear for a "good" reason than to work through uncomfortable tension at home. And how could anyone blame them for being involved in church ministries? But I knew these men and their families well, and I knew that they were avoiding problems, not primarily desiring to be of extra service in the church.

We can use so many things to avoid resolving marital issues, but to have an "A" kind of marriage, we must be devoted to developing and maintaining a comprehensive unity in every area of our lives.

"ONE-FLESH QUOTIENT" INVENTORY

To help couples with unity, I have developed what I call a "One-Flesh Quotient" Inventory that I believe can be helpful in evaluating how well a couple is doing in the area of oneness. In order to make improvements in this area, I recommend that you first take some time to go through this inventory together and really evaluate how you and your spouse are doing.

Instructions: Since you've read these chapters about becoming one flesh, it's now time to do some further evaluation and application using the following "One-Flesh Quotient" Inventory. Spend some time reflecting on each of the nine areas listed below to evaluate the oneness quotient of your marriage. Put a check mark in the appropriate column. Honestly facing reality is the beginning of involvement. Take all the areas in which one or both of you see need for improvement and think, discuss, plan, and pray about what you can do to promote improvement.

Oneness Area	Both Desire Improvement	Husband Desires Improvement	Wife Desires Improvement	Both Satisfied
1. Cognitive	_____	_____	_____	_____
2. Emotional	_____	_____	_____	_____
3. Social	_____	_____	_____	_____
4. Work	_____	_____	_____	_____
5. Spiritual	_____	_____	_____	_____
6. Physical	_____	_____	_____	_____
7. Sexual	_____	_____	_____	_____
8. Aspirational	_____	_____	_____	_____
9. Crises/Trials	_____	_____	_____	_____

List the areas in which both of you desire improvement and discuss what you will do to bring it about (for suggestions, see How To Develop Unity Exercise on pages 57–60).

_____

_____

_____

_____

_____

List the areas in which both of you are satisfied with your oneness quotient, praise God for His blessing in these areas, and continue what you are doing.

_____

_____

_____

_____

_____

To make all this very practical and therefore helpful, I also recommend that you go back over the things discussed in this chapter about why oneness in marriage is so rare. As a couple, spend some time answering and then discussing your answers to the following questions:

1. How much have you been influenced by the ideas of the world? (Little, somewhat, or very much?)

2. How much have you allowed yourself to be exposed to the ungodly counsel of the world, and how much have you listened to? (Little, somewhat, or very much?)

3. How much are you failing to consistently study God's Word and to read good biblically based material? (Little, somewhat, or very much?)

4. How much thought and attention do you give to the depth of your own selfishness? In other words, how much do you think about how selfish you are? (Little, somewhat, or very much?)

5. How much have you thought about and anticipated the inevitable development of disagreements and trials? Do you expect them to come? Disagreements will happen; are you prepared for them? (Little, somewhat, or very much?)

6. How much have you sought after what appeared to be a painless solution to marital problems—having an extramarital affair in any of the forms discussed? (Little, somewhat, or very much?)

God desires for His people to be one flesh in marriage. He purposed this characteristic from the very beginning of creation. As we strive for and work toward this type of relationship, we will experience more and more of God's blessing in our lives.

9

BE A BARGAIN

"Then the LORD God said, 'It is not good for the man to be alone; I will make him a helper suitable for him' " (Gen. 2:18). The last purpose of God for marriage that I want to discuss is that of completion and complementarity. If someone desires to remain sweethearts with his or her mate for a lifetime, that person must commit to completing and being completed by the spouse.

From the words of Genesis 2:18, we learn that God decided at the very beginning that there was something lacking in a man alone, and so He created a woman to complete the man. In Ephesians 5:25–26, we see that there must be deficiencies in the woman as well, since husbands are commanded to sanctify their wives, as Christ did the church, with the washing of water with the Word. In marriage, then, both spouses ought to be committed to helping the other in areas of deficiency and difficulty. This is the goal of completion.

Many couples have never thought about the idea of completing their mates because they have always been focused on receiving, not giving, in marriage. This often goes all the way back to the process of looking for a mate. Few people look for a spouse with their focus on what they can offer the other person. Rather, they are focused on looking at what the other person can offer them, which means that they are getting married for the wrong reasons. Their primary focus in getting married is on what the other person can do for them. Their main concern is on being ministered to by the other person rather than on ministering to the other person.

Throughout history, and still today, people have gotten married for the wrong reasons. Even many Christians get married for insufficiently biblical reasons. In some countries, marriage remains a bargaining process between families, as it often was in biblical times. In Genesis 24, Eliezer bargained for a wife for Isaac. Later, in Genesis 29, Jacob bargained with Laban for Rachel.

In some places in the past and even today, people with certain economic or social status marry only people of like status. That was true in Europe just a few centuries ago and is still true in such places as India, where social and economic status remain rigidly defined within that society's caste system. It is customary in India and some other countries for the father of the bride to provide a certain amount of money—a dowry—to the father of the groom. On both sides, families are seeking a bargain for their investment.

I recently finished reading a secular book called *The Namesake*[1] in which the author described the marriage of an Indian couple. According to custom, the marriage was arranged by the families, and each family positioned itself to get the best bargain out of the arrangement. In America, there is usually no obvious bargaining process, but that does not mean that the search for a bargain is not a part of American marriages as well.

What I mean by this is that most people, whether they admit it or not, are thinking more about getting than they are about giving when they get married. In other words, they are looking to get a bargain, not to be a bargain. Some people marry to get away from a bad home situation. Some marry to gain social status. Others marry because it seems expedient—they want a partner to share expenses, be their personal cheerleader, provide companionship, and take care of them. Some get married in an attempt to get an ego boost. They think that being married will help them to feel better about themselves. They are concerned that if they don't marry, others will think it must be because they aren't attractive, desirable, and worthwhile. Well, in their minds, marriage will fix all that.

Some people marry to solve personal problems. They are lonely and insecure, and getting married provides them with affirmation and protection from the rest of the world. Some people marry simply because they desire biblically legitimate sex. And some people marry because they want a caretaker, someone who will provide for them and take care of them.

None of these reasons are what God had in mind when He instituted marriage, and if we want to remain sweethearts with our spouses for a lifetime, we must be devoted to the purpose of more fully completing our mates. In other words, we must strive to *be* the bargain, not to *get* the bargain. In marriage, as in every other area of life, God wants us to "do nothing from selfishness or empty conceit, but with humility of mind regard one another as more important than yourselves; do not merely look out for your own personal interests, but also for the interests of others" (Phil. 2:3–4). In marriage, as well as in other areas of life, we should follow the example of our Lord Jesus Christ, who "did not come to be served, but to serve, and to give His life a ransom for many" (Mark 10:45). In marriage, as well as in other areas of life, we should remember that "it is more blessed to give than to receive" (Acts 20:35).

This, of course, does not mean that thoughtfulness, assessment, and evaluation of the strengths and weaknesses of the people involved should not be engaged in as they make the decision to marry. Nor does it mean that consideration should not be given to common interests and other compatibility issues. It does mean, however, that once that assessment and evaluation have occurred, the focus should primarily be not on being served, but on serving; not on how the other person can complete you, but on how you can complete the other person.

Being a bargain for the other person, ministering to the other person, should occupy your thoughts and conduct. When this is the main focus of the individuals who are married, they are operating according to God's blueprint for the marriage relationship. And the result will most certainly be, as we have previously noted in the Scriptures that were quoted, the blessedness that God promises to people who relate to others in this way.

Being companions, raising godly children, serving as colaborers, exalting Christ, developing comprehensive oneness, and each mate completing the other—these are the purposes of God for marriage. Christian husbands and wives must be wholly committed to pursuing these purposes in their marriages. It is possible to remain sweethearts for a lifetime. The good thing of marriage can remain a good thing and get even better, but only if we go about it in God's way.

APPLICATION
AND DISCUSSION

By this time, the question you should be asking is this: how can we strengthen the completion aspect of our marriage?

Please discuss and reflect on the following recommendations.

1. First, spend some time honestly evaluating the reasons that you and your spouse had for getting married. When I did that some time ago, I realized that my reasons for marrying my wife were not as biblical as they should have been. I married Carol because I thought she was a bargain (which she was and is!), but that should not have been my primary reason for marrying her. Though we were both Christians at the time and thought that it was God's will for us to get married, we were not yet really thinking biblically about marriage and God's reasons for it. Later, when we understood that our motives for getting married on July 6, 1957 were not entirely godly, we had to repent and commit ourselves to a marital lifestyle of being more concerned about serving than being served. Thank God for Proverbs 28:13 and 1 John 1:9.

2. Study Philippians 2:3–4: "Do nothing from selfishness or empty conceit, but with humility of mind regard one another as more important than yourselves; do not merely look out for your own personal interests, but also for the interests of others." Make a list of all the ways in which you can fulfill this command toward your spouse. How can you show regard for your mate above yourself? Think of ways to better serve and encourage your mate. Plan on doing at least one or two things each day that you are not now doing, and then keep a daily record of the times when you actually do these things. Continue to do this for a few weeks. Use your daily record to check up on yourself and evaluate how you are doing in this area of completion.

3. Make a list of all of your mate's strengths and weaknesses. Everyone has strengths and weaknesses. Prior to marriage, we tend to minimize the weaknesses and maximize the strengths. After being

married for a while, many people seem to reverse that order. Now's the time to be realistic on both sides of these issues. In marriage, the husband and wife should each be dedicated to serving the other person by helping him or her to develop and use the person's strengths and to overcoming or reducing his or her weaknesses. Doing this will never become a reality until there is an honest and accurate assessment.

4. Having done this, go on to identify ways in which you can help your mate to fully develop and use his or her strengths and improve his or her weaknesses. A study of the one-anothering commands in Scripture (there are fifty-eight in all) can be a great help in discerning ways to really help each other. Having a better understanding of all the things that God has commanded us to do for "one another" will help one spouse to better help the other become the person that God wants him or her to be. Complete the one-anothering assignment found at the end of this chapter. This study contains only a sample of the Bible's one-anothering passages, but it will give you a start on studying some of them. List the various one-anothering commands, determine what each of them means and demands, evaluate yourself in terms of how well and how frequently you are doing these things, and ask your mate to do the same. As you study, identify specific ways in which you are fulfilling these commands and specific ways in which you and your mate might improve your one-anothering ministries to each other.

"COMPLETING ONE ANOTHER" STUDY[2]

The Bible has a lot to say about how we should relate to one another. We often fall short in our relationships with other people because we are selfish. Study the following passages to draw out the principles that God wants you to apply in your relationship with your mate and note how you can implement these principles.

	God's Command	How I Can Implement It with My Mate
John 13:34–35		
Romans 12:16		
John 13:34–35		
Romans 13:8		
Romans 14:13		
Romans 14:19		
Romans 15:7		
Romans 15:14		

	God's Command	How I Can Implement It with My Mate
Galatians 5:13	_____	_____
	_____	_____
	_____	_____
Galatians 5:26	_____	_____
	_____	_____
	_____	_____
Galatians 6:2	_____	_____
	_____	_____
	_____	_____
Ephesians 4:2	_____	_____
	_____	_____
	_____	_____
Ephesians 4:25	_____	_____
	_____	_____
	_____	_____
Ephesians 4:32	_____	_____
	_____	_____
	_____	_____
Colossians 3:9	_____	_____
	_____	_____
	_____	_____
Colossians 3:13	_____	_____
	_____	_____
	_____	_____

	God's Command	How I Can Implement It with My Mate
Hebrews 10:24	_____	_____
	_____	_____
	_____	_____
James 4:11	_____	_____
	_____	_____
	_____	_____
James 5:16	_____	_____
	_____	_____
	_____	_____
1 Peter 4:9	_____	_____
	_____	_____
	_____	_____
1 Peter 5:5	_____	_____
	_____	_____
	_____	_____
1 John 1:7	_____	_____
	_____	_____
	_____	_____

10

YOUR SPOUSE, A PRIORITY

In 2 Timothy 3:16–17, Paul wrote, "All Scripture is inspired by God and profitable for teaching, for reproof, for correction, for training in righteousness; so that the man of God may be adequate, equipped for every good work." One of the good works for which God desires to equip us is that of being the kind of spouses that He has designed us to be. That equipping, as Paul pointed out, takes place through the Scripture—by studying, understanding, and applying the Word of God to our lives. God's blueprint for marriage is revealed in His Word, and so it is to the Word that we again turn to explore the second *P* in remaining sweethearts for a lifetime: being committed to the *priority* of the marriage relationship.

The book of Ephesians provides a good picture of the order of importance in which our relationships should be. Chapters 1 to 3 talk about our highest priority: our relationship with the Lord. In chapters 4 through 6, Paul explains how we should relate to the different people in our lives. After giving some general principles for interpersonal relationships in chapter 4 and the beginning of chapter 5, Paul gets very specific about the most important relationships. Starting in Ephesians 5:22, Paul gives some guidelines for the husband–wife relationship. This is followed by commands for the parent–child relationship (6:1–4) and then, finally, for relationships between employees and employers in the workplace (6:5–9).

Paul uses this deliberate ordering to emphasize that the most important human relationship one has is with one's mate. After God, marriage is first, children are second, and work is third. We know that this order is deliberate because Paul repeats it in both Colossians and 1 Timothy. In 1 Timothy, Paul includes this ordering in the qualifications for church leadership. He begins by writing: "An overseer, then, must be above reproach, the husband of one wife" (1 Tim. 3:2). In verse 4, he mentions children, and finally, in verses 6–7, he talks about relationships with other people.

When Paul wrote "the husband of one wife," he was not primarily talking about being monogamous or not being divorced. By including this in the context of church leadership qualifications, Paul was emphasizing the fact that men who desire leadership roles are to be to their wives everything that God desires them to be because they will be examples to other men in the church. How they love, lead, and serve their wives will be observed by others and must be above reproach. Pastors and elders do not just verbalize the Word of God; they exemplify it by their lives as well.

This passage indicates that if a man is not properly relating to his wife, he has no business being a part of the teaching and leading ministry of the church. This is important because it shows us how vital the marriage relationship is. It is not that Paul was holding pastors and elders to a higher standard of conduct than that for other men in the church, but rather he was pointing out to all men how supremely important their relationship to their wives is. Because it is so important, pastors and elders should be visible, exemplary examples for the church in this matter.

Other passages in Scripture refer to the supremacy of the marriage relationship as well. In Titus 2:4, Paul said that older, godly women should "encourage the young women to love their husbands, to love their children . . ." Again, the marriage relationship comes first. In Genesis 2:24, when God established marriage, He said, "For this reason a man shall leave his father and his mother, and be joined to his wife; and they shall become one flesh." This command makes it clear that the husband–wife relationship takes precedence over the parent–child relationship because children are told to leave their parents, be joined to their mates, and become one flesh. Nowhere in Scripture are spouses ever commanded to leave each other.

LEAVING FATHER AND MOTHER

In his book *Solving Marriage Problems*, Jay Adams wrote, "Perhaps the most difficult of all relationships to deal with is the in-law relationship. It's true that you marry the family. Unlike other situations, you cannot simply avoid your in-laws."[1] Indeed, all the way back in Genesis, the Bible shows us that in-law relationships can cause problems for couples. Jacob had difficulties with his father-in-law, Laban (Gen. 31), and also with his brother Esau and his wife (Gen. 27:46).

God, the Author of marriage, anticipated this difficulty. He knew that the matter of leaving father and mother would be difficult, and so He included a command regarding this aspect of marriage in His very first statement on the subject. I believe that most of us do not really understand what leaving father and mother entails. In my experience as a counselor, I have found that though most people would deny that they have any problems in this area, the matter of leaving is one of the most significant and problematic in marriage relationships.

Leaving father and mother is a very broad concept that involves far more than most people think. Before we discuss what leaving *does* mean, let me point out two things that leaving does *not* mean. First, leaving father and mother does not mean that adult children stop honoring their parents. There is no time qualification in the fifth commandment. It does not mean that married children should stop listening to their parents, either. Proverbs 23:22 warns against this: "Listen to your father who begot you, and do not despise your mother when she is old." And in Mark 7, Jesus rebuked the Pharisees for finding ways to avoid honoring or caring for their parents.

Second, leaving father and mother does not simply mean moving out of the parents' house. Children can move three or three thousand miles away from their parents and still not have really left them as God intended. In fact, parents may even be dead, yet their children have not left them. After preaching on this subject some time ago, I was approached by a sixty-five-year-old man who had been married to his wife for forty years. He said to me, "I understand now why my wife and I have had so many problems in our relationship. My wife has never really left her mother and father." Though his wife's parents were long dead, the fact that she had never truly left them was still causing problems in their marriage. In my years of counseling, I have encountered this problem many times.

What leaving *does* mean is that certain aspects of the parent–child relationship before marriage must be put off after marriage. (The concepts of putting on and putting off will be explained in the next chapters.) This principle applies to both parents and children alike. Some of these aspects are fairly obvious and some are not. At the same time, certain other things must be put on in terms of the parent–child relationship after marriage. It is vitally important, for the sake of attaining and maintaining a godly marriage relationship, that young couples (the ones who are leaving) and older couples (the ones who are letting them leave) rightly understand this concept of leaving father and mother.

APPLICATION AND DISCUSSION

1. What is the scriptural basis for saying that after your relationship with God, your marriage should be a priority issue in your life?

2. Why do you think Jay Adams says that the most difficult of all relationships to deal with is the in-law relationship?

3. Study Genesis 29 to 32 and note everything you can about the relationship of Jacob with his father-in-law, Laban. How would you describe this relationship? What do you notice about the way that Jacob treated his father-in-law? What do you notice about the way that Laban treated his son-in-law? Would you say that this was a good relationship? Why or why not?

4. Study Exodus 18:1–27 and notice how Moses and his father-in-law, Jethro, related to each other. How would you describe this relationship? What do you notice about the way that Moses treated

his father-in-law? What do you notice about the way that Jethro treated his son-in-law? Would you say that this was a good relationship? Why or why not?

5. What is meant by the statement in this chapter that leaving father and mother involves more than most people think?

6. According to this chapter, what doesn't leaving father and mother mean?

7. Do you have any problems with your in-laws or parents that have affected your marriage relationship?

8. What are the common mistakes that in-laws (children and parents, brothers-in-law, sisters-in-law, etc.) make?

9. What advice would you give to someone about the way that married people should relate to their parents or in-laws?

10. What should and should not characterize the relationship of married people with their parents or in-laws?

11

LEAVING INVOLVES
PUTTING OFF

To leave father and mother, as God intends, involves both putting off and putting on certain things in terms of the parent–child relationship. I want to focus first on the putting-off aspects of this concept.

First, we must leave behind an inordinate dependency relationship with our parents when we get married. Growing up, all children have a legitimate, appropriate dependence on their parents. Babies can do virtually nothing for themselves and depend on their parents for everything. My three-month-old granddaughter spends most of her day either eating or sleeping, but she cannot get herself into bed or get food for herself. She depends on her parents to change her, fix her food, and feed it to her. But as children get older, they learn to do more and more things for themselves and become less dependent. When we get married, we leave that kind of dependence behind.

A woman once told my wife that even though her mother was dead, she still thought constantly about what her mother would say or do in certain situations. When she went shopping, she would think about whether or not her mother would approve of what she had bought. If she thought that her mother would not approve of some behavior, she usually would not do it. If she did it anyway, she would feel very guilty about it. That type of life is parent-centered and demonstrates that this woman has never really left her mother.

Leaving also means that we must put off the natural, imitative, or reactionary relationship that we have with our parents. In other words, we should not do things automatically the same way that our parents did just because that is what we are used to. On the other hand, we must not automatically do things differently just to be different. I have met people who have said things such as, "My parents always made me go to Sunday school and I hated it, so I'm not making my kids go." Not liking something that our parents made us do is not, in itself, a valid reason for not doing it ourselves.

This means that we must be prepared to examine the things that we do to see whether they are biblical and to determine whether they are pleasing to God and beneficial for our family. Is something we're doing commanded in Scripture? Is it an issue of preference? Is it best for our family? These are questions that should be asked and carefully answered. Doing something or not doing something simply because it is the way our parents always did it is not a legitimate reason and does not demonstrate proper leaving of father and mother as God commanded.

Another aspect of leaving is putting off an inordinate reliance on our parents' approval for our security and happiness in life. Some people, even as adults, are devastated if their parents do not agree with them or approve of what they are doing. In a similar vein, leaving our parents means that we are more concerned with fulfilling our mates' desires than we are with meeting our parents' desires. I have heard a number of women say something like this: "If his mother wants him to do something, he goes right over and does it, but if I need something done, forget it." Being more concerned with what our parents think than with what our mates think is not leaving father and mother as God intended.

Leaving father and mother also involves putting off a close and exclusive confidence with our parents. In other words, our parents should not be the only ones that we share all our secrets with anymore. Many, many times in my counseling experience I have encountered situations in which the wife shares everything with her mother—any little difficulty with her husband, anything he did or did not do that she thought he should or shouldn't have done—and then wonders why her mother has such a bad opinion of her husband. I am sure that there are men who share this problem as well, but this aspect of leaving parents seems to be especially a problem with some women. Spouses who do this have not truly left father and mother as God has commanded.

Leaving our parents means being willing to give up our traditions regarding family structure and function, if those traditions are not commanded by Scripture. For example, my wife and I were raised in very different types of families. I grew up on a farm with parents who had very little education. My wife's parents were very well educated (her father was a lawyer and a professor of law in a law school), and their family structure was quite different from mine. When we got married, we discovered that although both of our fathers had been the heads of their homes, the different ways in which our fathers had exercised their leadership informed our individual ideas of headship and submission in the family.

From the beginning, we both agreed that I ought to be the head of the home and that Carol should be in submission to me. Without knowing it, however, our definitions of leading and submitting had been influenced not only by Scripture, but also by the ways that our parents did things. Over time, we came to see that not all of our ideas were as biblical as we had first thought or pretended them to be. And so we had to carefully reexamine our family structure—how we related to each other, how we raised our children, how we made decisions, how we handled conflicts, how we communicated, how we spent our money, etc.—in light of God's Word.

Even something as seemingly minor as vacations was something that we had to work through together. Until I was married, I never took a vacation in my life. Farm families worked all the time, most days of the year. We took a little time off on Christmas morning, but then we went back to work. In Carol's family, vacation was a family ritual. Because her father taught in law school for many years, they often spent their summers in the Pocono Mountains. While her father taught a law-review course, the rest of the family enjoyed a relaxing vacation.

As a result, Carol's perspective on taking time off was much different from mine. When we went on vacations together, my suitcase was full of books. To me, it just seemed wrong to relax and enjoy spending time with my family because all I knew from my childhood was work. We had to work through this issue and many other areas of family structure to determine what we were going to do in our family based on the Word of God, not on what our parents had done.

Another aspect of leaving is putting off the tendency to play the blame game. As long as we are blaming our parents for our deficiencies—not enough love, encouragement, opportunities, material goods, etc.—we are not leaving them as God intended. A related aspect is leaving behind all the bitterness and resentment we have carried with us from childhood. No parents are perfect in the way that they raise their children, and we must be willing to be tenderhearted and forgiving as Christ commanded. If we carry anger or resentment toward our parents with us into marriage, we are not leaving them as God intended.

APPLICATION
AND DISCUSSION

1. Review this chapter and list everything that it says is included in the putting-off aspect of leaving.
2. Have you and your mate ever had a conflict between the two of you because of the way in which you or your spouse was relating to your parents or in-laws?
3. How is it possible to continue to be tied to your parents in an unbiblical way even though they are dead or live many miles away?
4. Have either of you ever thought that the other person was more devoted to and more concerned about his or her parents than about you?
5. Evaluate yourself and your mate in terms of how well you have accomplished the putting-off aspects of leaving. Use this rating scale: Excellent; couldn't be better = 4; Good, but needs a little

fine-tuning = 3; Fair; needs some changes = 2; Poor; needs many changes = 1; Terrible; couldn't be worse = 0.

6. Are there ways in which you need to make some changes in the putting-off aspect of leaving? What are they?

7. What can you do to improve your relationship with your mate by changing the way in which you relate to your parents or in-laws?

12

LEAVING INVOLVES
PUTTING ON

In the Bible, change is always a two-step process. It always involves putting some things off and putting other things on. The Bible teaches us that when we are saved, we must put off the ways of the flesh and put on the fruits of the Spirit. We have discussed the things that need to be put off in terms of leaving father and mother. What things do we then need to put on?

First, leaving our parents means putting on a peer relationship with them. This replaces the dependency relationship that we had as children, which we are to put off. As we become friends with our parents, we begin to contribute to their lives as they continue to contribute to ours. For example, when not doing seminars or teaching elsewhere, my wife and I attend Grace Fellowship Church of the Lehigh Valley and assist our youngest son, Josh, who is pastor there. When at home, I also function as a pastor working with him. My wife and I respect him greatly and are receiving great benefit from him as he teaches us the Word of God. When we have an issue that we are wrestling with, we go to our son and receive counsel from him. We relate to one another as peers now because he is no longer under our authority.

Leaving father and mother also involves accepting responsibility for making our own decisions. We have put off the need for our parents' approval, the tendency to imitate them out of habit, and the former submission to their desires so that we can now examine our choices in light of God's Word for ourselves. Though there is still a place for our parents' counsel—they should remain advisers and resources to us throughout our lives—our decisions must now be made because we are sure that they are what God wants for our family. Leaving means that we learn to look at our parents objectively, evaluate their strengths and weaknesses, and love them anyway because God has given them to us.

Another aspect of leaving means putting on the willingness to honestly and respectfully discuss our family backgrounds with our mates without becoming defensive. As we have already discussed, family history has an impact on us as adults and on our expectations in marriage. When I do premarital counseling, I do a Family of Origin study with the couple so that they have the opportunity to work through and evaluate their family backgrounds together. Taking some time to do this before marriage helps young people to avoid major problems later because they already know about and have dealt with some of the things that can cause friction.

Leaving father and mother also means putting on a determination to make one's mate, rather than one's parents or anyone else, the most significant person in one's life. And finally, one must be prepared to treat the parents of one's mate with the same respect and honor as one treats one's own parents. When two people get married, they each gain a new set of parents—that is part of becoming one flesh. As they put off the exclusive parent–child relationship that they had with their own parents, they each must at the same time put on a proper and appropriate peer relationship with the mate's parents that places them on equal footing with the child's own parents.

Leaving father and mother as God intends is not a simple thing to do, as we can now see. It involves consciously—and with a concerted effort—doing many things that will help us to develop the type of relationship that God desires adult children to have with their parents. It is vitally important, however, that we be diligent about fulfilling God's first command to married people. God, who is the Author of marriage, knew from the beginning that the issue of leaving parents would be crucial to the success of the marriage relationship in the long run.

PRACTICAL GUIDELINES FOR LEAVING

How do we successfully implement the leaving process after we get married? First, I always tell young people that they must never allow their parents to demean their mate. If a mother, for example, accuses her daughter's husband of some wrongdoing, that daughter has a responsibility to respond to her mother by saying, "God says I am to reverence and respect my husband. If you have a problem with something he has done, you need to go and talk to him about it privately, as the Bible commands." On the other hand, a husband or wife must be very careful to never complain to his or her parents about the spouse because this can make it difficult for parents to love and respect their child's spouse as they should. In all things regarding their parents, husbands and wives should talk together and make mutual decisions about how they—as one flesh—will relate to them.

Second, one should always look for ways to commend and build up one's mate to one's parents. This means that, without being dishonest, one should look for every opportunity to extol the mate's virtues and avoid talking about negative things to one's parents. Since a married child's parents know the child better than they know the mate, they will get much of their opinion and regard for the mate from what they hear the child say. It is the child's responsibility to see that his or her parents' love and respect for the mate grows over time, to the extent that the child is able.

Third, the husband or wife should always make an effort to be sure that his or her mate feels included in family discussions and activities. Sometimes, without a spouse's even realizing it, his or her mate is left out when the family gets together. I have seen this happen on a number of occasions. The in-law is ignored in the conversation, which often revolves around "inside" family information. Being one flesh means that the husband and wife should function as a team in all things. This may require a concerted, special effort on the part of the biological child when his or her spouse is with the child's own family.

Fourth, it is important for the husband and wife to decide together what course of action to take when problems arise with a parent. Whatever the issue, it should be first taken before the Lord in prayer; then, if appropriate, counsel from another person may be sought out. When a decision has been made about how to handle the situation, we ought to respectfully go to our parent or parents and discuss it with them. If they disagree with us, we must also be ready to handle the conflict in a mature way, allowing them the right to their own opinion. Unless we are able to put these things into practice, we will still be functioning as children who have not left our parents.

APPLICATION AND DISCUSSION

1. Review this chapter and list everything that it says is included in the putting-on aspect of leaving.

2. Have you and your mate ever had a conflict between the two of you because you thought that the other person was not putting on something mentioned in this chapter?

3. What does and doesn't it mean to have a peer relationship with your parents? What is and isn't true in a peer relationship?

4. Evaluate yourself and your mate in terms of how well you have accomplished the putting-on aspects of leaving described in this chapter. Use this rating scale: Excellent; couldn't be better = 4; Good, but needs a little fine-tuning = 3; Fair; needs some changes = 2; Poor; needs many changes = 1; Terrible; couldn't be worse = 0.

5. Are there ways in which you need to make some changes in the putting-on aspect of leaving? What are they?

6. What can you do to improve your relationship with your mate by changing the putting-on aspects of the way in which you relate to your parents or in-laws?

7. Think of all the ways in which your families of origin were alike and all the ways they were different.

8. Discuss the ways in which the similarities have been of help to your relationship.

9. Discuss the ways in which the differences may have caused difficulties in your relationship.

13

THE PARENTS' SIDE
OF LEAVING

In the last chapter, we considered what it means for couples to leave mother and father and then drew out some of the practical implications for actually accomplishing this important biblical directive. In this chapter, we will discuss the flip side of the leaving endeavor by suggesting some practical guidelines for parents whose children have married and left the home geographically. These guidelines when followed can be very helpful in smoothing out the biblically commanded leaving process for married children.

I think it is very interesting that God made this statement about leaving father and mother to a couple who had neither children nor parents. What was His intention in giving Adam and Eve a directive that they could not immediately put into practice? I believe that God made this statement to them because He knew that they were going to have children and it would be their responsibility to teach them about marriage. It would be very important for Adam and Eve, as the first parents, both to model a godly marriage relationship and to allow and encourage their children to leave them and establish their own families.

In terms of a couple's letting their children leave them, first each spouse must make sure that the relationship with the other spouse is the primary, fundamental relationship in his or her life. This must be true both before and after the children have left home. Second, as they raise their children, they should be preparing themselves for the time when the children will leave. I have counseled women who had become depressed because the last child had left the house. They were so wrapped up in the lives of their children that when their children left, their purpose and meaning in life left as well. This occurred because they had not properly prepared themselves for this eventuality in life.

Third, parents must prepare and train their children for leaving. As they grow older, they should be expected to take more and more responsibility for their decisions and actions. Parents who make all the decisions for their children effectively cripple them. As a rule, parents should try to never make decisions for their children that their children are capable of making for themselves. What parents do need to do, however, is to teach them how to make decisions. Even when children are young, we should use every opportunity to teach them biblical principles for decision-making.

When we were living in Louisiana, one of my sons announced that he wanted to buy a dirt bike. Apparently, many of the other boys he knew were getting dirt bikes, and so he wanted one, too. So I said to him, "Okay, how are you going to decide whether or not you are going to buy a dirt bike?" I did not say "yes" or "no" to him because I thought this would be a good opportunity to teach him about decision-making.

I told my son that he and I should both think about it some. I also reminded him that I always wanted him to do everything to the glory of God, as 1 Corinthians 10:31 commands. I said that this means that whenever I have a decision to make, I evaluate the situation—small and large alike—in terms of whether or not it will help me glorify God. I asked him to think about whether a dirt bike would meet that criterion because the verse says, "Whether, then, you eat or drink *or whatever you do*, do all to the glory of God." As a "whatever you do," buying and owning a dirt bike is clearly governed by this command.

In order to get my son to think through this issue carefully and effectively, I asked him to make a list of ways that he could glorify God with a dirt bike and a list of possible ways that a dirt bike could hinder him from glorifying God. I wanted him to gather information and think through it properly before he made a decision. After making his list of pro and cons, he came back to me and said, "Dad, after thinking about it, I've decided that I shouldn't get a dirt bike." Without ever having to tell him no—and I probably would not have—I was able to help him make a decision not based on feelings but based on godly principles. Rather than making wise decisions for our children, we must teach them to do it for themselves.

Fourth, we must always keep in mind that our children have been lent to us by God. They are not our property. "Behold, children are a gift of the LORD, the fruit of the womb is a reward" (Ps. 127:3). Every time we look at our children, we ought to remind ourselves that they do not belong to us. There would be far less child abuse in this world if more parents really understood the fact that their children belong to God and that they are not entitled to their children or anything from them. Because they are only on loan to us, our relationship with them must change dramatically when they marry or reach a marrying age.

Fifth, we must be careful to give our children the right to respectfully disagree with us without being hurt or angry with them and without punishing them. On issues with no clear "thus saith the Lord," we should allow our children the right to disagree with us. And even if there is a clear commandment, we can allow them to disagree and then teach them why they are wrong without being overbearing or nasty. As parents, we ought to take these opportunities to help our children grow in wisdom, both by prayer and by demonstration.

For example, when one child wrongs another, the parents should explain to that child that he or she has sinned against God and against his or her brother or sister. Because of this, the child ought to pray and ask God for forgiveness and ought to apologize and ask his or her sibling for forgiveness as well. I do not believe, however, that it is of any value to force the offending child to go through the charade of saying that he is sorry when he really is not. If he is not sorry, it is an indication that he has not reached the point of even understanding or admitting that what he did was wrong. Helping him to grow in wisdom regarding his sin is far more important (and difficult) than simply forcing an obligatory "I'm sorry" out of him.

Sixth, parents should help a child leave by accepting their child's mate as an equal to their own child. In other words, parents should not be thinking about "my daughter" and "my son-in-law" in different categories of love and respect. When a child gets married, the family grows and parents must be willing to love, respect, and treat that new child as an equal to their biological child. I have no less regard for my daughters-in-law than I do for my own daughter, and Lord willing, if my daughter gets married someday, I want to look on her husband with the same regard that I do my own sons because they have become one flesh.

Seventh, we ought to seek to develop a proper peer relationship with our adult children. This means that our influence on our adult children ceases to include commands or demands and instead comes entirely by our example and, when asked, through limited counsel and advice. When our children do something that we do not approve of or agree with, we ought to make every effort to make our lives a model to them and to lift them up in prayer. We can ask God to cause them to be willing to ask us for advice, but we should never push our opinions or convictions on them.

It means that we should be careful to never do anything, such as criticizing or nagging, that would weaken the marriage relationships of our children. Instead, we ought to look for every opportunity to praise and encourage our children's spouses. And it also means that we should be careful not to abuse the hospitality of our children any more than we would that of our friends. Parents should have the same respect for the privacy of their children as they would for anyone else they know. In all things, we should act toward them with unconditional and unselfish love, never expecting or demanding anything in return. Helping our children to properly leave us at the appropriate time is an important part of keeping our own marriage relationship a priority as God intended.

APPLICATION AND DISCUSSION

Study the following biblical passages, noting their implications to the issue of extended-family relationships and responsibilities when the children become adults.

1. The passages in this section describe how the relationship and responsibilities change; identify what these verses teach about how marriage changes parent–child relationships.

   Genesis 2:24–25   Luke 2:41–45

   Mark 3:31–35   John 2:1–5

2. The passages in this section describe the continuing relationship and responsibilities; identify what these verses teach about continuing parent–child responsibilities after marriage occurs.

   Genesis 47:11–12   Proverbs 28:24

   Exodus 20:12   Proverbs 29: 3

   Exodus 21:15, 17   Proverbs 30:17

   Leviticus 19:3   Proverbs 31: 1–31

   Leviticus 20:9   Isaiah 49:15

   Deuteronomy 24:16   Ezekiel 18:19

   Deuteronomy 27:16   Micah 7:6

   Psalm 68:6   Malachi 1:6

   Psalm 103:13   Malachi 4: 4–6

   Proverbs 1:8, 9   Mark 5:19

   Proverbs 3:1, 2   Mark 7:6–13

   Proverbs 4:1–7:27 (Notice the words "my son" and what the son is being advised to do—notice also from the Proverbs 5:15–22 and other passages that the son may be a married person.)

   Proverbs 10:1–5   Luke 1:17

   Proverbs 15:20–27   John 1: 26–27

   Proverbs 17:6   1 Corinthians 4:14–17

   Proverbs 17:21   2 Corinthians 6:11–13

   Proverbs 17:25   Philippians 2:19–22

   Proverbs 19:13–14   1 Timothy 5: 1–10

Proverbs 23:22–28   2 Timothy 1:5

Proverbs 28: 7   Titus 2:3, 4

3. The passages in this section describe the general relationship and responsibility of believers to other believers. The point being that if believers have these responsibilities to others who are not part of the nuclear or extended family, how much more do we have similar responsibilities to our parents even if we are married?

Genesis 4:9   Ephesians 4:1–3

Genesis 4:9   Ephesians 4:25–5:2

Leviticus 19:32   Philippians 2:1–9

Proverbs 17:17   Colossians 3:8–15

Proverbs 18:24   1 Thessalonians 4:9

Romans 12:10   1 Thessalonians 5:11

Romans 12:16   1 Thessalonians 5:14–15

Romans 13:7–8   Hebrews 13:1–3

Romans 15:1–2   1 Peter 1:22

Romans 15:14   1 Peter 3:8

1 Corinthians 12:25–26   1 Peter 4:8–9

1 Corinthians 13:1–13   1 Peter 5:5–6

2 Corinthians 12:28–30   1 John 3: 16–17

Galatians 6: 1–2   2 John 4

Galatians 6:10   3 John 1–4

14

OTHER TYPES OF LEAVING

Leaving father and mother is an important part of establishing and maintaining a godly marriage. But other types of leaving must take place in order for marriage to be the priority that God desires it to be. In 1 Corinthians 7:33–34, Paul implied that marriage requires some major changes in our focus in life. In discussing the things that single people are free to do for the Lord, he intimated that married people must be focused largely on their relationship to each other.

When a person gets married, that person must leave behind anything that will keep him or her from becoming totally one with his or her spouse. One of these things is the previous identification as a single person. We have to train ourselves to stop thinking and talking in terms of "I" and "me" and start thinking and talking in terms of "we" and "us." When a married person fails to do this, it is an indication that he or she is still trying to carve out a niche for himself or herself as an individual. If marriage is a person's chief priority relationship, his or her independence in all things—time, money, friendships, desires, work, recreation, and the like—must be left behind. There is no room for "only me" in "one flesh."

How Are We Doing?

Take some time to think through the following questions as a means of evaluating how you are doing in this area of leaving. Then after you've made your evaluation, ask your spouse for his or her perspective on each of these questions and have your spouse give you the reasons for answering as he or she did. Make sure that you listen without interruption, without defensiveness, without excuse-making, without argumentation. Just listen and learn all you can about your mate's perspective, and then seek to change in whatever way would be in keeping with God's will for your marriage relationship.

1. Who means more to me: my spouse, my children, my parents, or my friends?

2. What means more to me: talking with my spouse or talking with someone else?

3. What means more to me: my spouse's opinion or someone else's opinion?

4. What means more to me: meeting my own desires or meeting the desires of my spouse?

5. Which would I rather do: pray with my spouse or pray in church/Bible study/by myself?

6. What means more to me: spending time with my spouse or spending time at work/hobbies/church activities?

7. What means more to me: the respect and appreciation of my spouse or that of my boss, parents, friends, or others?

8. What means more to me: my spouse's displeasure or disapproval or that of someone else?

9. In addition to thinking through these questions, I suggest that you seek out other ideas for improvement in the form of some good books on the subject of marriage. Proverbs 15:10 instructs us that "he who hates reproof will die," so it is important that we constantly search for ways to be corrected if we want to keep the marriage relationship alive and healthy.

In my book *Preparing for Marriage God's Way*,[1] I have an assignment called the In-Law Inventory. There are two parts to this exercise; one is designed for couples to evaluate how they are doing in terms of their relationship with their parents, and the other is designed for parents to evaluate their relationship with their married children. Also, chapter 1 of my book *Strengthening Your Marriage* is all about the principle of leaving, cleaving, and weaving in the marriage relationship. It would be a good Bible study for couples to do together.

10. Finally, you and your spouse need to sit down and discuss whether or not your marriage is the priority that it ought to be and how to go about making needed improvements and changes. Good communication is a key to a meaningful relationship. Studying these things that I've previously mentioned is a good first step, but it is only a first step. Following God's blueprint for marriage involves much effort, but the reward—a happy and secure marriage that lasts a lifetime—is far greater.

15

PURITY IS ESSENTIAL

I n 1953, the well-known sex researcher Alfred Kinsey reported that, according to his data, fifty percent of men and twenty-five percent of women admitted to having had extramarital affairs. That controversial report was published over fifty years ago, but more recent surveys indicate that the problem has only worsened. Sherry Hite, a modern sex researcher, claims that her findings reveal that sixty-six percent of men have had extramarital affairs. Recent political sex scandals in our nation's capital have prompted speculation that nearly half of the members of Congress have been involved in affairs outside of their marriage.

Other, much-publicized statistics agree with these figures. It is generally thought that as many as two out of three men and one out of two women have been unfaithful to their spouse at some time during their marriage. According to a survey by *Redbook* magazine, thirty percent of women admitted to affairs, and eighty-seven percent of those women admitted to having had premarital sex. Married women in the workplace were more likely to have affairs than were women who worked only at home. And nonreligious wives were twice as likely as strongly religious wives to cheat on their spouses. Some researchers predict that in time, fifty percent of all women will have engaged in extramarital sex.

All of this is in spite of the fact that another survey reports eighty-six percent of those questioned as believing that extramarital affairs are always or almost always wrong. Another eleven percent said that special circumstances must be considered, and only three percent said that affairs are never wrong. Apparently, what we say that we believe and what we do are often worlds apart.

Clearly, we are living in a time when impurity runs rampant. Sex, sex, sex . . . our culture is near the point of total saturation, and the cesspool is beginning to overflow. Books, magazines, television, movies, and billboards all display sex in living color because sex gets the ratings. It is the recurring theme in nearly every corner of the media. It is not a bit surprising that one of today's most popular television shows, *Desperate Housewives*, is centered on the salacious lives of a handful of unfaithful married men and women.

The fact that sexual immorality and impurity so pervades our culture should not actually come as much of a surprise to us. The Bible has much to say about sexual immorality almost from the beginning. The New Testament alone contains directives and warnings on this subject in nearly every book because sexual immorality was rampant in the culture of that day. Though we tend to think that things are much worse today than ever before, Ecclesiastes 1:9 is proved true in this area as well: "That which has been is that which will be, and that which has been done is that which will be done. So there is nothing new under the sun."

The fact that the Bible is filled with passages dealing with sexual immorality tells us two things. One, God knew from the very beginning that sexual immorality would be a problem for us; and two, God takes this sin very seriously. In 1 Corinthians 6:16, Paul used part of Genesis 2:24, "the two shall become one flesh," in the context of commands regarding sexual immorality. Throughout Scripture, God makes it very clear that we are to be sexually pure, and especially so in marriage.

Hebrews 13:4 has this to say: "Marriage is to be held in honor among all, and the marriage bed is to be undefiled; for fornicators and adulterers God will judge." The word that is translated "marriage bed" in this verse is the Greek word *koitus*, which refers to sexual intercourse. The writer of Hebrews was saying that God hates sexual immorality both within marriage (adultery) and outside of marriage (fornication).

Of the Ten Commandments, two refer to sexual immorality: "You shall not commit adultery," and "You shall not covet your . . . neighbor's wife" (Ex. 20:14, 17). Wives are specifically commanded in 1 Peter 3:1–2 to be chaste, which includes the idea of sexual purity. And husbands are told in Proverbs 5:15–18: "Drink water from your own cistern and fresh water from your own well . . . Let your fountain be blessed, and rejoice in the wife of your youth."

As we mentioned in the last chapter, sexual purity is part of being one flesh as God has commanded married people to be. So the third *P* to which we must commit ourselves in order to have God's kind of marriage is *purity* in the marriage relationship.

ASPECTS OF PURITY

Purity has several facets. First, there must be a commitment to sexual purity in our behavior. Husbands and wives must be careful what they do not only with their sexual organs but also with their hands, feet, eyes, and ears. In other words, purity should characterize everything done with the physical body. In Colossians 3:5, Paul wrote, "Therefore consider the members of your earthly body as dead to immorality . . ." The word translated "immorality" here is the Greek word *porneia*, which refers to any sexual activity outside of marriage.

The only place for men and women to find sexual satisfaction is within the marriage relationship, and anything else is a serious sin. As evidence of this truth, we can look to the Old Testament, where we find that only two types of sins merited capital punishment. One was murder and the other was sexual immorality. Few of us regard sexual sin as abhorrent as murder, but God clearly does.

I remember when a friend of mine in California found out that his brother, who lived on the East Coast, was involved in an adulterous affair. My friend got on a plane and flew out to see his brother. As they were talking, he asked his brother if he knew how serious his sin with this woman was. His brother, who had previously professed to be a Christian, replied that he didn't think it was very serious. My friend then said to his brother, "You know, if we were living in Old Testament times, instead of walking around with you today, I'd be attending a funeral and the funeral would have been yours. If we were living in Old Testament times, Scripture indicates that you could have been stoned to death for what you're doing." Because sexual immorality is so grievous a sin to God, we must be vigilant in maintaining our physical purity.

Second, a commitment to purity includes purity in our thoughts. The Bible has much to say about our inner selves. Proverbs 4:23 warns us, "Watch over your heart with all diligence, for from it flow the springs of life." Romans 12:2 indicates that God is concerned with our thoughts because He says that we are to be transformed by the renewing of our minds. Second Corinthians 10:3–5 commands us to bring every thought into captivity and make it obedient to Jesus Christ. And Psalm 19:14 includes this prayer: "Let the . . . meditation of my heart be acceptable in Your sight, O LORD . . ."

Going back to Colossians 3:5, Paul said to consider ourselves dead to "immorality, *impurity*." Impurity refers to sinful thoughts. Fantasizing, looking at pornography, and other sexual sins of the mind are as serious as actual immoral behaviors, not perhaps in their social consequences, but in their heinousness before God. Some may think that doing may be wrong, but that merely thinking immorality is in a different category. In His Sermon on the Mount (Matt. 5:21–30), Jesus who is God manifest in the flesh, declares that this is not so. According to Him, the person who looks on a woman in a salacious way and lusts after her in his heart is guilty of immorality.

In our day, the Internet is a source of particular temptation because it provides easy, cheap, and often anonymous access to pornography. Until I put a blocker on my computer, my e-mail account was bombarded daily with pornographic offers and solicitations. It is difficult for many people, Christians included, to avoid sexual sin when it is no more than a simple mouse-click away. When I was teaching at The Master's College, we found out that a few male students were using the computers to look at pornography. Because Master's takes this type of thing so seriously, these men were immediately told that they had to get into a counseling program or be expelled from the college.

Recently, when I was preaching on this subject in Mississippi, a man came up to me afterward and said, "I almost didn't come this afternoon, but I decided to come and I'm so glad I did because you spoke about an issue that I've been struggling with for many years." This man was probably in his sixties, a professing Christian, a church member, and married. We may think that this kind of sin is the province of social outcasts and pedophiles, but the truth is that it is all around us. Husbands and wives must be constantly on their guard against this sin and committed to purity in their thoughts.

Third, we must commit to purity in our affections and desires. Paul exhorts us in Galatians 5:16: "But I say, walk by the Spirit, and you will not carry out the desire of the flesh." One "desire of the flesh" is the desire for sexual immorality. Galatians 5:24 continues, "Now those who belong to Christ Jesus have crucified the flesh with its passions and desires."

APPLICATION
AND DISCUSSION[1]

1. Why should the fact that sexual immorality is running rampant in our society not come as a surprise to people who know their Bibles?

2. How many of the Ten Commandments refer to sexual immorality? Which ones?

3. What are some of the aspects of sexual purity that are mentioned in this chapter?

4. What commitments described in this chapter must we make if we are going to remain sexually pure?

5. Have you made these commitments? Which of them, if any, do you have the most difficulty keeping?

6. Do you recall any specific event or events that may have affected your sex life?

7. Word-association test: when you think of sex, what word or words come to mind?

8. What was your parents' attitude about sex?

9. What did you learn from your parents about sex? Did your parents enjoy sex?

10. Did your parents talk freely to you about sex? Did you talk to your parents about your sexual concerns? Ask them questions? Were you satisfied with the answers they gave?

11. What stirs up sexual guilt or shame in you now?

12. What does the Bible say about sex? Describe it as fully as you can. What are God's purposes for sex?

13. What is proper and improper in sexual relations? What would be wrong?

14. What were your expectations regarding sex, lovemaking, and intercourse before marriage? Are these expectations being fulfilled in your marriage? If not, describe.

16

EVERY MARRIAGE NEEDS
SOME HEDGES

In Colossians 3:5, Paul referred to the importance of sexual purity when he said to consider ourselves dead to "immorality, impurity, *passion, evil desire,* and *greed . . .*" The King James Version translates "evil desire" as "inordinate affection." Whatever stirs us up to think about or participate in sexual immorality must be put to death because it is contrary to God's plan for us. That last word, *greed,* is important for us to consider because it refers to the fact that people involved in sexual sin are not satisfied. When someone is not satisfied with his or her marriage relationship and looks outside of it for sexual fulfillment, that person is being greedy, which is exactly what the tenth commandment condemns: "You shall not covet . . . your neighbor's wife . . ." (Ex. 20:17).

In the last part of Colossians 3:5, Paul added one final, important thought: "and greed, *which amounts to idolatry.*" In Ephesians 5:5, Paul said much the same thing: "For this you know with certainty, that no immoral or impure person or covetous man, *who is an idolater,* has an inheritance in the kingdom of Christ and God." Sexual immorality is a form of idolatry. In other words, sexual sin is serious because not only does it affect the other people involved, but it demonstrates that we are in rebellion against God.

When my wife and I were living in California, we always passed the largest Hindu temple in Los Angeles on the way to our church every Sunday morning. Each time I passed it and saw the hundreds of people pouring in to worship their false god, I grieved for them. It was obvious to me that these people were bowing down to an idol. Sadly, what is often not obvious is how often we Christians bow down to false gods ourselves.

According to Paul, when we become involved in sexual immorality, we are in effect shaking our fists at God and saying, "I don't care what You think! I'm going to do what I want to do! This is more important to me than honoring and glorifying You." Putting anything in our lives ahead of God and failing to submit to His commands in all areas of our lives is idolatry. If indulging in sexual sin becomes more important than obeying God, sex has become our god. Though the world may call it an addiction or the result of bad genes, God calls it idol-worship.

In Matthew 5:28–30, Jesus said that just looking at a woman lustfully was equivalent to adultery. He went on to say that this sin was so serious that "if your right eye makes you stumble, tear it out and throw it from you; for it is better for you to lose one of the parts of your body, than for your whole body to be thrown into hell." In other words, we ought to loathe sexual sin so much that we are willing to do whatever it takes, no matter how painful or difficult, to keep ourselves from it.

Consider this analogy. Temptation to sexual immorality is like a murderer who knocks at the front door. If you knew that a serial killer was knocking at our front door, would you invite him in, get him a drink, and sit down on the couch with him? If he asked to stay, would you tell him that he could hide in the basement, out of sight, while you fed him the occasional scrap? Would you really imagine that he was not there to do you mortal harm? How foolish! No one would open the door even a crack for such obvious danger.

Sexual immorality is like that serial killer. When it comes knocking, we must not think that we can invite it in for a few minutes or even talk with it briefly at the door. We must not think that we can keep it in the basement, throwing it the occasional scrap of pornography or sexual fantasy. We cannot dabble with sexual sin any more than we can dabble with a murderer. Instead, we must bolt the door, lock the windows, and do everything in our power to see that this enemy is destroyed.

Clearly, we cannot afford to kid around, play around, or rationalize with sexual sin. Nor can we minimize it. In Colossians 3, Paul concluded his statement on sexual sin this way: "For it is because of these things that the wrath of God will come upon the sons of disobedience" (3:6). God's wrath is coming against sexual immorality because it is a very serious sin.

Destroying the enemy of sexual sin requires a steadfast, rock-solid, no-exceptions commitment to sexual purity. Joseph had this type of commitment to purity, demonstrated by his reaction to Potiphar's wife in Genesis 39. When Potiphar's wife tried to lure him into sexual sin, he replied, "How then could I do this *great evil and sin against God?*" (39:9). The Scripture says that this woman tempted Joseph "day after day," but he continued to resist (39:10). One day, when the house was empty, she grabbed him. What did Joseph do? "And he left his garment in her hand and fled, and went outside" (39:12).

Joseph did exactly what Paul advised Timothy to do when tempted: "Now flee from youthful lusts . . ." (2 Tim. 2:22). When temptation comes, we cannot allow ourselves to stick around and chat for even a moment. We need to put on our track shoes and get out of there as fast as our legs will carry us. We should have the same reaction as we would if clear, immediate, mortal danger were staring us in the face—because it is. If we fail to do this, we will be like the foolish young man in Proverbs 7:

> With her many persuasions she entices him; with her flattering lips she seduces him. Suddenly he follows her as an ox goes to the slaughter, or as one in fetters to the discipline of a fool, until an arrow pierces through his liver; as a bird hastens to the snare, so he does not know that it will cost him his life. (7:21–23)

BUILDING HEDGES OF PROTECTION

In his book *Loving Your Marriage Enough to Protect It*, Jerry Jenkins wrote about the need for Christians to put up what he called "protective hedges" around themselves to keep away sexual immorality.[1] He listed several hedges that we should put up, and in the next chapter I want to add two more. The first hedge that Jenkins talked about was being careful about never spending time alone with anyone of the opposite sex, even on business, especially if it occurs more than once with the same person.

Jenkins, who was the editor of Moody Press at the time, wrote that he occasionally had to meet for business lunches with women. He made it a practice to never go to lunch with a woman unless someone else was with him. If the other person canceled, he always called his wife and let her know what had happened. As a counselor, I always make it a point to have my wife join me in counseling a woman, and I prefer that her husband be present as well if he is able. This way, there is a hedge around me and the person that I am counseling.

Another hedge that Jenkins mentioned involves being careful about how and where someone touches a person of the opposite sex. A pat on the back, a handshake, a squeeze of the arm, a hug from the side may be appropriate with certain individuals. Full and lengthy embraces, kisses on the lips, caresses, and touching in any area that could have sexual connotations should be off limits in our culture for anyone to whom the person is not married.

Among his hedges, Jenkins also recommended that a man should be very careful about giving personal compliments to women who are not related to him. It is certainly proper for a man to express appreciation for a woman's character or service to him, but he should be careful not to comment on any aspect of her appearance or shape. Compliments about acts of kindness or godly attitudes are suitable as long as the motive for giving them is not manipulative or salacious. Saying something like "I appreciate the way you help your husband" or "how you exude a love for Christ" or "the godly way you relate to your children" would be in keeping with biblical parameters. Comments about how a person looks in shorts or a swimsuit or other clothing items would be inappropriate to make to anyone but a person's spouse or a close relative.

According to Jenkins, a commitment to abstain from anything that could be considered as flirting is another hedge that we should raise. This is somewhat related to the previous hedge, but includes other types of things as well. It is inappropriate to say things such as, "I wish my wife appreciated me the way that you do," "A goddess should look so good," "You are so sexy," "Being around you makes my day," "I wish my spouse listened to me or paid attention to me the way you do," "I miss you so much when you are gone," or "I just wish I could spend more time with you." Such statements qualify as flirting and should never come out of the mouth of a married man unless they are being spoken to the woman to whom he is married.

Some flirting is fine as long as it is sincere and as long as it is aimed at a spouse. In fact, when sincere and discreetly used, as is clear from the book of Song of Solomon, flirting can serve as a positive factor in developing and sustaining the sweetheart aspect of a marriage. Both husbands and wives might learn how to appropriately flirt with their mates by studying the Song of Solomon, which is a divinely inspired version of how married people should speak to and act toward each other in the physical, sexual area of their relationship. On the other hand, a high hedge of protection should be erected, and never taken down, against doing anything that could even vaguely resemble flirting with anyone but one's mate. At all costs, the purity that is essential to fulfilling God's blueprint for marriage must be maintained.

APPLICATION
AND DISCUSSION

1. What is meant by the statement that sexual immorality is idolatry?

2. What is meant by the statement that sexual temptation is like a murderer who knocks at your door?

3. What can we learn from the example of Joseph in Genesis 39 about how to overcome sexual temptation?

4. What are some of the hedges mentioned in this chapter that Jerry Jenkins says we ought to put up to guard the sexual purity of our marriages?

5. From the beginning of time, people have struggled with the problem of lust. Because every person is born with a sinful nature (Pss. 51:5; 58:3; Mark 7:21–23), lust has always been a problem for

us. With Faithful, a character in John Bunyan's *The Pilgrim's Progress*, we have often been confronted by what Bunyan calls Wanton (*wantonness* is another name for "lust"). Perhaps, in our day, there is one difference between what most people in the United States and many other countries face and what others have encountered in the past. That difference is that because of the modern media and literature venues, we have easier access to sexual images. Being true disciples involves dealing with and overcoming the lust that is already in our hearts but is inflamed by the society in which we live.

Lust comes to us in many forms. For the married man, lust may appear in the form of focusing on getting from, not giving to, his spouse. It may come in the form of basing closeness with one's wife on lust, not love. For the single man as well as the married man, lust may involve pornography, perversion, seeking physical pleasure and self-fulfillment rather than focusing on using the body to serve the Lord and other people. This tendency, if unchecked, develops into a pattern of engaging in mental as well as physical immorality as a life-dominating sin with powerful effects on a man's walk with God.

The Bible speaks extensively about lust (Greek *epithumia*, "desire," "longing for what is forbidden," and "passionate longing"). God tells us what we need to know about lust and how to have victory over it. And since lust is such a common problem, even among those who are disciples of Jesus Christ, we encourage you to carefully and prayerfully study the following verses that deal with the subject. Then complete the assignment at the end of the list. If sexual lust is a problem, I also encourage you to keep a lust journal, noting when you are tempted, what is happening when you're tempted, what you're thinking when you're tempted, what you want that you're not getting when you're tempted, what you think God would say about what you're being tempted to do, what you actually choose to do, and what you should do to overcome your lust until the pattern of your life has become righteousness. Commit yourself to turning and going the other direction. With the help of God's Spirit and His Word, you can have victory in this vital aspect of life.

Reflect on and discuss the meaning of these important biblical facts about temptation and lust:[2]

Matthew 5:27–28	"You have heard that it was said, 'You shall not commit adultery'; but I say to you that everyone who looks at a woman with lust for her has already committed adultery with her in his heart."
Romans 6:12	Therefore do not let sin reign in your mortal body so that you obey its lusts . . .
1 Corinthians 6:19–20	Or do you not know that your body is a temple of the Holy Spirit who is in you, whom you have from God, and that you are not your own? For you have been bought with a price: therefore glorify God in your body.
1 Thessalonians 4:3, 7–8	For this is the will of God, your sanctification; that is, that you abstain from sexual immorality . . . For God has not called us for the purpose of impurity, but in sanctification. So, he who rejects this is not rejecting man but the God who gives His Holy Spirit to you.
James 1:13–14	Let no one say when he is tempted, "I am being tempted by God"; for God cannot be tempted by evil, and He Himself does not tempt anyone. But each one is tempted when he is carried away and enticed by his own lust.
1 Peter 1:14–15	As obedient children, do not be conformed to the former lusts which were yours in your ignorance, but like the Holy One who called you, be holy yourselves also in all your behavior . . .

Since these facts are true, what wrong things must you not allow yourself to think and with what ideas must you fill your mind so that you can maintain the sexual purity of your marriage in keeping with God's blueprint? Make complete lists.

_____

_____

_____

_____

_____

_____

_____

_____

_____

_____

_____

_____

_____

_____

_____

_____

_____

_____

_____

_____

17

MORE ABOUT HEDGES

A commitment to sexual purity is an indispensable requirement for any couple who want to remain sweethearts for a lifetime. But what does that commitment involve? In the last chapter we mentioned four key elements of that commitment. Review them. In this chapter, we will mention several more key facilitators for enhancing your marriage through sexual purity. One practice I heartily recommend to couples who want an "A" kind of marriage is the frequent review and reflection on their marriage vows. My wife and I have an audiotape of our wedding service, and we used to listen to it together on our anniversary each year. Going to other people's weddings and attending marriage seminars are also good ways to reflect on the meaning of marriage and rededicate ourselves to our spouses. Along with that, we must spend both quality and quantity time with our spouses, continuing to cultivate the friendship we have with them. Building and sustaining good relationships takes a lot of weeding and cultivating and growth time.

A number of years ago, when I was teaching some missionaries in Europe about biblical counseling, my wife and I received a telephone call informing us that one of our good friends had just left his wife. This man was chairman of the deacons' board at his church, taught in the church, and was well versed in theology and Scripture. After speaking with his wife on the phone and grieving with her, I sat down and thought to myself, "If it could happen to him, it could happen to almost anyone."

I decided then and there to remake some personal commitments. I wrote out a statement to my wife that began, "I promise that with the help of God, I will never be unfaithful to you. I promise with the help of God that I will do whatever I can to change in any way that you want me to change, as long as it does not violate the will of God." At the end of the statement, I signed my name, dated it, and handed it to my wife. I told her that I was recommitting myself to the things that I had written, and asked her to do the same if she was willing. I was and she was! Whenever we hear about someone getting divorced that we never would have expected to, we are reminded of the commitment we made to each other that night.

STAYING PURE

To remain sexually pure, couples should make it a regular practice to follow the instructions of Philippians 4:8 in reference to their mates. In this verse, Paul said, "Finally, brethren, whatever is true, whatever is honorable, whatever is right, whatever is pure, whatever is lovely, whatever is of good repute, if there is any excellence and if anything worthy of praise, dwell on these things." Instead of allowing ourselves to dwell on the negative things, we should be reminding ourselves of, thinking about, and thanking God for all the positive qualities of our spouses. Every day we as married people should spend at least some time thinking about and reviewing the qualities that are found in our mates and in our marriage situation that are in keeping with Philippians 4:8.

A commitment to never complain about our spouses to anyone, especially to someone of the opposite sex, will be of great help for couples who are committed to remaining sexually pure. Unless we are discussing problems with a biblical counselor to whom we have turned for help, we should never talk about marital problems with a member of the opposite sex. As a general rule, we should avoid discussing marital problems with anyone—male or female—who is not qualified and willing to give us biblical counsel and advice.

A commitment to purity in marriage also requires that we commit ourselves to breaking the chain that leads to immorality at its earliest link. In other words, we have to stop ourselves at the very beginning of sin and not wait until the sin has had time to grow and develop into something large and difficult to handle. Adultery does not happen quickly; it is almost always a process. Those who do fall usually do not fall very far from where they have secretly and slowly been stooping. As Proverbs 17:14 notes, "The beginning of strife is like letting out water, so abandon the quarrel before it breaks out." In other words, the best and easiest time to stop a problem is when it has just started.

The Process Leading to Sexual Immorality

As I have counseled people involved in sexual immorality and adultery, I have come to see a common pattern in the road that people travel to sexual sin. The first step occurs when a person experiences a distressing or unpleasant event in life and does not receive adequate support or encouragement from his or her spouse. This is usually followed by the discovery of someone of the opposite sex who is friendly and attractive.

The third step occurs in the person's thought life as he or she begins to spend time thinking about the attractiveness of that other person. This is followed by time spent thinking about the negative and unpleasant aspects of the person's present circumstances and relationship with his or her spouse. The new person of interest is constantly compared with the spouse.

Fifth, the person goes somewhere and happens to run into the person of interest. There was no planning involved, just a coincidental meeting. Then the comparing to the spouse continues as the person starts to think how much better and happier life would be if his or her mate were like this other person. The process continues as the person starts to think about and plan for the next "accidental" encounter. When the meeting occurs, the person subtly seeks out the other person to engage him or her in conversation. As they go their separate ways, the comparing continues as the person thinks about how much more enjoyable the other person is than his or her spouse.

The planned, "innocent" encounters continue until it happens that the two are alone, and formerly innocent expressions of affection escalate to embracing and kissing. Then, especially if the two people are Christians, their consciences bother them and they decide not to let it happen again. They deliberately avoid each other for a time until their desire again takes over and they make plans to meet. In an effort to silence their consciences, they find ways to rationalize and minimize their sin by distorting Scripture, blaming their spouses for driving them to it, or even denying that it is wrong at all. They convince themselves that they are entitled to this happiness.

The desire for the other person grows and grows until the two can no longer contain themselves and they participate in sexual intercourse. Then, of course, they are conscience-stricken again, afraid of the consequences if they are found out, and vow never to do it again. Once the fire has been stoked, however, it is nearly impossible to go back. They make plans to meet as frequently as they can, all the while either becoming much more attentive to their mates to compensate, or avoiding them as much as possible.

Finally, someone becomes suspicious and starts to ask uncomfortable questions and even make accusations. When this happens, the adulterer often becomes defensive and strongly denies any wrongdoing. I once counseled a couple who had come to me because the wife suspected her husband, a pastor, of cheating on her. During our counseling, the man completely denied any wrongdoing and actually tried to counsel his wife during our sessions together. A year and a half later, after suffering a serious heart attack and almost dying in the hospital, he confessed his sin and apologized to me for his deception.

As in that instance, God usually orchestrates circumstances so that the truth is eventually revealed and the adulterer is found out. When this happens, the two people decide one of three things. One, they may decide to continue their relationship and remain married if their mates allow it. Two, they may decide to continue their relationship and end their relationships with their spouses. Or three, they may decide to repent, ask forgiveness, break off the adulterous relationship completely, and get help.

This process has taken place countless times in the lives of believers and unbelievers alike. In the book *Lasting Love*, by Alistair Begg, a friend of Begg's described how the process went for him:

A new woman came to work in our office. We struck up an acquaintance and began to talk to each other over coffee. In time, she began to share the problems in her marriage, and we found that we were both in a position of drifting away from our spouses. We actually found that we communicated better together than with our own spouses. We looked for reasons to be together and found that we shared similar interests and hobbies. I had no ulterior motives, no sinister plans, but I enjoyed our time together as friends. We saw each other every day for a few moments, and once a week we went to lunch. In time, I began to compare Elaine with my wife. I saw so many positives in Elaine. The more I compared, the more defects I saw in my wife. And one day it hit me: I was in love with another woman. Me!

No! I'm a married man with three children. I'm chairman of our church board. This happens to other people, but not me. Why did I let myself get into this mess? I felt confused, my work suffered, my relationships suffered. I tried to stop the involvement. Some weeks I didn't see Elaine that much; other weeks I saw her every day. I had to. Last week it happened. We made love. I am so torn up right now. What do I do?[1]

This is a man who did not put up hedges. He did not make any attempt to break the chain at its earliest link. He put himself in an extremely dangerous position and then seemed surprised that he ended up exactly where he was headed. We must not fool ourselves. We are all capable of doing the same thing, and unless we are careful to protect ourselves, we may very well end up where he did.

APPLICATION AND DISCUSSION

1. What are some other ways that we can reinforce our commitment to purity in marriage? First, I encourage you to write out a statement indicating your commitment to purity, date it, sign it, and

review it regularly. Show it to your mate and discuss it together. It might resemble the one I wrote and signed and asked my wife to read and sign when we were in Europe and heard the news about how a professing Christian who was very close to us was leaving his wife. Putting your commitment down in writing and signing and reviewing it can be a tangible way of solidifying that commitment.

2. Second, take some time to write out a list of the terrible consequences of immorality. Most people do not think ahead about where they are going when it comes to sin. Many delude themselves into thinking that they are the only ones who will get away with it. We may be sure, however, that our sins will find us out. As Scripture teaches, the wages of sin is death—death to a marriage and, for some, even physical death.

   Some time ago, I sat down and in a very short time made a list of thirty-four consequences of sexual immorality; I am sure that even more could be added. For example, an adulterous husband violates his wife's trust in him as a faithful husband. Sexual sin poisons God's beautiful design for the marriage union. It introduces physical impurity, putting both spouses at risk for sexually transmitted diseases. Sexual immorality demolishes the one-flesh relationship between husband and wife, as the adulterer withholds the attention, respect, and service due his or her spouse. Moreover, an adulterer cultivates a pattern of deception as he or she engages in lying and deception to cover up the sin. Still further, the person seriously damages his or her imagination, burning into the mind pictures and sensations that will rule him or her in the future. The person who participates in ungodly sexual relations will develop a seared, hardened conscience as he or she lives a life of duplicity and rationalization and in so doing will grieve and quench the ministry of the Holy Spirit and become insensitive to the teachings of God's Word.

   In addition to all that, the person's children are corrupted as well. The weak moral character of the adulterer reinforces weak moral values in his or her children. If the adultery is exposed, children may become bitter both toward the sinning parent and toward

God. Potentially, sexual sin may be reproduced in the lives of the children when they are grown.

As we discussed earlier, sexual sin is idolatry. Those who choose to worship at the altar of self and of pleasure will surely reap the terrible consequences of their terrible sin. I encourage everyone—married and single alike—to do the biblical thing as frequently reflected in the book of Proverbs and in many other passages of Scripture of thinking about consequences of our behavior. Again and again, the Bible encourages us to think about not just present pleasure, but future consequences (Prov. 7; Gal. 6:7–8; Heb. 13:4). Thus, as a deterrent to the temptation to sexual immorality either in thought or in action, I encourage you to do some serious thinking about consequences, write them down, and then frequently review the results of sexual sin. Discuss and add your ideas about the negative consequences of sexual immorality to those that I have mentioned. Review this list regularly. In addition to this negative-consequences list, make another list of the benefits of purity as well, and review these often to be reminded of the blessings of obeying God's plan.

3. Third, do a study on sexual relations in marriage together with your spouse. Chapter 6 of my book *Strengthening Your Marriage* contains such a study. Renew your marriage vows with your spouse frequently. It would also be helpful to do the study on sexual immorality found in volume 1 of my book *A Homework Manual for Biblical Living*.

4. Fourth, find a godly person who will hold you accountable for your actions. In our church, we have men's groups that meet on weekdays. The groups are each led by an elder, and the men in each group are able to study the Word of God together, share their struggles, pray for one another, and hold one another accountable for their responsibilities to their families, their spouses, their jobs, and the Lord. If you are serious about protecting yourself from sexual sin, ask someone to keep you accountable on a regular basis.

5. Fifth, stay away from people, places, and activities that will cause you to be tempted. Do not do what the young man in Proverbs 7 did: "Suddenly he follows her as an ox goes to the slaughter, or as

one in fetters to the discipline of a fool" (7:22). Learn from David's mistake in 2 Samuel 11. Determine in your heart that, with God's help, there is no other option for you than purity. Make a steadfast, deliberate commitment in all areas of life—behavior, thoughts, and desires—to God's blueprint for marriage.

18

GOOD MARRIAGES REQUIRE SOME PERSPIRATION

We have all heard the expression "No pain, no gain." As in most other areas of life, improvement and success in marriage require effort. Therefore, we must be willing to commit ourselves to the fourth *P* of a godly marriage: *perspiration* (i.e., a willingness to put forth a strenuous effort). Good marriages do not just happen; they exist only when people are willing to roll up their sleeves and put effort into making their relationship what God wants it to be. According to Proverbs 14:23, "In all labor there is profit, but mere talk leads only to poverty." Men and women who talk about wanting a good marriage but refuse to do anything about it will merely reap what they have sown: nothing or worse.

We might think of the marriage relationship as being like a garden. A good garden requires constant attention. There is fertilizing, planting, watering, weeding, thinning, and harvesting to be done if it is to be a success. When we were living in California, we had the opportunity to go up to Victoria Island and see the Butchart Gardens. These gardens were some of the most beautiful, immaculate, and carefully tended that I have ever seen. But regardless of whether the garden is on Victoria Island or in our backyard, if it is ignored, it will quickly turn into a messy patch of weeds.

WORKING THROUGH THE DIFFERENCES

Why does a good marriage require so much work? There are two basic reasons. First, husbands and wives are different. Aside from the obvious physical differences, they are usually different in such things as their family backgrounds. For example, my wife was raised in the city by well-educated, affluent parents, and I was raised on a country farm by uneducated, relatively poor parents. At the beginning of our marriage, this great difference in our backgrounds provided the context for marital problems that we never anticipated early on. Because of a lack of the right kind of premarital counseling, the thought that our differences in background could cause any problems never entered our minds. After all, we were both Christians who loved each other and were committed to structuring our lives and our marriage according to Scripture. How naive we were; we had no idea that working through these differences would require so much work.

Most husbands and wives are also different in their personalities and personal tendencies. Some people are fast thinkers and talkers, and others are slow. Some people are outgoing and some reserved. Some are adventurous and some cautious. Some are logical and some sentimental. Some are flexible and some rigid. No couple is completely alike in every aspect, and quite often the husband and wife are different in many. This also provides a context for difficulties and conflicts.

Men and women are different in terms of their genders as well. Their physical bodies are different, and their brains work differently. In the book *Recovering Biblical Manhood and Womanhood*, by John Piper and Wayne Grudem, a scientist named Dr. Greg Johnson documented at least six major differences between men and women. According to Dr. Johnson, there are what he calls ethological differences, non-nervous-system differences, peripheral-nervous-system differences, limbic-system differences, cerebral-organization differences, and stress-management differences between men and women. In this essay, Dr. Johnson clearly makes the point that men and women might find themselves at odds with each other in plenty of areas simply because of the way in which they are made. Understanding these differences and keeping them in mind should be of practical assistance for husbands and wives as they relate and respond to one another.[1]

Another major difference between men and women is in the area of relational tendencies. Generally speaking, research and observation has led students of gender differences to conclude that these relational differences manifest themselves in some of the following ways. Most men tend to concentrate on one task at a time, while women balance many tasks simultaneously. Women tend to be more compliant with rules than men. Among children, boys tend to be more adventuresome, curious, and willing to take risks than girls. Most females, at any age, are more nurturant than are most males. One of the strongest fears of many women is lack of relationship. Lack of achievement or failing is one of the deepest fears of many men. Most women tend to have more friends in whom they confide than do men. Men tend to be more exploratory, adventuresome, and risk-taking than most females. They are more inclined to value freedom, independence, and competition, and to possess a desire to "prove themselves" by being daring.

These are a few of the generalized differences between male and female. The generalizations have exceptions, but nonetheless they are usually true. And being aware of these differences can be helpful to the way in which husbands and wives understand and relate to one another.

Husbands need to learn that their wives are not necessarily going to think and act the way they do, and vice versa. Anne Moir and David Jessel explained this idea further in their book *Brain Sex: The Real Difference Between Men and Women*:

> Men are different than women. They are equal only in their common membership of the same species: humankind. To maintain that they are the same in aptitude, skill, or behavior is to build a society based on a biological and scientific lie.

The sexes are different because their brains are different. The brain, the chief administrative and emotional organ of life, is differently constructed in men and in women. It processes information in a different way, which results in different perceptions, priorities, and behavior.

In the past ten years, there has been an explosion of scientific research into what makes the sexes different. Doctors, scientists, psychologists, and sociologists working apart have produced a body of findings which, taken together, paints a remarkably consistent picture, and the picture is one of startling sexual asymmetry.

It is time to explode the social myth that men and women are virtually interchangeable, all things being equal. All things are not equal, all things being equal.[2]

In a book entitled *You Just Don't Understand: Women and Men in Conversation*, researcher Dr. Deborah Tannen added her perspective on the differences between men and women in this way:

I am joining the growing dialogue on gender and language because the risk of ignoring differences is greater than the danger of naming them. Sweeping them under the rug doesn't make it go away; it trips you up and sends you sprawling . . .

Pretending that men and women are the same hurts women, because the ways they are treated is based on norms for men. It also hurts men who, with good intentions, speak to women as though they were men, and are nonplussed when their words don't work as they expected, or even spark resentment and anger . . . If we recognize and understand the differences between us, we can take them into account, adjust to [them], and learn from each other's styles.[3]

And so the husband and wife must realize that they have much work to do if they wish to maintain a harmonious, one-flesh relationship with each other even though they differ so fundamentally.

The second major reason that the marriage relationship requires so much work is sin. Husbands and wives are sinners who are prone to selfishness, as Isaiah 53:6 reminds us ("each of us has turned to his own way . . ."), and this selfishness results in a power struggle. He wants his way; she wants hers. James 4 talks about this source of conflict: "What is the source of quarrels and conflicts among you? Is not the source your pleasures that wage war in your members? You lust [strongly desire something] and do not have . . . You are envious and cannot obtain . . ." (James 4:1–2). We respond to minor differences with major selfishness because we are sinners. We may be saved sinners, and we may even be growing more and more into the likeness of Christ, but none of us has arrived in this world at the place where we no longer struggle with the remnants of indwelling sin in our lives (Rom. 7:21–25; 8:13; Phil. 3:12–14; 1 Tim. 1:15). Unfortunately, because we still have to regularly deal with the problem of not doing things out of selfishness or empty conceit (Phil. 2:3), and because we don't always have the servant mind or attitude of Christ (Phil. 2:5), we don't always respond to our differences in a godly manner.

This remaining propensity toward selfishness in which we esteem ourselves better than others and are more concerned about our own interests (ideas, perspectives, desires, etc.) provides the context in which coldness, apathy, bitterness, anger, wrath, distancing, conflicts, disappointment, lack of harmony, and major marital unhappiness may occur (Phil. 2:3–4). To prevent this from happening, the husband and wife must be willing to put forth a regular and strenuous effort, in Paul's words, to put to death the deeds of the body, by the help and power of the Holy Spirit who dwells in them, so that they and their relationship might live (Rom. 8:13). Because they have been raised from spiritual death through Christ, they can and they must put to death their ungodly passions, their ungodly desires, and their greed for power or control or having their own way, and do so regularly and with much dedication, if they and their relationship are going to be pleasing to God (Col. 3:1–5).

Putting our selfishness, ungodly passions, and desires to death will not automatically or easily occur. It must be done by the power of the Spirit of God and in the power of our risen Christ. In and of ourselves, we can never kill our selfishness, but the good news is that we don't have to do it by ourselves (2 Cor. 9:8; Phil. 4:13). By God's grace and the empowerment of the Holy Spirit, we can and we must work hard at overcoming ungodly mental, attitudinal, and behavioral responses to our differences. Unless we do this, we will never achieve a proper one-flesh relationship with our spouses.

One counselor has said:

Is the cup of your marriage half-empty or half-full? The thing to do is to recognize that the time spent in your present relationship is an investment to be nurtured. Your marriage is like a good retirement plan: as long as you keep the deposits flowing, the account grows. The marriage develops like compound interest over time. Small investments of love and nurture reap great dividends in relational happiness. No one in their right mind would squander a solid investment account that has been growing through the years to take up a shaky, speculative venture. It doesn't make good sense. If the grass is greener on the other side of the fence, you should try watering your own. There is no easy road to authentic relationship. It takes hard work. If you feel the pleasure has gone out of your marriage, or the romance, or that the marriage is not meeting your basic need for encouragement and love, then you have to work at it. I'm sorry, but there's no other way. The only action that makes sense is to dig in and recommit yourself to your present marriage.[4]

J. R. Miller has observed:

In China, the bridegroom does not see the bride until she is brought to him on his wedding day, closely veiled and locked up in a sedan chair. The key is handed to him when the chair reaches his house and he unlocks the door, lifts the veil, and takes his first look at his treasure. Brides and bridegrooms with us are not usually such strangers . . . They see each other's face often enough, but it is doubtful whether as a rule they really know much more of each other's inner life. Even without any intention to hide their true selves, or to appear veiled, it is only after marriage that their acquaintanceship becomes complete. There are graces of character and disposition that are then discovered for the first time. And there are also faults, peculiarities of habit, of taste, of temper, never suspected before which then disclose themselves. It is just at this point that one of the greatest perils of wedded life is met.

Some are disappointed and discouraged by the discovery of these points of uncongeniality, these possibilities of discord, concluding at once that their marriage was a mistake and must necessarily be a failure. Their beautiful dream is shattered and they make no effort to build it again. But really, all that is needed is wise and loving patience. There is no reason for discouragement—much less despair.

The present duty is unselfish love. Each must forget self in devotion to the other. Each must blame self and not the other when anything goes wrong . . . There must be the determination on the part of both to make the marriage happy and to conquer everything that lies in the way.[5]

In one of Howard Shneider's comic strips, Eek and Meek were having a discussion about marriage. Eek said to Meek, "Good marriages are made in heaven. They come in kits." To which Meek wisely responded, "Well, it's true that good marriages are made in heaven and they may come in kits. But they still have to be put together here on earth." Eek and Meek were both right. Good marriages do occur because God has brought two people together. But this fact does not obviate the hard work of two people who have been joined together by God to develop and sustain the harmony and unity of their marriage relationship on earth. That won't happen by chance; it will happen as two people willingly work hard at developing and sustaining that relationship. As the title of this chapter suggests, good marriages require some perspiration. And the question is: can what you are doing to promote your marriage relationship be rightly called work?

After reading this chapter, sit down together and pray for God's help to be honest and constructive in answering the following questions. I suggest that you and your mate evaluate the areas in which you have already worked on improving your relationship. Then identify the areas in which you still need to do some work. Discuss each question carefully, with each of you giving your perspective on the appropriate answer. Then summarize what you have learned, thank God for the positives in your relationship, confess your failures, and make plans for the what, how, and when of improvement.

1. Do we need to work harder at communicating effectively? How do we need to improve in this area of our relationship? Have we really been working hard at this important marriage component?

2. Do we need to work harder at having a regular and effective family devotional time? Are we praying together as we should?

3. Do we need to work harder at being each other's companion?

4. Do we need to work harder at preventing and resolving conflict? Are there unresolved conflicts in our relationship?

5. Do we need to work harder at being united in our child-rearing efforts? Are there differences between us about how to discipline the children?

6. Do we need to work harder at being kinder and more gracious to each other?

7. Review the material covered in the preceding chapters and evaluate your "perspiration quotient" on each of the *P*s of a good marriage that have been presented so far. Use the rating scale of Excellent, Good, Fair, Poor, or Nonexistent to evaluate how hard you are working on each of the items included in the commitment to the first *P*, the *purposes* of God. Next, what about the second *P*, the *priority* of your relationship? Then evaluate your perspiration quotient in terms of your efforts involving the third *P*, the *purity* of your relationship.

8. Discuss the specific reasons for assigning the ratings you did. Finally, decide what steps you are going to take to improve the

areas that need to be improved and commit yourself to a greater degree of perspiration (work) in these areas. Doing this will help you to remain real sweethearts for a lifetime.

9. For more help on how to deal with the selfishness that hinders relationships, follow up this study by reading the book written by my son and me entitled *A Fight to the Death: Taking Aim at Sin Within.*[6]

19

TILL DEATH US DO PART

The *permanence* of the marriage relationship is the fifth *P* that requires our attention in order to have the kind of marriage that God desires us to have. Scripture makes it quite clear that God wants the marriage relationship to be permanent: " 'For I hate divorce,' says the LORD, the God of Israel" (Mal. 2:16). "Hate" is strong language. In addition to hating divorce itself, God also hates the things that cause it. Three times in Malachi 2, God says that the person who seeks a divorce is "deal[ing] "treacherously" with his spouse. Again, why such strong language? It is because the husband and wife have made a commitment—a vow—before the Lord that they are now breaking.

R. C. Sproul has explored this issue at length:

In order to gain a better understanding of the content and meaning of the marriage vows, let us again look briefly at the vows contained in the United Presbyterian Book of Common Worship. Most marriage vows correspond to these: "I, _____, take thee, _____, to be my wedded wife (or husband); and I do promise and covenant; Before God and these witnesses to be your loving and faithful wife in plenty and want; In joy and sorrow; In sickness and in health; As long as we both shall live."

What is promised in these vows? Two things: love and fidelity . . . What about fidelity? It means maintaining the honor of the marriage by keeping the terms of the covenant. This is why marital infidelity is so serious. It cuts at the heart of the marriage contract. It violates the deepest part of the commitment.

Under what circumstances are the vows to be maintained? The first vow mentioned is "in plenty or in want." The vows are to remain intact regardless of the financial circumstances of the marriage. The commitment is not to depend on money. If poverty comes, the one does not have the right to seek another partner who can provide a better financial situation or offer more luxury. Nor can one dissolve the covenant when great riches suddenly come, seeking another partner more accustomed to a higher standard of living.

The second circumstances are joy and sorrow. Being married to a person who does not bring the level of joy desired is not an excuse to leave the marriage. If tragedy strikes the home, bringing grief, there is still no reason to walk out. The third circumstance that is mentioned is that of health. When the fine physical specimen you married is ravaged by age or disease, these are not grounds for breaking your promise. When your wife becomes forty years old, you cannot trade her in for two twenty-year-olds.

These vows do not specifically state every possible circumstance that might arise and affect the marriage. The wedding ceremony would last for hours if every eventuality were dealt with explicitly. But the spirit of the vows contains implicitly all of these possible circumstances. What the vows are expressing is a promise of love and fidelity in all kinds of circumstances.

The vows involve a lot more than a present declaration of love. A person must not enter marriage saying, "I love you today, but I might not tomorrow." Nor, "I promise to love you if everything goes well." The vows are not merely a declaration of present love and fidelity, but a declaration and commitment to future love and fidelity. Many of you who are reading this book took those vows a long time ago. What was future then is present now.

What is the duration of the obligation to keep the vow? Is there an annual review clause in the marriage? Can one commit himself for five or ten years? Not by these vows. The vow here is, "as long as we both shall live." The commitment of marriage is a commitment for a lifetime.[1]

When the Pharisees asked Jesus about divorce, Jesus answered them, "Have you not read that He who created them . . . said, 'For this reason a man shall leave his father and mother and be joined to his wife, and the two shall become one flesh'? So they are no longer two, but one flesh. What therefore God has joined together, let no man separate" (Matt. 19:4–6). Paul reaffirmed this admonition in 1 Corinthians 7:10–11: "But to the married I give instructions, not I, but the Lord, that the wife should not leave her husband . . . and that the husband should not divorce his wife."

If we desire to have an "A" kind of marriage, we have to look on our marriage as being on the twentieth floor of a building from which there is no exit. If a fire breaks out, there are no windows to jump out of, no skylight to climb through, and no staircase or elevator to take to the bottom. We have only two choices: one, we can burn to death (allow the problem to overwhelm and consume us); or two, we can put the fire out.

Scripture has made it clear that as far as God is concerned, the only acceptable choice is the second. Husbands and wives need to work through their problems and difficulties with the Lord's help. Anything short of that is disobedience. As we discussed in the previous chapter, this means that we must be willing to work.

Harold Myra explained what commitment really means in an essay found in his book *Love Notes to Jeanette*. He wrote the following to his wife, Jeanette:

"You know it could happen to us," you said to me, sitting in your favorite chair as we sipped coffee, digesting the news of the latest couple splitting up. "No matter how great we think we have it, if all those people can break up, it could happen to us. We're humans like them. It is possible."

I did not answer for a while. We were both incredulous at the news. Men and women of maturity, decades-long marriages—so many have exploded one after another. Almost every week, another set of names. Not him! Not her! They're too sensible, too solid.

"You're right," I finally admit. We have never joked about divorce, never brought it up as an option. We declared total commitment to each other and must reaffirm that always. But maybe realizing that it could happen to us helps us make sure it will not.

How terrible to think of an argument some day when one of us feels the need for the ultimate weapon. "Well, obviously there's no sense staying together. We're just hurting each other, just keeping each other trapped." Those are words mouthed in kitchens and bedrooms of "mature" Christian homes.

What do we mean by commitment? How do we keep our love alive? How do we make love grow from early blossoms to summer fruit? Remember how our love began? Years ago, I offered you my arm that September night we first went out. You reached for it as we leaped a puddle together. Then you walked just close enough to show you liked it. I glimpsed your face under the streetlight, excitement splashing gently on it . . . No commitment—just beginnings.

My arm pulled you that January eve tight beside me in that car. Midnight. Time to leave. "Good night" wasn't enough and our lips touched gently in a kiss as light as angel cake. "I like you," it said, but nothing more.

November air had rough-scrubbed our faces, as we wrestled playfully in your parents' farmhouse. That moment I knew and breathed into your hair, "I LOVE YOU."

The words exploded around us. They meant far more than "you're nice." They meant commitment.

Your words came back to me in firm, sure sounds: "I love you too." And our kiss of celebration was the beginning of a new creation.

Yes, I chose you. Out of all the lovely girls I knew, I chose you. How marvelous are the women of planet earth, hair flaring in the wind, rich browns and golds, a thousand delicious shapes, girls who laugh saucily, girls who read Browning, girls who play sitars, girls who fix carburetors.

Of all those fascinating possibilities, I chose you. Decisively. Permanently. Is that self-entrapment? Was a commitment made in youth to bind me a lifetime?

Ah, but it was as strong as birth, a fresh creation, soon to be a new flesh, you and I as one. We chose each other. We created something new under the sun. You to shape me and I you, like a Luther Burbank original. We, our own new creation to produce fruit wholly unique, UNIQUE IN THE UNIVERSE!

Then the wedding, flying rice and honeymoon, days and nights together. Two persons as unalike as birch and cypress had chosen each other. The heavens laughed and the sands of earth lay ready for the tender feet of our newborn self. Does time change all that? Were we naïve? Now, after we've loved, argued, laughed, given birth, what does it mean when I hold you and say, "I love you"? Without the young-love ecstasy, is it required rote? Or is it a reaffirmation of our new creation?

"I love you." My temples don't pulse as I say it. My body doesn't ache for coupling, not as it did. Yet the words carry more fact than ever they did in courtship. They embrace a million moments shared. Standing together atop Cadillac Mountain and aching to absorb the blue-green beauty . . . Or angrily expounding to each other in the kitchen about our particular stupidities, then sharing a kiss ten hours later . . . Bonding moments, holding us together. How easily those bonds could be tyrannical. "You always forget. You never think." And bitter moments bite into their flesh with binding ropes that tie them to the time and place instead of to each other.

Yet bonds can be a thousand multi-colored strands of sorrow, joy, embarrassment, of anger, laughter shared, as we watch God maturing us, as we gently tell each other of our joys, our fears, even of our fantasies.

Rope is rope. Experiences are much the same. Crabby days, laughing days, boring days, we'll go through them in love by commitment to each other. Sharing, forgiving, not blaming, not hurting. Yet when we do hurt we ask forgiveness, so the ropes will bind us together.

For if they don't, they'll wrap around our throats so that each struggle will tighten the noose, and we'll have to reach for the knife to cut the bonds.

"I love you." It sounds trite, but not if it's remembering the thousands of strands of loving each other when we don't feel loving, of holding each other, . . . of getting up in the morning thousands of times together and remembering what we created the day we first said, "I love you." Something permanent and growing and alive.[2]

That is commitment. Being committed to the permanence of marriage means embracing all kinds of days—good, bad, and even terrible—and working through each one in love.

APPLICATION
AND DISCUSSION

1. Review Harold Myra's piece of prose about commitment and answer the following questions:

   a. What does Myra suggest is lacking when people get a divorce?

   b. What does Myra mean by the word *commitment*? What adjectives does he use in connection with *commitment*? What other words or concepts does he associate with the word *commitment*?

   c. What does Myra suggest is required in order to keep the commitment we make when we get married? What must people do if their marriage relationship is to be sustained over a long period, according to Myra?

   d. What does Myra suggest are the enemies of a longtime relationship?

   e. What ideas in this piece of prose impress you the most?

   f. Does your commitment to your mate resemble the commitment illustrated in Myra's piece?

g. If someone were to carefully observe your marriage relationship, what evidence would convince that person that your commitment to each other is a solid and permanent one?

2. Read again the marriage vows mentioned in this chapter; then reflect on their meaning. What should a vow to be a loving and faithful wife and husband in plenty and in want, in joy and in sorrow, in sickness and in health, as long as we both shall live look like in actual practice? Is that your attitude and commitment? Reaffirm that commitment by reading the vows to each other. Then close in a prayer of commitment to fulfill those vows, seeking God's help to do so.

20

THE MOST IMPORTANT
FACTOR

God's blueprint for marriage requires that we commit ourselves to one last *P*: the *preeminence* of Christ in the marriage relationship. We will never be able to fulfill the other five commitments—purpose, priority, purity, perspiration, and permanence—if Jesus Christ is not first in our lives and loves. Jesus Christ alone gives us the power to do the things necessary to have godly marriages.

Scripture clearly teaches that Christ's place is first in all things. In Colossians 1:18, Paul said, "He is the beginning, the firstborn from the dead, so that He Himself will come to have first place in everything." If Christ is first in everything, then He must be first in a couple's marriage. "But seek first His kingdom and His righteousness . . ." was Christ's command in Matthew 6:33. And in Psalm 127:1, Solomon wrote, "Unless the LORD builds the house, they labor in vain who build it . . ."

Christ's preeminence is the essential key to fulfilling the five previous commitments because when God commands us to do something—and all the things we have discussed are biblical commands—

He alone is the One who can give us the power to obey. This is our hope and confidence as believers because we know that we can do nothing to please God on our own.

Psalm 112:1 says, "Praise the LORD! How blessed is the man who fears the LORD, who greatly delights in His commandments." Psalm 128:1 echoes this idea: "How blessed is everyone who fears the LORD, who walks in His ways." And Ecclesiastes 12:13 says, "The conclusion, when all has been heard, is: fear God and keep His commandments, because this applies to every person." These three verses all exhort us to first fear and then obey. We cannot walk in God's commandments unless we have a deep, reverent love for the Lord. He must reign in our hearts as Lord of all before we can have any hope of doing what He says.

SIGNPOSTS OF CHRIST'S PREEMINENCE

What does it look like to have a marriage in which Christ is preeminent in the lives of both husband and wife and in their relationship? The first signpost is that we will look exclusively to God as our director. In other words, we will constantly be asking the Lord, "What do You want us to do? How should we raise our children? How should we use our time? How should we use our resources for Your glory?" What God thinks about every area of our lives will be what we desire to know most each and every day.

Second, we will be looking to God as our audience. This means that He is the One that we want most to please by what we do. If no one else is pleased by our actions, but the Lord is pleased, then we are satisfied. If others like what we are doing, but God does not, then we seek to do better. As Paul said in 2 Corinthians 5:9, "Therefore we also have as our ambition, whether at home or absent, to be pleasing to Him." Our greatest ambition should be to please God in all that we do.

The third signpost of Christ's preeminence is that we will rely on God as our enabler. Recognizing that nothing we can do on our own can please God, we must depend solely on the enabling power of the Holy Spirit to obey. And fourth, we will love God's Word, love His church, love to fellowship with His people, and delight in the service to which He has called us.

Fifth, making Christ preeminent means that we will seek God's glory above all else. Paul expressed this desire in Philippians 1:20: "my earnest expectation and hope [is] that I will not be put to shame in anything, but that with all boldness, Christ will even now, as always, be exalted in my body, whether by life or by death." To this end, we will want to know and do God's will above all else so that He will be glorified in everything that we do.

RECOGNIZING THE OBSTACLES

As much as we may wish to make Christ preeminent in our marriages, numerous obstacles present themselves. Knowing what these obstacles are, preparing for them, and working at overcoming them are essential to realizing this goal for the marriage relationship. First is the obstacle of pride. Our sinful nature does not wish to exalt anyone or anything above ourselves. Second, the selfish desire for instant gratification hinders our progress in making Christ preeminent. In an age of instant everything, it can be difficult to focus our energy and desire on heavenly things, which often do not yield instant or even tangible results.

Third is the obstacle of busyness with other things. In our high-speed society, it is easy to become so consumed with the everyday tasks of life—the demands of jobs, children, and other commitments—that we fail to take time to do the things that will make Christ preeminent in our lives. Also present in our lives are people who pressure us and make demands of our time and resources, pulling us away from God.

Some years ago I counseled a man about this matter of making Christ preeminent in his life. I told him that part of this would involve investing time in personal devotions each day and attending church on Sunday. When I finished, he said to me, "I don't have time for that." I asked him why, and he explained: "I just started a business, and it takes all my time to keep it going. I work at the business all day, and then I do the paperwork and keep the books at night. I don't have time for anything else."

At that point I looked at him and said, "You mean you don't make time." "No, I don't have time," he insisted. I repeated my point and then continued, "You are making a choice to say that this business is more important than anything else. It's not because you don't have time. You have time for your business, but you don't have time for God? You have to decide whether you are going to obey God and do what He wants, or obey yourself and do what you want. The Bible says to seek first the kingdom of God and His righteousness and He'll help you take care of all the other things. In reality, you are unwilling to trust God in this matter." Sadly, what was true of that man is so often true of us as well.

Fourth is the obstacle of an undisciplined, lazy lifestyle. When we lack self-control, organization, and diligence, we tend to structure our lives more around what we feel like doing than what we ought to do. Because of our sin nature, all of us are lazy to some extent. Following Christ requires a great deal of work and effort on our part for which we must discipline ourselves.

Fifth, we are sometimes hindered by the example of others around us who are not making God preeminent in their own lives. Many people in our churches do not, in reality, desire to please Christ above all. They do their Christian duty on Sunday, but they live for themselves the other six days of the week. If we measure our Christian zeal by the standard of these "Christians" around us, we will be tempted to think as they do—that making Christ preeminent in all things is not important.

Sixth, we can be hindered by unbiblical views of the Christian life. Some people have the idea that everything should be easy. "Let go and let God," they say. If it requires struggle and difficulty, it must somehow be wrong. Or some people are so consumed by trials and temptations that they get distracted from trusting God. They are so wrapped up in their pain that they forget that God is in control.

Seventh, we may be hindered by our own spiritual inadequacy. Maybe we feel as though we cannot understand Scripture. "I try to read my Bible, but I don't get anything out of it." Perhaps we are feeble in prayer. "I pray, but nothing ever happens." Rather than making excuses for ourselves, we should make an effort to improve. We may need to study more or talk to others about how to read and understand Scripture or how to pray more effectively.

It has been said that the greater the goal, the higher the obstacles. Making Christ preeminent in our lives is perhaps the highest goal there is, so it should not surprise us when we are faced with many obstacles. Overcoming them will not be easy or quick, but it will be a struggle well worth the effort for its eternal and immeasurable reward.

APPLICATION
AND DISCUSSION

1. What does this chapter indicate is the most important factor for developing and sustaining a good marriage relationship?

2. Why is this the most important factor in having a deep, lasting, and fulfilling marriage?

3. When Christ is preeminent in a marriage relationship, what does that marriage look like? What will the husband and wife do? Reflect on each of the signposts mentioned in this chapter.

4. Evaluate yourselves in terms of whether you exhibit the signposts indicating that Christ is preeminent in your marriage relationship. Use this rating scale: Excellent; couldn't be better = 4; Good, but needs a little fine-tuning = 3; Fair; needs some changes = 2; Poor; needs many changes = 1; Terrible; couldn't be worse = 0.

5. What obstacles to making Christ preeminent are mentioned in this chapter?

6. Can you think of any other obstacles?

7. Have you allowed any of these obstacles to hinder you from doing what is necessary to make Christ preeminent?

8. If so, which ones are most problematic?

Join with your mate in reading through and then verbally making the following Agape Commitment to each other. Read through it to each other aloud, fill in the blanks, sign the commitment, and frequently review it.

A G A P E   C O M M I T M E N T   F O R   R E M A I N I N G   S W E E T H E A R T S   F O R   A   L I F E T I M E

I, _____, do this day, _____, renew my agape commitment (vow) to you, _____, to permanently love you according to the commandment of our great God and Savior, in order to please Him and follow in the more excellent way. I make this commitment to God and to you, trusting that He will enable me to love you in the following way until death us do part.

1. I choose to be permanently committed to you with agape love, to a selfless, sustained, like-minded, oneness relationship, and to a pure and fervent love;

2. I choose to be committed to love you with vulnerable love regardless of your response;

3. I choose to be committed to a releasing love, a love that gives you total freedom—to be who God made you to be (not who I think you should be), to share yourself and life with me in your unique way; I hold you with an open hand;

4. I choose to be committed to an affirming love, with the purpose of building you up as a person; to be good for you all your days, to strengthen your hands in the Lord; to encourage and motivate you to increasing obedience and closeness to our Father;

5. I choose to be committed to a profound love, as deep a love that is possible for two redeemed sinners to share, with sensitive, tender, free expression, both verbally and physically, in the way most fulfilling and meaningful to you, choosing to meet your need before my own;

6. I choose to be committed to a totally open, sharing love, by unrestrainedly communicating with you on a regular basis in the way that meets your heart's longings, by attempting to keep in touch with your needs as well as my own so that nothing will hinder our oneness—never hiding my hurts, needs, or longings from you;

7. I choose to be committed to an active, available love, to always be there for you, to actively listen to you, praying regularly for your specific needs, giving you affection and closeness, and planning shared times of fun that we can both enjoy;

8. I choose to be committed to honoring you as very special, by treating you as a priceless treasure given me by a loving heavenly Father, showing you deep respect, carefully handling your reputation, and publicly and privately affirming the abilities that God has given you by encouraging you and giving you freedom to grow in them;

9. I choose to be committed to a forgiving love, never keeping account of wrongs, always communicating hurts in a loving, reconciling manner as quickly as possible, not letting the sun go down on my wrath.

To you, my lover and friend, I commit myself permanently, with great joy and gratitude for the priceless privilege of being your mate, in the sight of our great God and Savior, who handpicked you for me with tenderest love as a gift from His great heart to mine long before the world began.

Signature _____ Date _____

21

OVERCOMING OBSTACLES
TO CHRIST'S PREEMINENCE

We know that the road is going to be rough, so how can we prepare ourselves for it? What can help us to make Christ preeminent in our lives and in our marriages? First, we must understand that it is important. This may sound simple, but it is a crucial point. If we don't think that making Christ preeminent is important, we will not make time for it and we will not put our energy into it.

As I discussed in my book *Preparing for Marriage God's Way*, the most important relationship in one's relationship with a spouse is one's relationship with God. A right relationship with God will give us the power, motivation, and strength to rightly relate to our spouses and others. Nothing is more practical and more critical than our relationship with the Lord.

Sadly, many Christians fail to recognize this truth. A number of years ago I had a weekly television program called *Solving Life's Problems God's Way*. At one point, when we were dealing with the topic of conflict resolution, I began the program by talking about how a right relationship with Jesus Christ was the most important factor in conflict resolution.

The moderator, a man named Chris, then turned to me and said, "That's great, but now let's get down to something that's really practical." Much to his surprise, I continued by calmly but forcefully repeating my point. I said, "Chris, there is absolutely nothing more practical than what I've been talking about." When we are deeply and rightly related to Christ, many potential conflicts are prevented, and those that do arise die away quickly and quietly. In all things, Christ must be at the center.

PRACTICAL HELPS
TO MAKE CHRIST PREEMINENT

A right relationship with God does not just happen. It is something that must be carefully cultivated, actively pursued, and stubbornly protected. It requires having the proper tools—a good Bible, commentaries, study guides, prayer notebooks, etc.—and it requires making an investment of time and effort. As Solomon counseled his son, "Make your ear attentive to wisdom, incline your heart to understanding; for if you cry for discernment, lift your voice for understanding; if you seek her as silver and search for her as for hidden treasures; then you will discern the fear of the LORD and discover the knowledge of God" (Prov. 2:2–5).

You can do many other things to make Christ preeminent in your marriage. Get involved in common ministries. Find ways to serve the Lord together. Purchase and read good biblical literature that will provide food for your soul. Listen to edifying tapes in the car, whether it be preaching, teaching, or good Christian music. Attend conferences that are spiritually challenging and encouraging. Keep a common prayer list with your mate and set aside time to pray together. Develop relationships with other godly people, especially couples. Make it your aim to spend more time with godly people who will challenge you, mentor you, support you, and encourage you than with people who will merely entertain you.

As Christians, we should all be involved in three kinds of relationships. We should have relationships with people who are more mature in Christ than we are so that we can learn from them. We should also have relationships with people who are on basically the same level as we are so that we are both giving and taking equally in the relationship and holding each other accountable. And we should have relationships with those who are less mature in Christ than we are so that we can serve them and help them to grow.

The practice of periodically planning for and enjoying a mini-honeymoon can also be a means of enhancing, enriching, and sustaining a deep, satisfying, God-honoring marriage. Getting away by yourselves for a few days, a weekend, or even just one day when rightly used can be a real relationship-deepener and booster. You'll greatly benefit from a time for the two of you to get away together in order to talk and enjoy each other's company, spend time in the Word of God together, read books, participate in recreation, and pray together without interruption or distraction. This will provide refreshment to you both spiritually and in your marriage relationship. So get out your calendar and begin to plan the when, what, and how of your next (or perhaps first) mini-honeymoon after the honeymoon. And if you can't afford the time or money to actually go someplace, at least begin to schedule in evenings or afternoons when you will give focused attention to your mate and your relationship.

Final Thoughts on
the Six *P*s of Marriage

As Christian husbands and wives, none of us should ever have to wonder, as Ann Landers did, "How did it happen that something that started out so good, turned out so bad?" We have been given God's blueprint for marriage in the Bible. If we commit ourselves to God's purposes for marriage, the priority of the relationship, the purity in marriage, the perspiration required to maintain it, the permanence of the relationship, and the preeminence of Christ in all things, then we will find, as I have, that marriage gets better and better with each passing year. Are you committed to following the six *P*s of a godly marriage? If you truly want to have an "A" kind of marriage, may God challenge and help you to pursue them.

1. Join with your mate in taking and discussing the following "Six Ps of a Good Marriage" Inventory. For you and your mate to remain sweethearts for a lifetime involves making and keeping certain commitments. Please complete this inventory, evaluating your perspective on your own and your mate's commitment quotient for each of the six Ps. Use an S for rating yourself and an M for rating your mate's commitment, or use your initials.

   a. After you and your spouse have each completed this inventory, spend some time discussing how and why you scored the inventory items the way you did.

   b. After you complete the inventory and discuss your ratings, go on to talk about how you can and will improve in any of the areas needing improvement.

"S I X P S O F A G O O D M A R R I A G E" I N V E N T O R Y

4 = very strong;   3 = somewhat strong;   2 = weak;   1 = very weak

Commitment Items

_____ 1. The Purposes of God for the Marriage Relationship

_____ 2. The Priority of the Marriage Relationship

_____ 3. The Purity of the Marriage Relationship

_____ 4. The Perspiration Required for a Good Marriage

_____ 5. The Permanence of the Marriage Relationship

_____ 6. The Preeminence of Christ in the Marriage Relationship

2. To help you become more specific in the evaluation and improvement of your marriage relationship, complete and then discuss the following "Rate Your Marriage" Inventory. Use this inventory to

discuss areas in which you are doing well and areas in which you need to improve. Use this rating scale:

4 = usually; 3 = often; 2 = sometimes; 1 = seldom; 0 = never

"RATE YOUR MARRIAGE" INVENTORY[1]

_____ 1. Does the fact that Jesus Christ is Lord manifest in practical ways in your marriage?

_____ 2. Do you use the Bible to determine your convictions, decisions, and practices in your life in general?

_____ 3. Do you use the Bible to determine your convictions, decisions, and practices in your marriage?

_____ 4. Do you and your spouse study the Bible and pray together?

_____ 5. Do you and your spouse worship God together in a Bible-believing church?

_____ 6. Do you and your spouse serve God together in a Bible-believing church; do you have common ministries?

_____ 7. Do you and your spouse seek to please each other?

_____ 8. Do you admit it and ask your spouse for forgiveness when you have done something wrong?

_____ 9. Do you grant forgiveness when your spouse asks for forgiveness?

_____ 10. Do you allow your spouse to disagree with you without becoming upset?

_____ 11. Do you allow your spouse to make a mistake without becoming nasty or punishing him or her?

_____ 12. Do you mainly focus on the things you appreciate about your spouse and freely express your appreciation?

_____ 13. Do you communicate with each other on an in-depth basis?

_____ 14. Do you feel free to express your opinions and ideas with your spouse?

_____ 15. Do you welcome your spouse's opinions and ideas?

_____ 16. Do you share your plans, aspirations, and desires with your spouse?

_____ 17. Do you share your feelings with your spouse?

_____ 18. Do you share your likes and dislikes with your spouse?

_____ 19. Do you feel free to express your fears, joys, frustrations, problems, and annoyances with each other?

_____ 20. Do you welcome what your spouse shares with you?

_____ 21. Do you and your spouse understand each other when you try to express yourselves?

_____ 22. Do you do many different things together?

_____ 23. Do you enjoy being with each other? Do you have fun together?

_____ 24. Do you have many common interests?

_____ 25. Do you show love to each other in many practical ways?

_____ 26. Do you still court each other by occasional gifts, unexpected attention, etc.?

_____ 27. Do you pray for each other?

_____ 28. Do you support and seek to encourage each other?

_____ 29. Do you anticipate and enjoy sexual relations with your spouse?

_____ 30. Are your sexual desires compatible?

_____ 31. Do you freely discuss your sexual desires with your mate?

_____ 32. Do you think your spouse is concerned about your views on sexual relations?

_____ 33. Do you agree about the way in which money should be spent?

_____ 34. Do you think your spouse is concerned about your views regarding the way in which money should be spent?

_____ 35. Do you agree on how to bring up children?

_____ 36. Do your children know that it is foolish to try to play one of you against the other—for example, that if Dad says "no," Mom will agree?

_____ 37. Do you refuse to lie to your spouse or deceive him or her in any way?

_____ 38. Can your spouse put full confidence in what you say, knowing that you are telling him or her the truth?

_____ 39. Do you relate well to your in-laws?

_____ 40. Do you refuse to allow your parents to interfere in your relationship with your spouse?

_____ 41. Does your spouse have reason to believe that you have really left mother and father in all the ways previously mentioned in this book?

_____ 42. Do you show respect to your spouse?

_____ 43. Are you glad to introduce your spouse to friends and associates?

_____ 44. Do you seek to change your specific habits or behaviors that may cause discomfort to your spouse or displease him or her?

_____ 45. Do you make your relationship with your spouse a matter of priority?

_____ 46. Do you agree with your spouse about the roles and responsibilities of the husband and wife?

_____ 47. Are you willing to face, discuss, and look for biblical solutions to any problems you may have without blowing up at or attacking the other person, dissolving into tears, running away, or becoming abusive in any way?

_____ 48. Do you maintain your own spiritual life and cultivate a deep and meaningful relationship with the Lord through regularly spending time in Bible study and prayer?

_____ 49. Do you keep short accounts with God, regularly examining yourself and confessing and forsaking your sin?

_____ 50. Do you memorize and meditate on Scripture and on living a life in accordance with God's Word?

Part 2

THE FULFILLED AND FULFILLING HUSBAND

WAYNE A. MACK
WITH
JOSHUA MACK

22

HUSBANDING INVOLVES
BEING A REAL LOVER

To begin this chapter of this sweetheart book, let's consider the following case study of a man who was experiencing difficulties in his marriage and in so doing learn something about what men must do to be the fulfilled and fulfilling husbands that God wants them to be.

Eight days after Christmas, Phyllis announced to Frank, her husband, "I'm leaving you. I'm thinking about getting a divorce. I waited to tell you so that I wouldn't spoil your holiday." The announcement struck Frank like lightning out of the blue. Until that moment, he had thought that they had an ideal marriage. When he met with his pastor for the first time, he described the situation this way:

"Pastor, I don't know what's gotten into Phyllis. She just told me that she's leaving me and thinking about getting a divorce. I don't have any idea why she's so unhappy. I love her deeply. We've been married twenty-eight years now, and I think we've had a really good marriage. We rarely argue and we never fight. I've never hit her, I don't yell at her, I'm not critical, and

I've always been an easygoing guy. Over the years, I've asked little more of her than to make the meals, wash the clothes, keep the house, take care of the kids, and be there when I need her.

"When I'm done with work, I head right for home, and that's where you'd find me every night. I haven't run around like other guys. I'm satisfied to stay home, read the newspaper, watch television, and work in my shop or out in the yard. I don't have to be around people all the time, and I certainly haven't wasted our money going places or buying frivolous things that none of us really need.

"Phyllis and I are both Christians. We're both church members who have attended the service of the church regularly. We have three lovely children who are all walking with the Lord. With all of this going for us, I just don't understand what could have gotten into Phyllis. I have no idea what she is so unhappy about. I just don't know what's going on. I've tried to be a good husband, but for some reason she's not satisfied. She refuses to talk, and she absolutely refuses to come with me for help.

"Pastor, please help me. I don't want to lose Phyllis. I love her. What do you think is going on? Why is she acting this way? What is she so unhappy about? What can I do to change her mind?"

From this case study, it is obvious that Phyllis and Frank's marriage is in real trouble. Phyllis is very unhappy—so desperate that she is willing to do something drastic to change her life. Frank is very confused. He was not in touch with how Phyllis was doing in their relationship, and so he was caught off guard by her announcement.

GOING WRONG ON TWO LEVELS

Where did things go wrong for this couple? We can answer that question on two levels. Ultimately, Phyllis is unhappy because she is trusting in Frank to bring her happiness. The Lord warns us not to do this: "Cursed is the man who trusts in mankind and makes flesh his strength . . . " (Jer. 17:5). Trusting in another person is futile because we are all sinful and incapable of satisfying the needs of another. And yet, as God says in Jeremiah 2:13, we so often do it anyway: "For My people have committed two evils: they have forsaken Me, the fountain of living waters, to hew for themselves cisterns, broken cisterns that can hold no water." Frank is a broken cistern who cannot meet the needs of Phyllis's heart.

On another level, however, we could also infer from the case study that Frank is not doing his part to be a fulfilled and fulfilling husband to Phyllis. Frank, as is the case for all husbands, needs to do three primary things for his wife in order to be a godly husband. Ephesians 5:25–33 lays out the first of these:

> Husbands, love your wives, just as Christ also loved the church and gave Himself up for her, so that He might sanctify her, having cleansed her by the washing of water with the word, that He might present to Himself the church in all her glory, having no spot or wrinkle or any such thing; but that she would be holy and blameless. So husbands ought also to love their own wives as their own bodies. He who loves his own wife loves himself; for no one ever hated his own flesh, but nourishes and cherishes it, just as Christ also does the church, because we are members of His body. For this reason a man shall leave his father and mother and shall be joined to his wife, and the two shall become one flesh. This mystery is great; but I am speaking with reference to Christ and the church. Nevertheless, each individual among you also is to love his own wife even as himself . . .

THE PRIMARY RESPONSIBILITY

What responsibilities does a husband have toward his wife, according to Scripture? The first thing, as indicated by this passage, is that husbands are to love their wives. Three times in these verses, Paul instructed husbands to love, and this is their primary responsibility toward their wives.

Concerning the husband's responsibility to love his wife, J. R. Miller has offered these thoughts:

> Each member of the household has a part in the family life and the fullest happiness and blessedness of the home can be attained only when each one's part is safely fulfilled. If any one member of the family fails in love or duty, the failure mars the whole household life, just as one discordant note in a company of singers spoils the music—though all the others sing in perfect accord. One person cannot alone make a home what it ought to be, what it might be.
>
> One sweet spirit may spread through the home the odors of love, even though among the other members, there is bitterness and strife, just as one fragrant flower may spread through a hedge of thorns a breath of perfume. The influence of one gentle and unselfish life may also in time soften rudeness and melt selfishness and pervade the home life with the blessedness of love.
>
> Yet still it is true that no member of a household can make the household life full and complete. Each must do a part. The husband has a part all his own which no other can do . . . There is one work which covers all as far as the husband's responsibility and the word is love.[1]

In order to be the fulfilled and fulfilling husband that God desires him to be, Frank needs to learn how to be a really good lover for his wife. Through my counseling and personal experience, I believe that many husbands have very little idea what it means to love someone as God desires. Some men, if they were asked, would say that loving their wives means making love to them—having sex. Others would say that love is a warm feeling toward their spouses, or intense physical attraction.

Some would say that love is something that one simply falls into and, by extension, can fall out of as well. When it happens, there is no controlling it, and when it is gone, there is nothing to be done to get it back. Or, like Frank, some would say that love is being there—being faithful, not being critical, providing for needs.

Wrong ideas about what love is abound. Frank seems to have accepted some of these ideas and, in order to save his marriage, is in need of some instruction on biblical love. To some extent, I suspect that many of us have also accepted some of these ideas and are in need of that instruction as well.

In the next few chapters, we will consider several reasons why husbands fail to love their wives as God commands. Then, having examined and evaluated our failings, we will spend the rest of this section for husbands looking at the three aspects of our responsibility toward our wives: being a godly lover, leader, and learner.

APPLICATION AND DISCUSSION

1. This chapter began with the case of Phyllis and Frank, who were experiencing some serious difficulties in their marriage. Frank asks, "What do you think is going on? Why is she acting this way? What is she so unhappy about? What can I do to change her mind?" This chapter suggests that these questions could be answered on two levels. What are those two levels? Explain them.

2. This chapter states that Frank, as is the case for all husbands, must do three primary things for his wife in order to be a godly husband. It also suggests that Phyllis is threatening to leave him because he is failing to fulfill that threefold responsibility. What does this chapter indicate is the primary responsibility in which Frank is failing?

3. How do we know that love is a very important aspect of being a fulfilling and fulfilled husband?

4. On what Scripture is this statement about the importance of husbandly love based?

5. What are some of the wrong ideas about love that are prevalent in our society?

6. From the account about Frank found at the beginning of this chapter, what do you think was Frank's concept of what it means to love Phyllis?

7. If someone were to ask you whether you love your wife, how would you answer?

8. If your answer is "yes," what do you mean when you say you love your wife? How do you define the word *love*?

9. What are you doing that communicates love to your wife? (Ask her!)

10. What do you do that communicates a lack of love to your wife? (Ask her!)

11. How can you improve as your wife's lover?

12. How would your wife like for you to improve as a lover? (Ask her!)

23

WHY DO HUSBANDS FAIL TO LOVE?

The well-known Hollywood performer Cher once said, "The trouble with some women is that they get all excited about nothing . . . and then they marry him." While I normally do not listen to much that Cher has to say, this time she has a point. Many husbands are failing their wives. Even many Christian husbands are not the husbands that God desires them to be. They are failing in the most fundamental of ways because they are not fulfilling the primary responsibility that God has given them in marriage.

Certainly, a husband might give any number of different excuses for failing to fulfill his chief duty to his wife. One excuse he cannot give, however, is that God's instructions are too complicated. Paul sums up the most essential duty of husbands to their wives very simply in Colossians 3:19: "Husbands, love your wives and do not be embittered against them." While there is much to that command, it is not difficult to understand. The husband's primary responsibility to his wife can be expressed in one word: *love*.

I have yet to meet a husband—and I have met a lot of husbands— who did not know that he was supposed to love his wife. I have had a number of counseling sessions with hardheaded husbands, but I have never had a husband, no matter how hardheaded, act surprised when I explained to him that God wanted him to love his wife. Yet I have known many husbands, like Frank mentioned at the beginning of the last chapter, who were failing to do just that.

If God's instructions are so simple and so familiar, why are they so difficult for so many husbands to obey? In this chapter and the two that follow, I want to examine six reasons that many professing Christian husbands fail to love their wives. I hope that by understanding what prevents husbands from truly loving their wives, we will have a better understanding of what it takes for us to love our wives as Paul commands in Colossians 3:19.

Reason 1: Insincere Faith

Without a doubt, Frank Abagnale (not to be confused with the Frank in the last chapter) will go down in history as one of the greatest con artists of all time. Abagnale ran away from home at the age of sixteen and, in order to support himself, decided to impersonate people with real jobs rather than getting one himself. He started by posing as an airline pilot. After that, he attempted to pose as a doctor and then a lawyer. He was actually quite successful, and a movie was recently made about his uncommon life.

Our society tends to honor con men such as Frank Abagnale, but con men do not deserve our respect. Abagnale wanted all the benefits that airline pilots, doctors, and lawyers receive, but was not willing to do the necessary work to deserve those benefits. So instead of actually becoming a pilot, doctor, or lawyer, he took the easy route. He went out and bought himself a uniform and started to pretend.

Unfortunately, many professing Christians are doing the same thing in their relationship with Christ. They are pretenders. Although they confess with their mouths, "Jesus is Lord," they have never truly submitted to Him in their hearts, and thus they have never been born again. They have simply put on the "uniform" and started to pretend. Whether they realize it or not, they are putting on a con.

The first reason that many professing Christian husbands fail to love their wives is that they are not genuinely Christian husbands. While a con artist such as Abagnale may have been able to talk like an airline pilot or doctor or lawyer, he was not any of those things. He could not really do the work of a pilot, doctor, or lawyer. Likewise, the person who is pretending to be a Christian may talk like a Christian and fool people into thinking he is a Christian, but he is not and therefore he is not going to be able to truly "do the work" of a Christian. He will never be able to love his wife in the way God commands unless he is born again.

One look at the context of Colossians 3:19 makes it clear that Paul was speaking to men whom he considered to be believers—the genuine article. Paul was addressing men whom he considered to have been "circumcised with a circumcision made without hands" (2:11), who had "died with Christ to the elementary principles of the world" (2:20), and who had "been raised up with Christ" (3:1).

I point this out because Scripture makes it clear that genuine biblical love is a fruit of the Spirit: "But the fruit of the Spirit is love . . ." (Gal. 5:22); and an evidence of new life in Christ: "Beloved, let us love one another, for love is from God; and everyone who loves is born of God and knows God" (1 John 4:7). It is also a confirmation that God Himself dwells in us: "if we love one another, God abides in us" (1 John 4:12). If a husband consistently fails to love his wife in the way that God describes, it may be an indicator that he is a pretender and not a genuine believer.

Any husband who is having trouble loving his wife needs to begin by examining his profession of faith. If he is a genuine believer, there is hope. He can love his wife as God commands. He may struggle doing it, but he can do it because he has all the resources that he needs in Christ. But if he is not a genuine believer, any attempt to obey Paul's command in his own strength will ultimately fail. His relationship with his wife cannot be right until his relationship with Christ is right. A husband cannot con his way through this command.

REASON 2: THE WRONG BOSS

The second reason that many professing Christian husbands fail to love their wives is that they have forgotten that Christ is Lord—their

Lord. Though I want all husbands to enjoy a happy marriage relationship with their wives, my primary concern is much greater than that. Above all, I wish to demonstrate the difference that the lordship of Christ should make in the way that we relate to our wives.

As we read through Colossians 3:18 and following, we find one description of Jesus coming up repeatedly: "Lord." The word *Lord* means "Master." When Paul said that husbands were to love their wives, he was telling Christian husbands what their Master wants from them. A godly marriage relationship is not just a matter between a husband and his wife. First and foremost, it is a matter between a husband and Jesus.

What does this mean? This means that the husband is not the final authority in the home—Jesus is. Too many husbands act as if Paul's exhortation about loving their wives were simply a nice piece of advice. But Colossians 3:19 is not advice; it is a command. Loving one's wife is not an option; it is an act of obedience.

It is easy for us to treat Jesus as one old employee of mine once treated me. This woman had the hardest time remembering that I was her boss. No matter when I scheduled her to come in, she would come to work when she wanted to. No matter what I asked her to do, she would sit down and do whatever she thought was most important.

I would talk to her about coming in late, and she would respond, "Oh, thank you for telling me about that; I understand, and I'll do better." And then, in spite of our talk and what she'd said, she would come in late anyway. Or I would talk to her about not doing what had I asked her to do, and she would say, "Oh, I shouldn't have done that. I'm sorry about that." And then she would do what she wanted to do anyway. What amazed me was that she seemed genuinely confused when I fired her months later.

Many husbands treat Jesus like that. In their heart of hearts they think that they are the boss. As a result, they do not pay much attention to what He has to say. Although Jesus tells them that loving their wives is their primary duty as husbands, they act as though it were not an important priority at all.

Though they know very well what Jesus commands them in Ephesians 5:25 and Colossians 3:19, "Husbands, love your wives . . . ," they act like that employee of mine. They simply nod their heads, go out, and do their own thing. They make their work a priority, or being respected by other people a priority, or getting their wives to do what they want a priority. Instead of turning to Jesus and receiving from Him the agenda for their lives and marital relationships, they make up their own agenda and follow that instead.

If we are true believers in Christ, we do not get to set the agenda for our lives. We are not self-employed; we belong to Jesus. We are here on earth to represent Him in everything that we do and say. Again, we must consider the context of this command to love in Colossians 3:19. In verse 17, Paul wrote, "Whatever you do in word or deed, do all in the name of the Lord Jesus, giving thanks through Him to God the Father." We relate to our wives for Christ, not for ourselves. Therefore, we must pay attention to what Jesus wants. Our Master has spoken, and He says that we need to make a priority of loving our wives.

APPLICATION
AND DISCUSSION

1. What is the main duty of a husband to his wife?
2. What excuses do husbands sometimes give for failing to fulfill this duty?
3. What excuse can't husbands use for failing to fulfill this biblical duty?
4. What was the point of the Frank Abagnale story?
5. What does it mean that some husbands are pretenders in their relationship with Christ?
6. Why is being a real Christian absolutely essential if a husband is to fulfill his main duty to his wife?
7. What does the lordship of Christ have to do with a husband's fulfilling his main duty to his wife?
8. Have you ever tried to justify your failure to love your wife or anyone else? What reason or excuse have you used?

24

MORE REASONS FOR HUSBANDS' LOVE FAILURES

I f an employee at a fast-food restaurant showed up to work an hour late, was half-asleep during most of his shift, and paid little attention as he made burgers throughout the day, how would his boss react? His boss might not be happy, but it would hardly compare to how the chief of surgery would react if one of his doctors showed up for surgery an hour late, was half-asleep throughout the operation, and paid little attention as he worked on his patient's heart.

REASON 3: IRRESPONSIBILITY

The doctor's negligence would be so much more serious than the fast-food employee's negligence because the stakes were so much higher. Most doctors understand that and thus take their responsibilities seriously. Unfortunately, many Christian husbands do not. The third reason that many professing Christian husbands fail to love their wives is that they do not take their responsibilities seriously enough.

When it comes to obeying Colossians 3:19, which says that husbands are to love their wives, many professing Christian men have no idea just how high the stakes really are. The stakes are so high because, as we have seen in the last chapter in Colossians 3:17, we as believers are representatives of Christ in all that we do and say. That means that the way in which we relate to our wives should represent Christ to our wives, to our families, and to the watching world.

Paul explained this principle in Ephesians 5:23–25: "For the husband is the head of the wife, as Christ also is the head of the church, He Himself being the Savior of the body. But as the church is subject to Christ, so also the wives ought to be to their husbands in everything. Husbands, love your wives, just as Christ also loved the church and gave Himself up for her . . ."

God has so designed the marriage relationship that the way in which the husband relates to the wife and the wife to the husband is to be a picture of the way in which Christ loved the church and the church submits to Christ. Therefore, we men must never minimize our responsibility to love our wives and act as if it were an issue of little importance. We are representatives of Christ. In marriage, we husbands have the wonderful privilege of representing Christ and His love for the church through our love for our wives.

Further, the stakes are high because Colossians 3:18 indicates that the husband has been placed in a position of leadership in his home. As a leader, he has a tremendous impact on his entire family by the way in which he relates to his wife and then to his children. The husband sets the course for everyone in his home.

It is instructive that Paul never commanded husbands to lead their families, only to love. One reason why he does not command this is that husbands do lead their families, whether they like it or not. As Paul reminded in Ephesians 5, God has placed the husband as the head of the home. Because of this, someone once said that husbands were in a place of "inescapable leadership," so Christian husbands cannot really refuse to lead. It may be poor leadership, perhaps even in the wrong direction, but no matter what they do or wherever they go, they remain as the heads of their families.

That is how God designed marriage. Therefore much hinges on whether we set the pace by obeying Paul's instructions in Colossians

3:19 or not. Failing to take seriously this command to love our wives is like flipping a lighted match onto a pile of kindling in a forest on a hot, dry summer day. We may rightly say that it was only a small spark we let fly, but we can be sure that the consequences of that little spark will be devastating. Our failure to lead our wives in the way God desires will have harsh consequences. We must take our responsibilities seriously. The stakes are high.

REASON 4: WILLFUL IGNORANCE

The fourth reason that many professing Christian husbands fail to love their wives is that they are not willing to learn how to love their wives. Many men treat Colossians 3:19 the way that Tim "The Tool Man" Taylor from the television show *Home Improvement* treated instructions for construction projects. When someone would start to give Tim advice about how to do a project, he would listen to the first sentence and then, before he got sufficient "how to" instructions, would immediately go to work trying to complete the project. In this sitcom, Tim didn't see any point in waiting for instructions because he was confident that he already knew how to do the project. When he actually got into the project, however, about midway through he would realize that he should have listened more closely because he really had no clue what he was doing.

Likewise, many men sit in church and listen to sermons about loving their wives but never really hear them. They listen to the first sentence and then figure that they already know the rest and can take it from there. These men treat loving their wives as a "do-it-yourself" project. Because of that, it is no surprise that they have troubles.

Suppose I had decided to purchase a piece of land and build a house for my family. Though I had no talent for tools (none at all), for some reason I determined to build this house on my own. And even knowing my own lack of talent and expertise, I did not buy a book about building houses. In fact, I did not even talk to anyone about how to build a house because I had decided to do it all on my own. Obviously, in this type of situation the consequences of my willful ignorance would be dire. If that house ever got built at all, no one would want to live in it because it would be so poorly constructed.

Yet that is exactly what so many men do when it comes to loving their wives. Though they were never taught how to love a woman as God desires them to, they insist on doing it on their own. They never ask for help; they never seek out instruction. It is no wonder, then, that their families are crashing down all around them.

As Solomon explained in Proverbs 10:8, "The wise of heart will receive commands, but a babbling fool will be ruined." The instructions that Paul gave to us husbands in Colossians 3:19 will not do us any good if we refuse to listen.

APPLICATION
AND DISCUSSION

1. In the context of love failures, what is the point of the illustration that compares a fast-food worker to a surgeon?

2. Why do we say that the stakes are so high when it comes to the matter of a husband's loving his wife?

3. What does the fact that we are representatives of Christ have to do with a husband's love for his wife?

4. Evaluate and discuss the statement that "the husband sets the course for everyone in his home." Do you agree or disagree? Why?

5. What does "husbands are in a place of 'inescapable leadership' " mean? Do you agree or disagree? Why?

6. What is the point of the Tim "The Tool Man" illustration? What did Tim do that is comparable to what some husbands do?

7. If husbands are to fulfill their main responsibility to their wives, what must they be willing to do?

8. Are you willing to do this? How will you begin?

25

EVEN MORE REASONS FOR HUSBANDS' LOVE FAILURES

REASON 5: UNGODLY LOVE

The fifth reason that many professing Christian husbands fail to love their wives is that they do not have a biblical understanding of love. When Paul commanded husbands to love their wives in Colossians 3, he was not talking about a worldly kind of love. Ephesians 5:25–33, a portion of Scripture that we will examine very carefully in the next few chapters, expands on the idea presented in Colossians 3:19. Here, Paul explains exactly the kind of love that he is talking about: "Husbands, love your wives, just as Christ also loved the church and gave Himself up for her" (Eph. 5:25). In other words, husbands are to love their wives as Christ loves us. Unfortunately, many husbands love their wives according to the world's definition of *love* instead.

What does ungodly love look like? A husband's love is not a godly love when he says that he loves his wife, but he is not willing to make any personal sacrifices for her. He does not think about her interests. He is so consumed with himself that he rarely stops to think about what she might want or need. On her birthday, he cannot understand why she shows so little enthusiasm for the new fishing rod he got her. He is like the husband who said to me, quite sincerely, "My wife and I would get along great if she would just do what I want."

Christlike love is sacrificial by definition: Christ loved the church and gave Himself up for her. Jesus put our interests above His own interests. More than that, our interests were His interests. As husbands, we cannot be primarily concerned about our own selfish interests and expect to be able to love another person as Christ loves us. If we want to be imitators of Christ, as Scripture commands, we must love sacrificially.

Other husbands say that they love their wives, but then live with them on a merit system. This kind of husband loves his wife until she makes a mistake. Once she lets him down in any way, then she is treated differently.

It is very much like the way in which a friend of my father's used to treat waitresses. When he would go to a restaurant, he would put a couple of dollars down on the table and then look at the waitress and say, "That's your potential tip. Any mistakes and I'm going to start taking money away." Too many husbands are like that with their love and affection. "I'm putting it down on the table, and then I'll take a little bit away every time you mess up."

Christlike love is far different from that because, thankfully, it is not based on what we deserve. What we deserve is hell. Instead, as Romans 5:8 tells us, "But God demonstrates His own love toward us, in that while we were yet sinners, Christ died for us." Too many men love their wives according to the measure that their wives love them instead of loving their wives as Christ loved them.

Still others say that they love their wives, but then fail to express that love through action. They are lazy husbands. A few months ago my wife and I had the opportunity to walk through an old, abandoned junior-college building. It was a mess: rooms had been stripped to the bone, surfaces were moldy, windows were broken. It was cold, dark, and damp.

The real estate agent who was walking us through the building was in obvious dismay because she remembered what it had been like in its prime. But in just ten years, a great change had taken place in that old building. What was once a beautiful facility is now a nightmare, and all because of neglect. Many marriage relationships are like that old junior-college building because of the husband's neglect.

When Paul said, "Husbands, love your wives," he was giving a command. In other words, we have to do something. We have to act because Christlike love is active. Christ loved us and took action by coming to earth and giving His life for ours. Likewise, if we are going to love our wives as Christ loves us, it is not enough to merely say it; we must do something about it.

Finally, some husbands say that they love their wives, but then do nothing to seek their wives' spiritual good. Such a husband has never spent time thinking hard about how he can help his wife grow in Christ. He does not talk to her about spiritual things. He has never worked with her on issues in her life, nor has he gently confronted her when she sins. Many men are very careful and faithful to provide for their families' financial needs, but hardly ever think about how they can provide for their families' spiritual needs.

Again, Christlike love is vastly different. Paul said in Ephesians 5:26 that Christ gave Himself up for the church, "so that He might sanctify her, having cleansed her by the washing of water with the word." Christ loves us, so He made a great sacrifice to purify us. If we love our wives, we are going to do the same. We are going to be willing to make great sacrifices so that they might become more and more holy.

How do we do this? Loving our wives in this way means that we will take the lead when it comes to getting to church to hear the Word of God preached and to be around godly Christians. Scripture tells us that this is one of the ways that we grow spiritually, and yet so many husbands drag their families down because of their unwillingness to get out of bed and lead their families to church. The husband can have an impact on his wife's spiritual life in numerous other ways, and these will be discussed in later chapters.

Christlike love is far different from worldly love. Yet too often, Christian husbands apply worldly ideas of love to their marriage relationship. The kind of love that Paul was talking about in Colossians 3:19 is not something that one can fall in and out of, it is not based on the merit system, and it is much more than simply not giving one's wife a hard time, as poor Frank seemed to think. Instead of evaluating the way that we are loving our wives in light of the world's standards, we need to evaluate our love for our wives in light of Christ's standards. We will never walk in obedience to this command until we do.

REASON 6: UNGODLY RESPONSES

There are many myths about what makes a good marriage. One of the most common myths is that a good marriage is problem-free. But a good marriage is never without problems. Every marriage has them, and the final reason that many professing Christian husbands fail to love their wives is that husbands respond to those problems in a way that makes them worse.

As we discussed in earlier chapters, husbands and wives are different and we will disappoint each other at times. This is because we are sinners and we sin against each other. That is the reality of marriage in a fallen world—good marriages and bad marriages alike have problems. But one of the differences between a godly marriage and an ungodly one is the way in which those problems are dealt with.

A husband does not love his wife in a godly way if he responds to his wife's sin in ways that make the problem worse. Paul warned us about just such a wrong response when he ended his statement in Colossians 3:19: "Husbands, love your wives and do not be embittered against them."

Instead of biblically dealing with problems when they come up, many husbands allow those problems to fester in their hearts. They become bitter, and that bitterness is like venom, poisoning their love for their wives. They start doing things just to be difficult. Their voices have no softness or gentleness anymore. They take advantage of their authority by being overbearing and demanding.

The saddest thing about bitterness is that those who are bitter usually refuse to take any responsibility for their bitterness. Instead, they lay all the blame on their wives. Bitterness, however, is a response—and a bad one. Another person cannot make us bitter. According to Scripture, the husband has a responsibility (and thus an ability) to love his wife and not become bitter. This means that when she sins against him, he needs to choose to respond to her sin in a biblical way. He must be willing to forgive because if he does not, his ungodly response will destroy his marriage.

We might picture bitterness like a dirty diaper. Every time a wife sins against her husband, it is like a big, messy diaper. But instead of taking it out to the trash—forgiving his wife or being patient with her— many husbands just let that dirty, smelly diaper sit in the room with them. After a few years, there are hundreds of dirty diapers around the house, and the husband and wife wonder why their home life stinks.

The only way to avoid this kind of mess is to take out those dirty diapers, one at a time, as they are made. In the same way, we have to deal with sin biblically by addressing each issue in a proper way as it comes up. No, biblically dealing with sin is not easy. But if we are going to love our wives in the way God wants us to, we must live near the cross. In other words, we have to know how much Jesus loves us and how much He has forgiven us if we are going to love and forgive our wives.

In spite of what many have said, God designed marriage to be a good thing. If a couple is going to have a good marriage, one that glorifies God and brings them joy, then the husband's primary responsibility is clear: he must love his wife and refuse to become bitter. We have looked at the sin that keeps husbands from doing that. Knowing why many professing Christian husbands fail to love their wives ought to help us understand what it takes to truly love ours.

Husbands, if we are going to love our wives, we must first examine our profession of faith. One's relationship with his wife will not be right until his relationship with Christ is right. The husband must remind himself who is really boss. Loving his wife is not an option; it is a command. His relationship with his wife is not just about his relationship with his wife. It is about the husband's relationship with Christ. Are we husbands going to submit to Him, or not?

We must always remember the privilege that God has given us. We represent Christ and His love for us to a watching world. We need to put away our pride and seek out instruction. If we are going to obey Paul's command, we need to make a priority out of studying the Word and to develop relationships with other godly men who will help us learn how to love our wives.

Husbands, we ought to constantly bask in Christ's love for us. Understanding the way in which Christ loves us will help us model our own love after His. And we need to carefully guard our hearts against bitterness. We must not let anything poison our love for our wives.

Many husbands fail to fulfill their primary responsibility—namely, love—to their wives, but we do not have to be among them. Now that we have considered the six major obstacles to Christlike love—what a godly husband's love *should not* look like—we will examine Scripture in the next two chapters to find out what our love for our wives *should* look like.

APPLICATION
AND DISCUSSION

1. What additional reasons are mentioned in this chapter that relate to the love failures of some husbands?

2. What does ungodly love look like?

3. What does loving on a merit system look like? Give illustrations.

4. Ask your wife whether she ever thinks she is being loved on a merit system. What reasons does she have for her answer?

5. What does being a lazy husband look like? Give illustrations.

6. Ask your wife whether you ever seem to be a lazy husband when it comes to loving her. What reasons does she have for her answer?

7. What does the way in which we think about or respond to problems in marriage have to do with the husband's love for his wife?

8. How does the way in which some husbands respond to the sins of their wives or to relationship problems make matters worse?

9. How is bitterness related to love?

10. How does bitterness develop in a marriage relationship?

11. What effect does bitterness have on a marriage relationship?

12. How is bitterness like a dirty diaper?

13. What must be done if bitterness is to be avoided in a relationship?

14. In what ways does the information in this chapter relate to you? What instructions were given that you must implement in your relationship?

26

LOVING INVOLVES CHERISHING AND NOURISHING

Ephesians 5 reveals two key principles for loving our wives as God desires. One is described in verse 25, which we briefly discussed in the previous chapter and which we will study more fully in the following chapter. Another key principle is presented in verse 28, where we are told that husbands should love their wives as they love themselves. To begin, let's look at that principle: what does it mean to love as we love ourselves?

Verse 29 of this passage answers the question for us: "for no one ever hated his own flesh, but nourishes and cherishes it . . ." Loving our wives as we love ourselves means that, first, we will cherish her. In 1 Thessalonians 2:7, Paul used the same Greek word for *cherish* when he wrote, "But we proved to be gentle among you, as a nursing mother tenderly cares for her own children." How a nursing mother cares for her new baby is a wonderful picture of what it means to cherish someone.

First Peter 3:7 conveys this same idea: "You husbands in the same way, live with your wives in an understanding way, as with someone weaker . . . ; and show her honor as a fellow heir of the grace of life . . ." In both these verses we see the idea of communicating to the other person that she is important and deeply loved. In the case of Frank mentioned on pages 153 and 154, though he may not have beaten or mistreated his wife in any way, he seems to have failed to communicate to Phyllis how important she was to him. He did not actively cherish her.

It is important to note that when Peter uses the phrase "as with someone weaker," he is not referring to merely physical strength. Though men, on average, may have greater muscular strength than women do, there are other ways in which women are physically stronger than men. For example, it is well known that women have a higher tolerance for pain and usually live longer than men do.

Considering this verse within the greater context of chapters 2 and 3 of 1 Peter, I believe that Peter is referring to the biblical-authority relationship between husbands and wives. Because husbands have authority over their wives within the marriage relationship, a husband may be tempted to misuse his authority and abuse his wife. Peter was saying here that since that possibility exists, husbands ought to be especially careful in how they relate to their wives.

A person who is under the authority of someone else can be made to feel very useless and unappreciated if the one with authority is not considerate of the person's feelings and needs. A husband ought to put himself in his wife's place and ask, "How do I respond when I am under someone's authority? How do I like to be treated?" It is much easier to serve a grateful, appreciative, encouraging master than one who is critical or even just oblivious to the work being done. So it is with husbands and wives. Husbands need to communicate to their wives that they are extremely valuable and important to them.

In fact, I believe that much of the feminism in our world is the result of both the sinful hearts of women (pride makes us want to be our own boss) and, sadly, the reality that men do abuse women. Men have God-given authority over their wives, but some of them misuse that authority and are inconsiderate, insensitive, and unappreciative. They treat their wives as if their sole purpose were to satisfy and serve them. This has been true throughout history, and this sin on the man's part stirs up the natural sinfulness in the woman's heart.

Let's go back to the case of Frank again. If Frank is going to love his wife as he loves himself—if we are all going to love our wives as we love ourselves—then he must be careful to cherish Phyllis as God has commanded. This means that Frank must listen to her, thank her for the things she does for him, praise and encourage her, and regularly tell and show her how valuable she is to him.

WIVES REQUIRE NOURISHING

In addition to cherishing our wives, Paul said that we ought to love our wives as we love ourselves by nourishing them. The word that is translated "nourish" in Ephesians 5:29 is the same word used in Ephesians 6:4, where Paul said, "Fathers, do not provoke your children to anger, but bring them up in the *discipline* and instruction of the Lord." In the King James Version, this phrase is translated "the *nurture* and admonition of the Lord." This word is also used in the Septuagint (the Greek Old Testament) in Genesis 47:12, which says that Joseph "provided his father and his brothers and all his father's household with food . . ."

To nourish someone, then, means to provide for that person's needs. What needs do wives have? We can easily come up with a list of such obvious things as food, clothing, and shelter, which are certainly important things for husbands to provide, as 1 Timothy 5:8 points out: "But if anyone does not provide for his own, and especially for those of his household, he has denied the faith and is worse than an unbeliever."

But there is much more to it than that. The Scripture also indicates that husbands are to be shepherds of their families, including their wives. In Psalm 23 we find an excellent summary of the kinds of things that a shepherd does for his sheep. In looking at this psalm, consider what the shepherd does for his sheep in terms of how a husband might show love to his wife.

"The LORD is my shepherd, I shall not want. He makes me lie down in green pastures; He leads me beside quiet waters" (23:1–2). Husbands ought to provide comfort and safety. "He restores my soul" (23:3a). Husbands ought to make sure that their wives are spiritually refreshed. "He guides me in the paths of righteousness for His name's sake" (23:3b). Husbands need to provide guidance and direction.

"Even though I walk through the valley of the shadow of death, I fear no evil, for You are with me; Your rod and Your staff, they comfort me" (23:4). In Palestine, the Valley of the Shadow of Death was and is an actual valley through which shepherds would often lead their sheep. They would walk along a narrow cliff on one side of the valley that was so steep that if the sheep were to fall, they would be killed. It was often very dark in this valley, so much so that the sheep could not see the shepherd ahead of them. To reassure them, the shepherd would take his rod and tap the rocks beside him so that the sheep would hear and be assured that he was still with them. Husbands, as shepherds of their wives, likewise need to be encouraging, comforting, and sensitive to them.

"You prepare a table before me in the presence of my enemies; You have anointed my head with oil; my cup overflows. Surely goodness and lovingkindness will follow me all the days of my life, and I will dwell in the house of the LORD forever" (23:5–6). Here we see the idea of providing, protecting, tending to hurts, and blessing.

All of these things are part of the idea of nourishing. Husbands must recognize that their wives need more than food and clothing. They have emotional needs, social needs, intellectual needs, and on and on. In order to love our wives as we love ourselves, we must make it our aim to nourish them in every way.

LIVING IT OUT

What does this look like on a practical level? Nourishing and cherishing means that a husband will do things such as using terms of endearment when addressing his wife. It means demonstrating affection and expressing appreciation. It means enthusiastically cooperating with her on things that she wants to do. It means fulfilling her requests—fixing the drainpipe, taking out the trash, etc. And it means discerning and fulfilling her unspoken requests as well.

The following application exercise can be used to evaluate whether or not husbands are loving their wives as they love themselves by cherishing and nourishing them. Use this inventory as a way not only to gauge how you are doing now, but also to broaden your understanding of what it means to cherish and nourish so that you can be the fulfilled and fulfilling husband that God wants you to be.

"How to Be Your Wife's Lover" Inventory[1]

How do you rate as your wife's lover? What is your LQ (love quotient) in reference to your wife? How are you doing at being the lover that God wants you to be (Eph. 5:25–33; Col. 3:19)? Are you loving your wife autobiographically (i.e., the way you want to be loved), or are you loving her in the way that she wants to be loved? The following list will help you to assess your LQ and, perhaps, reaffirm that you are doing a pretty good job in this area or help you to understand some ways in which you can improve. Carefully read and think about every statement. Having done this, (1) put an "X" next to the expression of something you are already doing, (2) put a check mark next to the things you are not doing or doing poorly and infrequently, (3) put a "+" (plus) mark in front of any of the expressions that you think your wife would appreciate most, and (4) put a "−" (minus) mark in front of any of the statements that you think your wife would not appreciate at all. To get the maximum benefit out of doing this exercise, work through the inventory with your wife to get her feedback after you have done it by yourself and ask her for her perspective on each item. Then have her put a check mark in front of any of the ways of showing love that are especially meaningful to her.

___ I (never ___ , seldom ___ , sometimes ___ , often ___ , regularly/daily ___) use words of endearment with her, such as: *I love you, honey, darling, dear, sweetheart.*

___ I (never ___ , seldom ___ , sometimes ___ , often ___ , regularly/daily ___) let her know how much I appreciate her.

___ When I know she'd like for me to demonstrate my affection for her physically, I (never ___ , seldom ___ , sometimes ___ , often ___ , regularly/daily ___) do so by holding her hand ___ , taking her arm ___ , giving her a hug __ , giving her a kiss __ , putting my hand on her leg __ , sitting close to her __ .

____ I (never __ , seldom __ , sometimes __ , often __ , regularly/daily __) enthusiastically support and cooperate with her when she wants to do something.

____ I (never __ , seldom __ , sometimes __ , often __ , regularly/daily __) try to anticipate her desires and wishes.

____ I (never __ , seldom __ , sometimes __ , often __ , regularly/daily __) try to fulfill her spoken requests.

____ I (never __ , seldom __ , sometimes __ , often __ , regularly/daily __) try to fulfill her unspoken desires and wishes.

____ I (never __ , seldom __ , sometimes __ , often __ , regularly/daily __) enthusiastically share her hobbies and recreational preferences.

____ I (never __ , seldom __ , sometimes __ , often __ , regularly/daily __) invite her to join me in my recreational preferences.

____ I (never __ , seldom __ , sometimes __ , often __ , regularly/daily __) attempt to make her aware that I admire and respect her and am thrilled to be her husband.

____ I (never __ , seldom __ , sometimes __ , often __ , regularly/daily __) enthusiastically exercise leadership in family devotions and prayer.

____ I (never __ , seldom __ , sometimes __ , often __ , regularly/daily __) structure my time and use it wisely.

____ I am (never __ , seldom __ , sometimes __ , often __ , regularly/daily __) willing to work with her on projects in which she is interested.

____ I (never __ , seldom __ , sometimes __ , often __ , regularly/daily __) ask for her advice/counsel when I have problems or decisions to make.

____ I (never __ , seldom __ , sometimes __ , often __ , regularly/daily __) accept her counsel and follow through on it.

____ I am (never __ , seldom __ , sometimes __ , often __ , regularly/daily __) her best cheerleader and fan, enthusiastically expressing my appreciation, confidence, and respect for her as a person, for her accomplishments, and for her abilities.

___ When I sin or fail in any way, I (never ___ , seldom ___ , sometimes ___ , often ___ , regularly/daily ___) don't excuse myself, blame someone else, or defend myself, but take full and personal responsibility for whatever I have done that is wrong.

___ When I sin against her, I am (never ___ , seldom ___ , sometimes ___ , often ___ , regularly/daily ___) quick to ask for forgiveness.

___ When I sin against her, I (never ___ , seldom ___ , sometimes ___ , often ___ , regularly/daily ___) try to change my sinful thoughts, attitudes, feelings, words, actions.

___ I (never ___ , seldom ___ , sometimes ___ , often ___ , regularly/daily ___) share my thoughts and feelings with her.

___ I (never ___ , seldom ___ , sometimes ___ , often ___ , regularly/daily ___) patiently listen to her when she wants to share her concerns with me.

___ I am (never ___ , seldom ___ , sometimes ___ , often ___ , regularly/daily ___) willing to allow her to disagree with me without becoming upset about it.

___ I am (never ___ , seldom ___ , sometimes ___ , often ___ , regularly/daily ___) willing to calmly and respectfully discuss her concerns even if they involve my having done something she doesn't like or wants me to change.

___ I (never ___ , seldom ___ , sometimes ___ , often ___ , regularly/daily ___) put the best possible interpretation on something she says, does, or doesn't do.

___ I (never ___ , seldom ___ , sometimes ___ , often ___ , regularly/daily ___) willingly listen to her without interruption.

___ I (never ___ , seldom ___ , sometimes ___ , often ___ , regularly/daily ___) stop what I'm doing, thinking, or saying and give her my full attention when she wants to talk.

___ I (never ___ , seldom ___ , sometimes ___ , often ___ , regularly/daily ___) wait until I've heard whatever she has to say before I decide what she means by her remarks.

___ I (never ___ , seldom ___ , sometimes ___ , often ___ , regularly/daily ___) wait until I've fully heard what she has said before I plan my response to it.

___ I (never __ , seldom __ , sometimes __ , often __ , regularly/daily __) let her know by my words, actions, and attitudes that I enjoy being with her.

___ I am (never __ , seldom __ , sometimes __ , often __ , regularly/daily __) a fun person to be around.

___ I (never __ , seldom __ , sometimes __ , often __ , regularly/daily __) take life seriously.

___ I (never __ , seldom __ , sometimes __ , often __ , regularly/daily __) focus mainly on the things in life, in our own relationship, and in our relationships with other people that are right, just, lovely, honorable, pure, excellent, and worthy of praise.

___ I (never __ , seldom __ , sometimes __ , often __ , regularly/daily __) seriously consider what will encourage her when she is discouraged.

___ When I sense that she is discouraged, I (never __ , seldom __ , sometimes __ , often __ , regularly/daily __) make it a matter of prayer.

___ When I sense that she is discouraged, I (never __ , seldom __ , sometimes __ , often __ , regularly/daily __) seek God's direction and help and then do what I think will encourage her.

___ I (never __ , seldom __ , sometimes __ , often __ , regularly/daily __) join with her in her Christian service (ministry) opportunities.

___ I (never __ , seldom __ , sometimes __ , often __ , regularly/daily __) empathize with her when she is experiencing difficulties and let her know that she can count on me.

___ When she is honored in any way or accomplishes some task, I (never __ , seldom __ , sometimes __ , often __ , regularly/daily __) enter into her joy and seek to let her know how pleased I am.

___ I (never __ , seldom __ , sometimes __ , often __ , regularly/daily __) want to have mutual friends and join with her in doing things with these friends.

___ I (never __ , seldom __ , sometimes __ , often __ , regularly/daily __) make an effort to understand the nature of her work.

___ I (never __ , seldom __ , sometimes __ , often __ , regularly/daily __) discuss spiritual truths with her.

____ I (never __ , seldom __ , sometimes __ , often __ , regularly/daily __) discuss problems with her.

____ I am (never __ , seldom __ , sometimes __ , often __ , regularly/daily __) available to her when she desires sex relations.

____ I (never __ , seldom __ , sometimes __ , often __ , regularly/daily __) focus on what pleases her in sex relations.

____ I (never __ , seldom __ , sometimes __ , often __ , regularly/daily __) pamper her and make a fuss over her.

____ I (never __ , seldom __ , sometimes __ , often __ , regularly/daily __) refuse to nag.

____ I (never __ , seldom __ , sometimes __ , often __ , regularly/daily __) do not treat her like a child or an incompetent person.

____ I (never __ , seldom __ , sometimes __ , often __ , regularly/daily __) refrain from giving advice or telling her what to do when she already knows what needs to be done.

____ I (never __ , seldom __ , sometimes __ , often __ , regularly/daily __) take the initiative in seeking sex relations.

____ I (never __ , seldom __ , sometimes __ , often __ , regularly/daily __) seek to learn what pleases her in our physical relations.

____ I am (never __ , seldom __ , sometimes __ , often __ , regularly/daily __) willing to do whatever pleases her and is not sinful in sex relations or to refrain from doing what would be displeasing to her.

____ I (never __ , seldom __ , sometimes __ , often __ , regularly/daily __) respond warmly and enthusiastically to her physical expressions of affection.

____ I (never __ , seldom __ , sometimes __ , often __ , regularly/daily __) try to make sure that all problems between us are settled before we have sex relations.

____ I am (never __ , seldom __ , sometimes __ , often __ , regularly/daily __) willing to participate with her in doing new and different things (sexually and otherwise).

____ I (never __ , seldom __ , sometimes __ , often __ , regularly/daily __) seek to develop an interest in the things that interest her.

___ When we're apart, I (never ___ , seldom ___ , sometimes ___ , often ___ , regularly/daily ___) really miss her and look forward to seeing her again.

___ I (never ___ , seldom ___ , sometimes ___ , often ___ , regularly/daily ___) share with her what I'm reading or what is going on in my life.

___ I (never ___ , seldom ___ , sometimes ___ , often ___ , regularly/daily ___) tell the children and others about her good qualities or accomplishments.

___ I (never ___ , seldom ___ , sometimes ___ , often ___ , regularly/daily ___) refuse to complain or gossip to others about her.

___ When I have agreed to do something, I (never ___ , seldom ___ , sometimes ___ , often ___ , regularly/daily ___) do it.

___ When I have agreed not to do something, I (never ___ , seldom ___ , sometimes ___ , often ___ , regularly/daily ___) don't do it.

___ When I know that there is something she'd like me to do and I know it doesn't violate God's will for me, I (never ___ , seldom ___ , sometimes ___ , often ___ , regularly/daily ___) try to do it.

___ When I know that there is something she doesn't want me to do and I know it doesn't violate God's will for me not to do it, I (never ___ , seldom ___ , sometimes ___ , often ___ , regularly/daily ___) either don't do it or discuss it with her and seek to discern whether it is just a preference or more than that.

___ When she shares something with me and I know she wants me to keep it confidential, I (never ___ , seldom ___ , sometimes ___ , often ___ , regularly/daily ___) keep it confidential unless to do so would violate God's will and she or someone else would be hurt or really hindered by my keeping it confidential.

___ When we have serious and continuing problems or conflicts that we can't personally resolve, I am (never ___ , seldom ___ , sometimes ___ , often ___ , regularly/daily ___) willing to seek godly counsel to secure resolution.

___ I am (never ___ , seldom ___ , sometimes ___ , often ___ , regularly/daily ___) more interested in her opinion than I am in anyone else's opinion.

___ I am (never ___ , seldom ___ , sometimes ___ , often ___ , regularly/daily ___) willing to cover her faults (Prov. 10:12) and not allow them to influence my attitudes and actions toward her.

____ I (never ___ , seldom ___ , sometimes ___ , often ___ , regularly/daily ___) get great joy out of seeing her growing in her walk with God.

____ If I have a problem with her, I (never ___ , seldom ___ , sometimes ___ , often ___ , regularly/daily ___) pray about it and seriously consider what God would have me do before I do anything.

____ If I think something in her life is seriously hindering her in her relationship with or service to God and effectiveness with others, I am (never ___ , seldom ___ , sometimes ___ , often ___ , regularly/daily ___) willing to do the hard thing and gently and carefully bring it to her attention (Prov. 27:6–7).

____ I (never ___ , seldom ___ , sometimes ___ , often ___ , regularly/daily ___) pray for her throughout my day.

____ I (never ___ , seldom ___ , sometimes ___ , often ___ , regularly/daily ___) attempt to help her to make important changes out of love for God and her.

____ I am (never ___ , seldom ___ , sometimes ___ , often ___ , regularly/daily ___) ready to leave at the appointed time and am punctual in keeping time commitments we have made.

____ I am (never ___ , seldom ___ , sometimes ___ , often ___ , regularly/daily ___) lovingly honest with her and don't withhold the truth that may hinder our present or future relationship.

____ I am (never ___ , seldom ___ , sometimes ___ , often ___ , regularly/daily ___) willing to dream with her and join with her in discussing future plans and aspirations.

____ I (never ___ , seldom ___ , sometimes ___ , often ___ , regularly/daily ___) run errands gladly.

____ I am (never ___ , seldom ___ , sometimes ___ , often ___ , regularly/daily ___) willing to do fix-it jobs and respond cheerfully to her requests for help.

____ I am (never ___ , seldom ___ , sometimes ___ , often ___ , regularly/daily ___) willing to help with household chores (making beds, washing dishes, cleaning up, doing the wash, folding the clothes and putting them away, going to the cleaner's, shopping, putting clothes in hamper, helping the children with homework, etc.).

____ I (never ___ , seldom ___ , sometimes ___ , often ___ , regularly/daily ___) handle my areas of finances responsibly.

____ I (never ___ , seldom ___ , sometimes ___ , often ___ , regularly/daily ___) stay within the family budget and respect her concerns about finances.

____ I (never ___ , seldom ___ , sometimes ___ , often ___ , regularly/daily ___) refrain from making comments about our lack of extra money in such a way that she might think I am blaming her for all financial difficulties.

____ I (never ___ , seldom ___ , sometimes ___ , often ___ , regularly/daily ___) take care of the children so that she has free time.

____ I am (never ___ , seldom ___ , sometimes ___ , often ___ , regularly/daily ___) a good example to the children.

____ I (never ___ , seldom ___ , sometimes ___ , often ___ , regularly/daily ___) make plans carefully, prayerfully, and biblically.

____ I am (never ___ , seldom ___ , sometimes ___ , often ___ , regularly/daily ___) tender, gentle, polite, and courteous with her.

____ I (never ___ , seldom ___ , sometimes ___ , often ___ , regularly/daily ___) do not yell or scream at her.

____ I (never ___ , seldom ___ , sometimes ___ , often ___ , regularly/daily ___) refrain from being overbearing, pushy, or domineering.

____ I (never ___ , seldom ___ , sometimes ___ , often ___ , regularly/daily ___) ask for her prayers and assistance in overcoming sinful habits.

____ I (never ___ , seldom ___ , sometimes ___ , often ___ , regularly/daily ___) plan date nights, mini-honeymoons, or some kind of getaway for the two of us to be together without interference.

____ I (never ___ , seldom ___ , sometimes ___ , often ___ , regularly/daily ___) compliment her on her appearance or something she is wearing.

____ I (never ___ , seldom ___ , sometimes ___ , often ___ , regularly/daily ___) write love notes, send a card, make a special call, remember birthdays and anniversaries.

____ I (never ___ , seldom ___ , sometimes ___ , often ___ , regularly/daily ___) exercise biblical leadership with the children, seeking to avoid provoking them to wrath and to bring them up in the discipline and instruction of the Lord.

____ I have been and still am (never ___ , seldom ___ , sometimes ___ , often ___ , regularly/daily ___) willing to discuss child-rearing issues and practices with her.

____ I (never ___ , seldom ___ , sometimes ___ , often ___ , regularly/daily ___) protect and defend her (physically, emotionally, spiritually, socially) against all people, including family members, who seek to hurt her.

____ I (never ___ , seldom ___ , sometimes ___ , often ___ , regularly/daily ___) consider her to be my best earthly friend and seek to do those things that promote the continuance and development of our friendship.

____ I (never ___ , seldom ___ , sometimes ___ , often ___ , regularly/daily ___) remember to keep her informed about items that will involve and affect her (such as meetings, people, finances, work responsibilities, the car, working late, etc.).

____ I (never ___ , seldom ___ , sometimes ___ , often ___ , regularly/daily ___) maintain my own spiritual life through Bible study, prayer, regular church attendance, and fellowship with God's people.

____ I (never ___ , seldom ___ , sometimes ___ , often ___ , regularly/daily ___) provide some form of adequate health, life, and disability insurance.

____ I am (never ___ , seldom ___ , sometimes ___ , often ___ , regularly/daily ___) seeking to provide some form of support for her and the children in case I die or become incapacitated.

____ I (never ___ , seldom ___ , sometimes ___ , often ___ , regularly/daily ___) put the children to bed at night.

____ I (never ___ , seldom ___ , sometimes ___ , often ___ , regularly/daily ___) make sure that I'm available and that we make time to truly communicate on a regular (usually daily) basis.

____ I (never ___ , seldom ___ , sometimes ___ , often ___ , regularly/daily ___) yield to her desires and let her have her own way unless to do so would violate God's Word.

____ I (never ___ , seldom ___ , sometimes ___ , often ___ , regularly/daily ___) realize that I am to love her as Christ loved the church and do make a conscious effort to love her this way with a love that is sacrificial ___ , consistent __ , unselfish __ , gracious (not dependent on her performance) __ , committed __ , practical __ , permanent __ , purposeful __ .

Add to the previous inventory any other biblically consistent ways that you either do show love or think your wife would like you to show love.

_____

_____

_____

_____

_____

Go back over the previous inventory and any additions you have made and make a list of the ways that you will, with God's help, seek to express your love to your wife more fully.

_____

_____

_____

_____

_____

27

LOVING INVOLVES
FOLLOWING HISTORY'S
GREATEST EXAMPLE
OF LOVE

In the previous chapter, we looked at the first way in which husbands are to love their wives: as they love themselves. In Ephesians 5:25, Paul laid out a second way: "just as Christ also does the church." Christ's love for the church is a model for all husbands in the way that they love their wives. So what does it mean for husbands to love their wives in this way?

First, it means that we will love our wives graciously. Christ's love for the church is all of grace; we did nothing to deserve it: "But God, being rich in mercy, because of His great love with which He loved us, even when we were dead in our transgressions, made us alive together with Christ (by grace you have been saved) . . ." (Eph. 2:4–5).

Therefore, husbands ought to love their wives not "if . . ." or "when . . ." or "because . . . ," but *always*. This means that we will love them freely (not because they have earned it in any way) and volitionally (by choice). Love is not a feeling; it is a decision that we make every day. Every morning that we get up, we make a choice to love our wives, just as the Lord chooses to love us: "The LORD . . . set His love on you . . ." (Deut. 7:7).

Second, loving as Christ loves the church means that we will love our wives unendingly and faithfully. John 13:1 says that Christ "loved His own who were in the world [and] loved them to the end." And in Jeremiah 31:3, the Lord declares, "I have loved you with an everlasting love . . ." God's love for us will never fail, and our love for our wives should last as long as our wedding-day vow promised: until death us do part. Christ's love for us is also a faithful love. Romans 8:38–39 assures us that nothing can separate us from God's love in Christ Jesus. Again, as we vowed on our wedding day, our love should not depend on circumstances, but should remain true to the end.

Third, loving as Christ loved the church means that we will love our wives unselfishly. Our God is all-sufficient and needs nothing from us. He does not love us because He requires anything from us. He has all the glory in Himself that He could possibly need. The Father, Son, and Holy Spirit each honor each other and are complete in their relationship with each other. Anything that God does for us is purely for our benefit, not His: "For you know the grace of our Lord Jesus Christ, that though He was rich, yet for your sake He became poor, so that you through His poverty might become rich" (2 Cor. 8:9). We husbands must likewise love our wives without expectation or need of anything in return. As 1 Corinthians 13:5 reminds us, "[Love] does not seek its own . . ."

Fourth, to love as Christ loves, we must love our wives constructively. Christ's love is a purifying love. It sanctifies and cleanses us by the washing of the water with the Word. Christ's love works in us and makes us better. "Yet He has now reconciled you in His fleshly body through death, in order to present you before Him holy and blameless and beyond reproach" (Col. 1:22). The love of a husband, in the same way, ought to build up and edify his wife. John MacArthur explained:

> When a husband's love for his wife is like Christ's love for his church, he will continually seek to help purify [her] from any sort of defilement. He will seek to protect [her] from the

world's contamination and protect [her] holiness, virtue, and purity in every area. He will never induce [her] to do that which is wrong or unwise or expose [her] to that which is less than good. Love wants only the best for the one it loves, and it cannot bear for a loved one to be corrupted or misled by anything evil or harmful.[1]

Our love for our wives ought to help them grow and develop as persons and help them become more useful and fulfilled followers of Christ.

Fifth, a husband's love should be sacrificial, as Christ's was. Christ loved us and gave Himself up for us on the cross. He gave much more than just His time and energy; He gave His life. Again, John MacArthur on this point:

> A husband is not commanded to love his wife because of what his wife is or is not. He is commanded to love his wife because it is God's will for him to do so. It is certainly intended for the husband to admire and be attracted by his wife's beauty, winsomeness, kindness, gentleness, or any other positive quality or virtue. But though such things bring great blessing and enjoyment, they are not the bond of marriage. If every appealing characteristic and virtue of his wife disappears, a husband is still under just as great an obligation to love his wife. If anything, he is under greater obligation because [her] need for the healing and restorative power of his selfless love is greater. This is the kind of love every Christian husband is to have for his wife.[2]

As husbands, we need to think about how we are sacrificing for our wives. Are we willing to sacrifice our time, our interests, our feelings, and our desires for our wives? As a reflection of Christ's love, this is how we ought to love.

Sixth, if we are to love as Christ loved the church, we must love our wives especially. This means that our love for our wives is far above and beyond our love for anything or anyone else, save God. Our wives should be most special in our eyes, as Christ has a special love for His people.

Seventh, we ought to love our wives openly and aggressively. In other words, our love for them should not be passive or hidden. Just as God has openly declared His love for His people in His Word and shown it definitively by the death of His Son, we husbands ought to be willing to make our love widely and clearly known. Our children, our friends, our relatives—no one should ever have reason to question whether we have a passionate and abiding love for our wives.

Finally, when we love as Christ loved the church, we will love our wives forgivingly. Our Lord's forgiveness, thankfully, never runs out. We can never use up His forgiveness or exhaust His patience: "If You, LORD, should mark iniquities, O Lord, who could stand? But there is forgiveness with You . . ." (Ps. 130:3–4). In the same way, husbands must be willing to constantly forgive their wives. As sinners, we will always fail one another. And no matter how sanctified our wives are, they will disappoint us, provoke us, or offend us in some way from time to time. When we learn to love them as Christ does the church, we will be always be willing to forgive any wrong suffered.

APPLICATION AND DISCUSSION

1. You and your spouse should read the following account and then discuss how you would respond to this man. Decide on the approach you would take in helping the man—the questions you would ask him, the Scripture you would use, the statements you would make, the counsel you would give to the man and his wife. If you don't know what to say to him, reflect on what this chapter teaches about love, and if you still don't know how to respond to him, seek help from your pastor, an elder, or another biblically wise person.

   After reading this chapter, some husbands might respond:

   "What you say about the husband's love for his wife being like the love of Christ and not being based on performance sounds biblical, but it's not very realistic. I know that's what the Bible says, but you don't know my wife; she constantly nags me, she calls me bad names, she constantly finds fault, she doesn't listen to me, she doesn't keep the house clean, she puts me down in front of people and with the children, she withholds sex from me, etc. I mean, a man can only take so much; then he has to defend and protect himself. Maybe Christ could respond differently, but I'm not Christ. I'm only human, and as a human I can take only so much."

Having read and discussed this account with your mate and having determined how you would respond to this man, go on to discuss how this scenario and your responses to it apply to you and your marriage. Do you ever put the blame on your wife for your occasionally or perhaps even frequently unloving words, actions, reactions, or attitudes? Is your love for her based on her performance? Ask her whether she thinks it is. Ask her for the reasons for her answer.

2. Make a list of the eight ways mentioned in this chapter about how Christ loved us. Then use these characteristics of Christ's love to evaluate your love for your wife. For each of these eight characteristics, use this rating scale: Regularly = 4; Often = 3; Occasionally = 2; Seldom = 1; Never = 0. Support your evaluation by identifying specific things you have done.

3. Ask your wife to evaluate you on each of these eight characteristics and to mention ways in which she has seen you loving her or not loving her in each of these ways.

28

HUSBANDING INVOLVES LEADERSHIP

L oving our wives is the first of the two principles set forth in Ephesians 5. The second is leading. Ephesians 5:23 says that the husband is to function as the "head of the wife." We must learn to be godly leaders of our wives if we are to be the fulfilled and fulfilling husbands that God desires us to be.

It is vitally important that husbands have a biblical understanding of leadership in the home. Some men fail to be godly leaders by omission—by what they do not do. This seems to have been Frank's problem. Husbands who fail by omission are usually not very actively involved in family life. They essentially turn everything over to their wives—decision-making and problem-solving—and are there only to complain when things go wrong.

Other men fail to be godly leaders by commission—by what they do. They approach family leadership as a dictatorship and make all the decisions in the home. They are constantly telling and commanding rather than asking, appealing, or encouraging. They refuse to seek out and listen to their wives' counsel and perspective; they are harsh, demanding, demeaning, and inconsiderate. Some go so far as to be abusive, whether verbally, sexually, physically, or emotionally. They interpret any kind of disagreement as a lack of submission.

As a biblical counselor, I have worked with men—some of them pastors—who approached headship in this way. This is certainly not what God has in mind for husbands, as the Scripture indicates when it says that husbands are to be the head of their wives "as Christ also is the head of the church" (Eph. 5:23). Christ's leadership of His church is to be the model for all husbands as they lead their wives and families.

What does it mean to lead as Christ leads the church? It means first that our leadership will be others-oriented. Christ does not lead the church for His benefit, but rather for the benefit of His children. He is always thinking about and doing what is best for us. All of God's commands are actually invitations to fulfillment and blessing. "If you abide in Me, and My words abide in you, ask whatever you wish, and it will be done for you" (John 15:7). A Christlike husband is an others-oriented leader.

Christ's leadership was also sacrificial and selfless: "Christ Jesus, . . . although He existed in the form of God, . . . emptied Himself, taking the form of a bond-servant, and being made in the likeness of men. Being found in appearance as a man, He humbled Himself by becoming obedient to the point of death, even death on a cross" (Phil. 2:5–8). Christ endured ignorance from His followers, insults and indignities from many who listened to Him, rejection by both family and friends at various times, and the ultimate humiliation of the cross. Likewise, a Christlike husband will be a humble leader.

Godly leadership is goal-oriented. Christ's leadership has as its goal God's glory and bringing about His kingdom: "I glorified You on the earth, having accomplished the work which You have given Me to do" (John 17:4). It is not self-centered in any way. Christ's leadership is also by example. He picked up a towel and basin and washed the disciples' feet to demonstrate the humility and willingness to serve that are hallmarks of a godly leader. "If I then, the Lord and the Teacher, washed your feet, you also ought to wash one another's feet. For I gave you an example that you also should do as I did to you" (John 13:14–15). Christlike husbands will lead selflessly and by example.

To lead as Christ leads means that we will be good problem-solvers. Husbands must not abdicate their role in decision-making, nor should they simply point fingers at the source of a problem. Godly leaders work to solve problems. This also means that we will give relevant, appropriate, meaningful, and clear instructions to our wives and children, as Jesus did. He never sent His disciples out to accomplish a task without clear instructions regarding what they should expect and do: "And He summoned the twelve and began to send them out in pairs . . . He instructed them that they should take nothing for their journey, except a mere staff . . . but to wear sandals; and He added, 'Do not put on two tunics' " (Mark 6:7–9).

It also means that we will be good motivators and coaches. Christ often took time to explain to His disciples the reasons for obedience. When they would go out and minister to people, Christ would gather His disciples together afterward and discuss what had happened. He used every opportunity to teach them, correct them, and train them. "And He did not speak to them without a parable; but He was explaining everything privately to His own disciples" (Mark 4:34).

Leading as Christ did means that we will be effective managers. A good manager does not do the work of ten men himself, but rather enables ten men to work better than they could without his leadership. He delegates responsibility and authority as needed so that the work is done most effectively. Within the church, Christ has delegated both responsibility and authority to elders (Titus 1:5–9). To all His followers, Christ has laid out parameters in His Word, but gives us freedom within those parameters: "For you were called to freedom, brethren . . ." (Gal. 5:13). Likewise, Christlike husbands must be leaders who are willing to delegate their authority appropriately.

It also means that we will be available to our wives and generous with our time. Christ was with His disciples day and night. They ate together, traveled together, and probably slept together many times. From what we are told in the gospels, it would seem that Christ spent very little time alone. Though He would disappear at times to pray— often at night—the vast majority of His time was given to the disciples and others. Christlike husbands ought to give as much of their time as they can to their wives and children.

It means that we will provide our wives with the resources they require for fulfilling their responsibilities. A godly leader does not command his followers to make bricks and not give them straw and clay to do it. Likewise, in Christ we have everything that we need. As the Lord has promised us, "seek first His kingdom and His righteousness, and all these things will be added to you" (Matt. 6:33).

Godly leadership means that we will allow our wives to fail and to learn from their mistakes without insulting them or reminding them of their failures. A godly leader does not say, "I told you so! If only you had listened to me." Christ never berated His disciples for their many mistakes, but rather used those opportunities to teach and encourage them.

These are just a few examples of what it means to be a Christlike leader in the home. As husbands, we all have areas in which our leadership needs improvement. Whether we are not involved enough, over-involved, or just involved in the wrong way, we need to be constantly looking back to the example of Christ so that we can become more fulfilled and fulfilling husbands.

How to Be Your Wife's Leader[1] "Comparison of Role Concepts" Inventory

Now complete the following inventory, which will help you to discern your concepts of leadership. Each of you should first privately (separately) indicate whether you agree with, disagree with, or are uncertain about each statement. Having done this, you should then respectfully discuss why you answered each statement as you did and what you meant by your answer. Compare the way you answered with the material about leadership presented in this chapter and then answer this question: Does my answer line up with the biblical concept of leadership presented in this chapter? If so, how? And if not, in what way and why not?

Check the appropriate column

Agree Disagree Not sure

_____ _____ _____ To say "Nothing" when your mate asks you whether something is wrong is better than starting an argument.

Agree	Disagree	Not sure	
_____	_____	_____	"Fighting" is always wrong between mates.
_____	_____	_____	The Bible teaches that a wife must always obey her husband.
_____	_____	_____	It is the husband's role to determine the responsibilities of each mate.
_____	_____	_____	Strict discipline will produce well-behaved and well-developed children.
_____	_____	_____	Fathers should be disciplinarians.
_____	_____	_____	The man should be head of the home.
_____	_____	_____	It is a wife's responsibility to have a house neat and clean at all times.
_____	_____	_____	Since the wife is a responder, only the husband should initiate lovemaking.
_____	_____	_____	The husband should plan the budget and manage the money.
_____	_____	_____	A man should have one night out with the boys each week.
_____	_____	_____	Cooking is a wife's responsibility.
_____	_____	_____	A wife is as responsible for child discipline as a husband.
_____	_____	_____	The yard, painting, and maintenance is the husband's responsibility.
_____	_____	_____	Each mate should have the freedom to spend money as he or she chooses without consulting the other, as long as a limit has been agreed on.
_____	_____	_____	Leisure time and recreation should be spent together.
_____	_____	_____	To argue is human; therefore, arguing is part of marriage.

____ ____ ____ It is the responsibility of the wife to teach values to the children.

____ ____ ____ A wife should not work outside the home.

____ ____ ____ A husband should not be expected to wash dishes, scrub floors, etc.

____ ____ ____ Since a wife has more time with the children, she has greater responsibility for them.

____ ____ ____ When a wife has been blessed with a special talent, she should have a career to utilize it.

____ ____ ____ The Bible teaches that men are responsible for their jobs and women are responsible for home and children.

____ ____ ____ A joint checking account is the best way to handle money.

____ ____ ____ Marriage is a 50/50 proposition.

____ ____ ____ Marriage is a 100/100 proposition.

____ ____ ____ If a husband and wife have a major impasse on a major decision, the husband should take the responsibility for the decision and make it according to his thinking.

____ ____ ____ Husbands should babysit so that wives can go out with their friends.

____ ____ ____ It is a true saying that "women are more emotional than men."

____ ____ ____ Children can play a part in family decision-making as they grow up.

____ ____ ____ If the husband fails to take leadership, the wife must take over.

_____ _____ _____ Sometimes a wife must use her children as leverage to move her husband.

_____ _____ _____ A woman can mold her husband the way she wants him after they are married.

_____ _____ _____ Since a husband earns most of the family income, he should be more free to spend money on sports, cars, etc.

_____ _____ _____ Using sex as a bargaining tool is sometimes necessary when a mate does not respond to requests.

_____ _____ _____ The authority given to men in the home by God makes him the "general" and his wife an enlisted person who must take orders.

APPLICATION AND DISCUSSION

1. You and your spouse should read the following account and then discuss how you would respond to this man. Decide on the approach you would take in helping the man—the questions you would ask him, the Scripture you would use, the statements you would make, the counsel you would give to him and his wife. If you don't know what to say to him, reflect on what this chapter teaches about leadership, and if you still don't know how to respond to him, seek help from your pastor, an elder, or another biblically wise person.

   After reading this chapter, some husbands might respond:

   "My wife is constantly complaining about my lack of leadership in the home. She's constantly telling me that if I'd be the kind of leader that God wants me to be, we wouldn't have the problems we have in the area of finances or with the children. She wants me to take more leadership in the spiritual area. She frequently tells me about what other men are doing in this area and says that I ought to be functioning in the same way, but I'm just not the kind of person who can do what she wants me to do. I do the best I can, but it's not good enough. I don't have a Bible-college education or seminary training. I guess she wants me to be another John MacArthur, but I'm not like him or some of the other men she mentions."

Having read and discussed this account with your mate and having determined the appropriate way to respond to this man, go on to discuss how this scenario and your responses to it apply to you and your marriage. Do you occasionally or even frequently blame your wife for your lack of leadership? Is your leadership based on what you want or on what God wants?

2. Make a list of what this chapter says about what leadership isn't and what it is. Then for each of the factors involved in what true leadership as a husband in your marriage is, use this rating scale: Regularly = 4; Often = 3; Occasionally = 2; Seldom = 1; Never = 0. Support your evaluation by identifying specific things you have done.

3. Ask your wife to evaluate you on each of the leadership characteristics mentioned in this chapter and to mention ways in which she has seen you leading or not leading in each of these ways.

29

HUSBANDING INVOLVES
BEING A LEARNER

Ephesians 5 gave us two of the three important aspects of our role as godly husbands: being good lovers and good leaders. The third aspect is found in 1 Peter 3:7: "You husbands in the same way, live with your wives in an understanding way . . ." The King James Version translates that second phrase "dwell with them according to knowledge." Notice that this verse is given in the form of a command. In other words, for us to do anything less means that we are not only failing our wives but sinning against God. This is a matter of obedience, not preference, and it certainly does not depend on how worthy we perceive our wives to be of such treatment.

In my years as a pastor and counselor, I have heard many men complain, "I just can't understand women!" Why is this? Sometimes it is ignorance—we really don't know what to do or say. Sometimes it is because other men or even our parents have taught us wrongly. We have been told by the world that women are impossible to understand, and we have accepted this proclamation as the final word on the matter.

Sometimes it is simply laziness—we don't know because we have never bothered to find out. I once counseled a doctor whose marriage was falling apart. I challenged him in this area of studying and understanding his wife. This man, who had been willing to do all the work of getting a medical degree, said to me, "If I have to study my wife, it's not worth it." His career had been worth it, but apparently his marriage was not.

Sometimes selfishness and pride keep us from understanding our wives. We compare ourselves to others and think that we must be doing okay because we are doing better than someone else. Or, like that doctor, we would rather spend our time and energy on things other than our wives. Or perhaps we think that we have nothing to learn—we treat our wives as we would like to be treated, and if it's good enough for us, it must be good enough for them. I believe that many men are really not aware of the many differences between men and women and that they assume that we all think alike.

A COURSE OF STUDY

How do we live with our wives "in an understanding way," or "according to knowledge"? God has essentially sent husbands to school with this command. If we are to understand our wives, we must be prepared to study. While some subjects are easily mastered, we can be sure that this is not one of them. To really get to know our wives, we are going to have to be willing to put forth a great deal of time and effort.

When I first met my wife, she was twenty years old. I am seventy-one years of age now, so I have known her for fifty-three years. In that time, my wife has changed, as I have also, and so I am constantly having to learn new things about her. Some things about Carol are the same, of course, but many things are not. The things that concerned her at twenty were different from the things that concern her now in her sixties. This is a school from which we husbands never graduate until one of us passes away.

We husbands need to learn many things about our wives. Every husband should seek to identify his wife's gifts and abilities. He should also want to know her likes and dislikes, her fears and concerns, and her strengths and weaknesses. What brings the greatest joy to her heart? What encourages her? What are her aspirations? What frustrates her the most? How does she want to be helped? In what ways does she prefer to be shown love and affection? What does she think about the way you treat her, and how would she like to be treated differently?

Some time ago my wife and I were in Colorado Springs, walking along the main boulevard with another couple who lived in the area. We were going in and out of many of the tourist shops, our wives shopping and we following along. After following them around for while, I turned to my friend and asked him, "What are you learning about your wife right now?" He looked at me and asked, "What do you mean?" I answered, "What are you learning about your wife by watching her shop?" He replied that he had never really thought about it.

Moments like these can be wonderful opportunities for learning. For example, if a husband takes the time to observe his wife shopping, he might learn what she would really like for her birthday, instead of racking his brain the day before and coming up with something that is more about what he thought of than what would genuinely please her. And when he gives her that present that he learned about through watching her, she will not only be pleased with the present, but also be pleased that her husband took the time and made the effort to pay attention to what she wanted.

In Philippians 1:9, Paul prayed that "your love may abound still more and more in real knowledge and all discernment." Real love is based on real knowledge. If we want to really love our wives, we need to know them deeply so that we can be guided by wisdom as we seek to be godly husbands to them. Knowledge, discernment, and wisdom come only through a concerted effort to learn. Fulfilled and fulfilling husbands must be good learners.

Resultant Blessings

As with all God's commands, there is great blessing to be had in obedience. When we get to know our wives in a more intimate way, we will find that it is easier for our wives to submit to us, respect us, and enjoy being our helpmates. Being a better lover, leader, and learner will result in a happier marriage—one in which both husband and wife experience great fulfillment in each other.

Even more than blessing, though, is the promise in 1 Peter 3:7 that if we live with our wives in an understanding way, "[our] prayers will not be hindered." In other words, if we fail to obey God in this way, our relationship with God is going to suffer. God has made it clear in Scripture that our relationships with others, especially our family, are very important to Him. First Timothy 5:4 instructs us that we must "first learn to practice piety in regard to [our] own family . . . ," and 1 John 4:20 says, "If someone says, 'I love God,' and hates his brother, he is a liar . . ."

Lovers, leaders, and learners—these are the things that God has asked us to be as husbands. How do we respond to this challenge? Do we respond in pride by saying, "I'm already a good lover, leader, and learner. I don't need to work on anything"? Or do we respond with indifference and rebellion, saying, "I know what God wants, but I don't care. I'm going to do it my way"? Do we respond with discouragement and unbelief, saying, "I have been failing miserably in so many ways. I don't think I'm capable of being the kind of husband that God wants me to be, so why should I even try?"

Or do we respond with humility and faith by saying, "Lord, if that's what You want from me, that's what I'm going to do. You are my Lord, and I belong to You. You know far better than I do how I should live. Please forgive me for my failures in being a godly husband. Help me, by the power of the Holy Spirit, to become the husband that You want me to be. Help me to be a better lover, leader, and learner so that I can bring more glory to You and be a greater blessing to my wife. Lord, I rededicate myself to being a fulfilled and fulfilling husband according to Your Word." Are you ready to pray that prayer? May God give you grace and faith to hear His commands and live according to them.

"How to Be Your Wife's Lover, Leader, and Learner" Inventory

After reading the previous chapter, as a couple complete the following inventory. Set up a time or several times when you will work through these questions. The husband should try to answer the first question as he thinks his wife would answer it. Then the wife should answer it the way it really is. As you do this for each question, make sure to discuss the answer in accordance with biblical communication principles (Eph. 4:25–32): be honest; be self-controlled (not controlling or angry); make sure that your nonverbal behavior (facial expressions, attentiveness, eye contact, body posture) and content, manner, and tone of speech are wholesome, helpful, kind, gentle, and loving. Having answers to these questions will help the husband to be the lover, leader, and learner that God wants him to be, the very husband who will be both fulfilling and fulfilled. This questionnaire is designed to begin with low-level, non-threatening discussion and then proceed to deeper-level questions. When you have completed discussing all the questions, do the summary exercises at the end of the questionnaire. When used properly, this can be a fun and very helpful exercise that will help you to really be sweet-hearts for a lifetime.

Fifty Questions to Ask Your Wife

1. What are her five favorite foods, with the most favorite first?
2. What are her five favorite kinds of meals, with the most favorite first?
3. What are her five favorite desserts, with the most favorite first?
4. What are her five favorite restaurants, with the most favorite first?
5. What is her favorite color?
6. What are her five favorite hobbies, with the most favorite first?
7. What are her five favorite recreational activities, with the most favorite first?
8. What are her five favorite sources of reading, with the most favorite first?
9. What gifts does she like?
10. What is her favorite book of the Bible? Why?
11. What are her favorite Bible verses? Why?
12. What is her favorite song?
13. What makes her the most fulfilled or happiest as a woman?
14. What makes her the most fulfilled or happiest as a wife?
15. What makes her the most fulfilled or happiest as a mother?
16. What makes her saddest as a woman?
17. What makes her saddest as a wife?
18. What makes her saddest as a mother?

19. What is her greatest fear?
20. What are her other fears?
21. What does she look forward to the most?
22. How much sleep does she need?
23. What are her skills?
24. What is her spiritual gift?
25. What are her weaknesses?
26. What things (personal, home, car, etc.) need repairing?
27. With what chores and responsibilities does she like your help?
28. What caresses does she enjoy the most?
29. What caresses does she enjoy the least?
30. What actions of yours provide her with the greatest sexual pleasure?
31. What other things stimulate her sexually?
32. At what times does she need assurance of your love the most?
33. How can that love be shown?
34. What do you do that makes it uncomfortable or difficult for her to discuss certain things with you? What can you do that will make it easier for her to discuss and work on these areas or problems?
35. What concerns does she have that you do not seem interested in?
36. What things do you do that irritate her?
37. What desires does she have that the two of you haven't discussed?
38. What does she enjoy doing with you, with the most enjoyable first?
39. What things can you do to show your appreciation of her?
40. What varying desires (spiritual, physical, intellectual, social, appreciation, recreational, protection, etc.) would she like for you to meet? How?
41. In what ways would she like for you to protect her (physically, spiritually, socially)? How?
42. In what ways would she like for you to sacrifice for her?
43. As she thinks of you, what things does she think are first in your life? What does she think should be your priority? What other priorities would she like for you to have, and in what order?
44. What implied or unspoken desires and wishes of hers would she like for you to fulfill?
45. What concerns and interests of hers would she like for you to support? How?

46. How much time does she think the two of you should spend together each day?
47. What motivating factors would be helpful for you to use in helping family members to use their skills and develop their abilities? How could you improve as a motivator?
48. What can you do that provides the greatest comfort and encouragement for her when she is hurt, fearful, anxious, or worried?
49. What personal habits do you have that she would like changed?
50. In what ways does she see you demonstrating to her that she is a very important person who is as important as or more important than you are?

Summarize how you were impacted as you went through this exercise (what you felt, how you were responding emotionally and relationally):

_____

_____

_____

_____

_____

_____

Summarize what you learned about your mate that you didn't know before or ways in which your understanding of your mate was corrected or enlarged:

_____

_____

_____

_____

_____

_____

Part 3

The Fulfilled and Fulfilling Wife

Carol Mack

30

IS *SUBMISSION*
A DIRTY WORD?

Some time ago I heard a humorous true story about one woman's reaction to the teaching of Ephesians 5 at a wedding. During the ceremony, the pastor read from Ephesians 5. After the service, a woman in the receiving line asked the father of the bride about the passage. "I never heard anything like that in my whole life," she said. "Like what?" the father asked. "What the minister had to say about women," she answered. "What did he say about women?" he asked. She replied, "He said that women are supposed to submit to their husbands." The father said, "The pastor was just reading that from the Bible." "The Bible?" the woman asked. "Yes, Ephesians 5," he said, to which she replied, "When I get home, I'm going to cut that passage out of my Bible."

That woman was not the first to be bothered by Ephesians 5, nor will she be the last. This passage addresses the roles of both husbands and wives in marriage. In Part 2 of this book, husbands looked at their responsibilities to their wives as laid out in Ephesians 5:25–33. In Part 3, we will consider God's instructions to women, given in verses 22–24 and 33:

Wives, be subject to your own husbands, as to the Lord. For the husband is the head of the wife, as Christ also is the head of the church, He Himself being the Savior of the body. But as the church is subject to Christ, so also the wives ought to be to their husbands in everything . . . Nevertheless, each individual among you also is to love his own wife even as himself, and the wife must see to it that she respects her husband.

This is unquestionably a controversial passage of Scripture. I am sure that many women would like to cut it out of their own Bibles as well, at least at times, if not permanently. Sadly, in some ways it has actually become less controversial these days because so many people simply ignore whatever parts of Scripture they do not happen to like or agree with.

As some people read this passage, they say that it is obvious that Paul hated women. Others say that Paul was speaking within the context of his culture. They suggest that since others in the culture believed that women were inferior, he was afraid that if he said otherwise they would be prejudiced against the gospel of redemption that he was preaching. So he just went along with the popular view of his culture. Still others think that Paul has just been greatly misinterpreted. They tell us that Paul didn't really mean what many have interpreted him to mean. Some go so far as to claim that Paul's teaching on this subject was simply wrong.

But if we say that we believe all Scripture to be true and without error, we cannot ignore, explain away, dismiss, or in any way reinterpret Paul's teaching in this passage or any other. As 2 Timothy 3:16 says, "*All Scripture* is inspired by God and profitable for teaching, for reproof, for correction, for training in righteousness . . ." The teaching of Ephesians 5 is in the Bible because God wanted it there and because it accurately describes His will for husbands and wives.

And in fact, Paul had a very high regard for women. In several epistles, Paul commended specific women for their service and faithfulness in the church. But regardless of how Paul viewed women, we must ultimately deal with the fact that the teaching in Ephesians 5 is not merely the opinion of one man but is part of the Bible, which has been inspired by God and is therefore inerrant, infallible, and authoritative (2 Tim.

3:15–17). This means that if women who have confessed Jesus Christ as Lord want to glorify God and be fulfilled and fulfilling wives, they must learn how to "be subject to"—or submit to—their husbands as God desires them to do.

The Key to True Happiness and Fulfillment

In modern times, much scorn has been heaped on the word *submission*. Some people avoid the word altogether, and many others seem to feel a bit embarrassed when they do use it. Submission is widely considered to be a politically incorrect idea, and the term itself has almost become a "dirty word"—even by some in the church. The fact remains, of course, that it is a biblical word and, within the context of Scripture, correctly describes the proper relationship between wives and their husbands.

Why is there such distaste for the idea of submission? Women dislike this doctrine for two main reasons. The first is that our sinful human hearts naturally resist authority. This is true of women and men alike. We don't like someone else telling us what to do. As Isaiah 53:6 says, "All of us like sheep have gone astray, each of us has turned to his own way . . ."

When our youngest son, Josh, was three years old, he came up to me one day and said, "Mommy, when Daddy's here, he's the boss, right?" I answered, "Right," and was pleased that my son had figured that out. Then he said, "When Daddy goes out, then you're the boss, right?" "Yes," I said. "And when you go out and Chip is here, Chip's the boss, right?" "Yes." "When Chip goes out and Nathan's here, then Nathan's the boss, right?" "Yes." "And when Nathan's gone and Beth is here, then Beth is the boss, right?" "That's right," I said. Finally, Josh said, "I can't wait until everybody goes out and I'm the boss!" Even a three-year-old resists the authority of his parents and older siblings. How much more do we struggle with accepting authority as adults!

The second reason that women dislike this doctrine is that they misunderstand what it means. They misunderstand what the "headship" of the husband is, and they misunderstand what it means for wives to be in submission. They think that this doctrine gives men all the privileges and women all the dirty work. As far as they are concerned, submission dooms wives to a life of miserable slavery, and they are convinced that the only way to true happiness and fulfillment is by demanding the freedom to do whatever they want.

True happiness and fulfillment, however, come only through doing what God wants us to do. As Luke 11:28 points out, "blessed are those who hear the word of God and observe it." Do we want true happiness in marriage? If that is our desire, then the only way to realize it is to study God's design for the marriage relationship and, as wives, learn what it means to be in submission to our husbands as Scripture teaches.

DISCUSSION
AND APPLICATION

1. Why is Ephesians 5:22–25 such a controversial passage for some women?

2. Is it a controversial passage for you? Why or why not?

3. Why is it foolish for women to resist the teaching of this passage? What reasons would you give to someone who resents the idea of the wife's submission to her husband to help her to see the wisdom of God's perspective? Imagine that you are counseling someone who may have problems with the concept of the wife's role as presented in this passage. What, in specifics, would you say to her?

31

THREE FAMILY PLANS

Most homes in the world today operate according to one of two game plans. Despite their appearance in many Christian homes, neither is biblical. In this chapter, these two unbiblical family plans will be contrasted with the less common third family plan, which is biblical. In the first, family decisions are made by the spouse who thinks he or she is more qualified. This plan results in competition between the husband and wife. The husband is confused because he thinks he remembers hearing somewhere that he is supposed to be the head of the home, but it seems as though his wife is calling all the shots. Whenever he tries to make a decision, she overrules him. As a result, he is never confident that his wife will support his decisions, and so he increasingly backs off from taking leadership in the home.

My husband has counseled many men in this position. They get to the point of just saying: "It's not worth it. Everything I try to do just ends up in a fight. If she wants to run things, let her." Over time, the husband starts to resent his wife because she does not respect his desire to lead in the home. He grows more and more bitter toward her. Whenever she makes a mistake, he calls it to her attention in an attempt to gain whatever superiority he can.

Ultimately, this husband may go elsewhere to find the respect and fulfillment that he is not getting at home. He may find it in other male friends, sports, business, church work, or another woman. We know of a home that was run exactly this way, and the husband eventually found what he wanted in another woman. He was tired of being criticized, insulted, and unsupported, so he found someone who treated him better.

The wife in this kind of relationship is resisting her husband's authority because of her pride. She sees her husband make mistakes and thinks that she could do better. Thus, she deems herself to be more qualified to make the family decisions. She does not respect her husband and, in many cases, is afraid of his leadership. She discourages him from making decisions because she expects them to fail.

Paradoxically, as the husband pulls away from leadership, she resents him for it. When she makes a decision that turns out badly, she blames him for leaving all the decision-making to her. Eventually, she pulls away from him and runs elsewhere to find fulfillment—her children, outside activities, church work, or another man. The relationship dies as they both retreat into their own worlds and do their own things. No one finds happiness and fulfillment when the wife demands equal authority.

In the second game plan, the husband is clearly the leader of the home, but the wife is not truly his helpmate. She is the kind of person who describes herself as "just a housewife." She is very dependent, is very subjective, has very little emotional control, and cannot make decisions. She is passive and not interested in growing as a person. She sees her duty in life as raising the children, keeping the house clean, and attending to her husband's needs. As a result, she becomes a very boring person who lives a very dull life.

Living this way causes a complaining spirit to grow in her. She becomes the woman that Solomon described in Proverbs 21:9: "It is better to live in a corner of a roof than in a house shared with a contentious woman." Because the wife constantly complains, her husband starts to complain, too—mostly about her. It leads to a cycle of bitterness and heartache, neither of them enjoying the relationship.

I once heard a story about a couple like this. When the husband was in the army, serving overseas, his wife kept him updated on the affairs of the home. While he was risking his life daily to defend their country, his wife could do no better than to write him letters full of complaints about her life at home. He finally wrote her a letter and asked, "Please don't write so often. I want to enjoy the war in peace."

In neither of these two game plans does the wife find that she is fulfilled and fulfilling as a spouse. In the first, the wife fails mostly because of her lack of understanding about what it means to submit or her unwillingness to follow God's directives for marriage. In the second, she fails mostly due to her lack of understanding about what it means to be her husband's helper or again because of her unwillingness to follow God's directives for marriage. Both of these concepts—godly submission and being a helpmate—are central to becoming a fulfilled and fulfilling wife.

The third family plan is God's design for marriage as outlined in Scripture. The first concept—godly submission—is described in Ephesians 5, where Paul gave two commands regarding the wife's relationship to her husband. Verse 24 tells wives to be subject to their husbands, and verse 33 instructs wives to respect their husbands. In the next few chapters, we will study what godly submission looks like, and later we will spend some time considering what it means for the wife to be her husband's helper.

WALKING IN LOVE

In order to better understand the meaning of these two commands in Ephesians 5, we need to look at the context of these verses. Here's what the first two verses of this chapter say: "Therefore be imitators of God, as beloved children; and *walk in love*, just as Christ also loved you and gave Himself up for us, an offering and a sacrifice to God as a fragrant aroma."

In this chapter, Paul was describing what it means to be an imitator of Christ—to walk in love—and the verses that follow provide for us a more detailed picture of what walking in love looks like. We are all under authority of some kind, and part of walking in love means properly relating to authority. In this chapter, Paul gave a series of instructions about authority relationships—husband–wife, worker–master, child–parent—which all contribute to our understanding of biblical authority and submission to it.

Though some may find it difficult to imagine that love and submission go together, we have to look only as far as the Godhead to see that they do. First John 4:16 proclaims that "God is love." The three members of the Holy Trinity—God the Father, God the Son, and God the Holy Spirit—relate to one another in love. Yet we know that God the Son submitted Himself to the will of God the Father, coming to earth in the form of a man and dying on the cross for our sins.

As children of our heavenly Father and imitators of Christ the Son, we are called to a life of love and submission to God. As wives, we are further called to walk in love by submitting to our husbands. When we do so, we will find the true happiness and fulfillment that our hearts desire and that God desires to pour out on us.

DISCUSSION AND APPLICATION

1. What two unbiblical game plans for the home are mentioned in this chapter? Describe them.

2. What often happens when the marriage is conducted according to the first game plan?

3. Do you know of marriages that are being operated according to this game plan? What do you observe happening in those marriages?

4. What often happens when the marriage is conducted according to the second game plan?

5. Do you know of marriages that are being operated according to this game plan? What do you observe happening in those marriages?

6. Compare what is happening in your marriage to the two game plans just mentioned. Are there ways in which you are following game plan number 1 or 2?

7. What insights into the meaning of submission do we get from the context in which Ephesians 5:22 is found?

32

No, It Doesn't Mean . . .

Before we study what submission means, it is important to clarify what it does *not* mean. First, it does not mean that a wife must always answer her husband with "Yes, dear" whenever he asks her something. When I married Wayne almost fifty years ago, I was a Christian, but I did not know much about being a godly wife. We had no premarital counseling, so as a future pastor's wife who wanted to be a godly person, I prepared myself for a lifetime of "Yes, dear," because that is what I thought submission meant.

In the early years of our marriage, when Wayne would bring up an issue or ask me what I thought of something, I might have thought to myself, "That's a terrible idea and it will never work," but I would dutifully answer, "Yes, dear." A couple of months later, Wayne would find out that I hadn't really meant what I said at all because when things went wrong, I would say, "I knew we shouldn't have done that. I knew it wouldn't work out."

This happened a number of times before Wayne finally said, "You know what, you lied to me!" I was aghast that he would think such a thing of me, since I was trying so hard to be a godly wife. What did he mean that I'd lied to him? He explained, "You always tell me 'yes' when I ask your opinion about something, and then I find out later that sometimes you really mean 'no.' " He was right, and at that point I started to learn what biblical submission meant. And it did not mean always saying, "Yes, dear."

Submission does not mean a wife's putting her husband in God's place. Colossians 1:18 says, "He is also head of the body, the church; and He is the beginning, the firstborn from the dead, so that He Himself will come to have first place in everything." For husbands and wives alike, Christ always comes first. Even as we wives submit ourselves to the authority of our husbands, we do it for Christ's sake: "Submit yourselves for the Lord's sake to every human institution . . ." (1 Peter 2:13).

If a wife puts her husband above Christ, she is really making an idol of him, and that is sin. We are called to serve and please our husbands, not idolize them. When Abram asked Sarai to lie in Genesis 12, she should have said "no" because doing so would have been honoring to God. Instead, she put Abram in God's place and did what Abram asked her to do. A husband must never take the place of God.

Likewise, submission does not mean that we are to give in to every demand of our husbands. In Exodus 1:15–17, Pharaoh commanded the Hebrew midwives to kill all the baby boys that were born. The women disobeyed, and that was right for them to do because Pharaoh's command was not honoring to God. When Peter and John were asked to stop preaching and teaching the gospel, they replied, "We must obey God rather than men" (Acts 5:29). So also should a wife always obey God first. If her husband forbids her to attend church, pray, or read the Bible, or if he asks her to cheat or lie or otherwise sin in any way, she must obey God rather than obey him. Submission does not mean blindly obeying the husband's every command.

Submission also does not mean that we should believe that our husbands are infallible. In Luke 2, we read about Mary and Joseph's leaving Jesus in Jerusalem after the Feast of the Passover. Mary and Joseph were fallible parents—they did not make sure that their son was with them when they left for home. But Scripture tells us that after they returned and found him in the temple, "He went down with them and came to Nazareth, and He continued in subjection to them . . ." (Luke 2:51). Hebrews 13:17 commands, "Obey your leaders and submit to them, for they keep watch over your souls as those who will give an account." God has placed certain people in our lives to be authorities over us—parents, husbands, church leaders, government officials—for our protection, not because they are perfect.

Submission does not mean that women are less important than or inferior to men in any way. As we just mentioned, God has placed people in various positions of authority to accomplish His purposes. Each of us has a different role to play. The policeman who blows his whistle at me is not a better or smarter person than I. We are equal human beings before God, but I stop when he signals because he has been placed in a position of authority over me for my protection. Jesus was certainly not less important than His parents were, and yet He obeyed them.

In 1 Timothy 2:15, Paul said, "But women will be preserved through the bearing of children if they continue in faith and love and sanctity with self-restraint." In this verse, one of the things that Paul was teaching is that women have an extremely important role to play in the world—raising children. My husband has often cited a survey that was done among some of the world's most successful businessmen. When asked who had the most influence on their life to make them what they were, a vast majority of them said that it was their mother. Men and women have different roles to play in the family, but neither is less or more important than the other.

In some cases, it may be true that the wife is more gifted than her husband. She may have a better education, be more talented, or be further along in her spiritual life. A woman like this might be tempted to think that she is far more qualified to be in authority than her husband is. Again, however, we must look to the example of Jesus. Though He was vastly superior to His parents in every way, He submitted to them. Submission is not based on superiority; it is based on obedience to a command.

At the same time, submission does not mean that we let our gifts lie dormant and unused: "As each one has received a special gift, employ it in serving one another as good stewards of the manifold grace of God" (1 Peter 4:10). If God has given us certain gifts, He wants them to be used and will give us opportunities to use those gifts as He pleases. Proverbs 31 gives us a wonderful picture of a woman who used her gifts—sewing, cooking, buying and selling goods—for the blessing and benefit of her family. All believers—both men and women—should be using their gifts to God's glory as they have opportunity.

Likewise, submission does not mean giving up independent thought and becoming intellectually stagnant. Proverbs 31:26 commends the wise wife: "She opens her mouth in wisdom, and the teaching of kindness is on her tongue." In Proverbs 1:8, Solomon instructed his son, "Hear, my son, your father's instruction and do not forsake your mother's teaching . . ." Indeed, if Paul thought women were incapable of understanding, he would not have addressed them directly in his epistles. God gave women brains that He expects us to use whether we are married or not.

Submission does not mean that we give up all efforts to influence our husbands. The instruction of Colossians 3:16 is addressed to all believers, not just men: "Let the word of Christ richly dwell within you, with all wisdom teaching and admonishing one another . . ." In 1 Thessalonians 5:14, Paul wrote to all believers, "We urge you, brethren, admonish the unruly, encourage the fainthearted, help the weak, be patient with everyone." God has given us instructions on the *way* that we are to influence our husbands; we are not to ignore those instructions.

DISCUSSION AND APPLICATION

1. What wrong ideas about wives' submission to their husbands are discussed in this chapter? Make a list.

2. Besides the wrong views of submission presented in this chapter, can you add any other wrong views that you or others may have?

3. Discuss why each of these views is not really what the Bible means by submission. Give biblical reasons demonstrating that they are erroneous.

4. Why are these wrong views problematic? What impact have these unbiblical views had on marriages and outreach efforts to others?

5. Have you (husband or wife) held any of these unbiblical views of submission? Go over the list one by one and evaluate.

33

WHAT KEEPS WIVES FROM DOING IT?

Women fail to be submissive to their husbands for basically two reasons. The first is fear. Fear or intimidation should never be a part of biblical submission. In fact, Scripture instructs us *not* to be fearful: "The fear of man brings a snare . . ." (Prov. 29:25); "There is no fear in love; but perfect love casts out fear . . ." (1 John 4:18). And in 1 Peter 3:1–6, wives are specifically instructed to be submissive, chaste, respectful, and gentle, and to "do what is right without being frightened by any fear." We are commanded to submit to our husbands *without fear*.

Fear can affect women in either of two ways: it can make them unsubmissive or it can make them overly submissive. Some women allow fear to get in the way of submission. They think, "If I submit, what is he going to do? He may waste our money. He may make bad decisions for our family. What will happen to me if I submit?" On the other hand, some women submit because they are afraid of what will happen to them if they do not. "What will he do to me if I say 'no' to him?" I have heard many women say, "I submit, but it's just because I don't want to find out what he'll do if I don't."

Scripture instructs us not to live in fear. Wives should not be afraid to submit, nor should they submit because they are afraid. First Peter 3:5 says, "For in this way in former times the holy women also, who hoped in God, used to adorn themselves, being submissive to their own husbands . . ." The word *hope* in this verse means "trust." If God is truly our God, we will not be anxious about what might happen if we submit and what might happen if we do not submit to our husbands, because we are confident in the Lord. When we live in fear, we demonstrate our lack of trust in God.

It is never appropriate for a wife to put herself in God's place and fail to submit because she is afraid that her husband's decision is poor or irresponsible. His decision may very well fail, but the wife must always remember that her husband's failure is within God's providence. God may allow him to fail in order to teach him, and far be it from anyone to get in the way of his spiritual growth. Though the means of growth may involve pain for both husband and wife, the reward will be for both of them as well.

True, sometimes our husbands will make bad decisions that affect us. My husband is a very wise man and I trust him, but that is not what gives me confidence. What gives me confidence is that I know my God will take care of me and is more than big enough to handle any problem that comes my way. I know of a woman who submits to her husband very graciously and lovingly and demonstrates a tremendous attitude of confidence in the Lord. One would never guess that she is actually living on the brink of poverty because her husband keeps making poor decisions with their finances.

Why does she continue to support and submit to him? She does it because she trusts in God, not her husband. As difficult as her life is, she knows that she serves a great God who loves her far more than she loves herself. She firmly believes that Romans 8:28 is as true for her as it is for any of God's other children: "And we know that God causes all things to work together for good to those who love God, to those who are called according to His purpose." We, too, need to remind ourselves that no one loves or cares for us more than God does. Our confidence is secure in Him alone.

Our attitude should be the same as that of this woman, who wrote:

There is nothing—no circumstance, no trouble, no testing—that can touch me until first of all it has gone past God, past Christ, right through to me. If it has come that far, it has come with a great purpose which I may not understand at that moment. But if I refuse to become panicky, as I lift up my eyes to Him and accept it as coming from the throne of God for some good purpose of blessing to my heart, no sorrow will ever disturb me, no trial will ever disarm me, no circumstance will cause me to fret, for I shall rest in the joy of what my Lord is and that is the rest of victory.

The second reason that women fail to submit to their husbands is selfishness. Selfishness is the source of much sin in our lives. It is also a major barrier to biblical submission for most women and must be dealt with daily. It is a remnant of the "old man" within us, which we must constantly put to death by the power of the Holy Spirit. In a later chapter, we will look at some of the practical ways in which selfishness manifests itself in our attitudes, words, and actions.

Sometimes we may be tempted to disguise our selfishness as fear, saying that we are afraid of what our husbands are going to ask us to do. Though we may say aloud that we are afraid that they will ask us to do something sinful, what we are really afraid of, if we are honest, is that they will ask us to do something that we just don't *want* to do. In the next section, we will discuss the proper steps to take when really faced with a sinful request, but we must be very careful to discern between what is sin and what is simply not our preference.

SEEKING PROTECTION IN A GODLY WAY

Submission does not mean that wives should do nothing to protect themselves from unreasonable husbands. We are not called to sit idly by, saying, "Here I am. Wipe your dirty boots on me." Rather, wives need to examine their motivations and be sure that everything they do in relation to their husbands is done because they love and trust God, not because they are afraid.

In addition to this, if a husband is abusive or leading inappropriately in some way, anything the wife does—talking to him, getting counseling—should be motivated by love for her husband, not concern for herself. A man who abuses his wife is certainly not glorifying God, and it is right that his wife should want him to change. As long as her motivation is a desire to do what would please the Lord most, then she should use whatever resources God has given her to influence her husband and protect herself.

If our trust is in the Lord as it should be, we have powerful weapons with which to protect ourselves. Second Corinthians 10:4 confirms this fact: "for the weapons of our warfare are not of the flesh, but divinely powerful for the destruction of fortresses." Ephesians 6:10–18 says that we are protected by the whole armor of God: truth, righteousness, the gospel of peace, faith, salvation, the Spirit, and prayer.

The godly wife must learn how to respond rightly when her husband sins against her. Romans 12:17–21 reminds us that it is wrong to repay his evil with evil: "Never pay back evil for evil to anyone . . . If possible, so far as it depends on you, be at peace with all men" (17–18). And it instructs us how to respond when we are wronged: "Never take your own revenge . . . 'But if your enemy is hungry, feed him, and if he is thirsty, give him a drink; for in so doing you will heap burning coals on his head.' Do not be overcome by evil, but overcome evil with good" (19–21).

Sometimes husbands do act like their wives' enemies. I know of a woman whose husband often came home drunk. He would wake her at two or three in the morning and demand that she cook him a meal. Night after night, she did it—and did it with a sweet spirit. Finally one night he asked her, "Why do you treat me so well?" She answered, "Because if you're not saved, this is as good as it's ever going to get for you. So I'm trying to make it good for you while you're on earth because you have nothing to look forward to but an eternity in hell." It was not easy for her to live that kind of life, but by the grace of God she was able to overcome evil with good.

In addition to living a godly life and doing good in return for evil, a wife must also learn how to make a godly appeal to her husband when he is in the wrong, using sweet speech to persuade him. Proverbs 15:1

teaches that "a gentle answer turns away wrath," and Proverbs 25:15 says that "a soft tongue breaks the bone."

Many years ago, our daughter Beth was living with us while attending graduate school. I remember driving my youngest son, Josh, to school one day when he turned to me and said, "I just don't think it's fair." "What's not fair?" I asked. He continued, "In the morning, when Beth is still asleep and I'm getting ready for school, you're always saying, 'Be quiet; Beth is sleeping.' But at night, I go to bed a long time before she does and I don't hear you saying, 'Be quiet; Josh is already in bed.' "

"You're right, Josh," I said. "And I never realized that. I am really sorry; please forgive me. I need to change because that isn't fair and it's not right." When I finished, I noticed that he still had a grouchy-looking face, so I said, "What's the matter?" He answered, "It's really hard to be mad when you ask for forgiveness." I thought about that moment in relation to Proverbs 15:1. There are so many times when a gentle answer can put out a fire and a harsh one can stir it up. We have a choice in how we respond to our husbands.

So how does a wife go about rebuking her husband when he has done something that is definitely wrong? Galatians 6:1 instructs all believers: "if anyone is caught in any trespass, you who are spiritual, restore such a one *in a spirit of gentleness* . . ." Ephesians 4:15 says to "[speak] the truth in love," and Matthew 18:15 says, "If your brother sins, go and show him his fault in private . . ." This is a time when the wife needs to confront her husband and, in a loving and gentle way, tell him that what he is doing is wrong and needs to change. The teaching in Matthew goes on to tell us that if the husband does not listen to the wife, she is to take others with her to confront him. If it got to that point, this would mean getting the pastor of the church involved.

When serious abuse is involved, the woman should follow the procedure laid out in Matthew 18:15–17 in terms of what to do when she has been repeatedly and abusively sinned against. She should first of all examine herself to make sure that she is personally following the instructions of Matthew 7:2–6, Romans 12:14–21, and 1 Peter 3:1–6. She should also turn to the elders of her church for direction, support, and protection. She should suggest to her husband that they should both go for biblical counseling to improve their relationship. And if he rejects her suggestion about mutual counseling, she should personally seek counseling from godly and biblically wise elders or people suggested by the elders for the guidance, objectivity, support, and protection that she needs (Prov. 12:15; 15:22; Eccl. 4:9–12; Col. 3:16).

In Scripture, pastors or elders are called "shepherds," and shepherds are responsible to do what they can to provide protection, provision, support, comfort, and guidance to the sheep in the presence of their enemies (Ps. 23:1–6; Ezek. 34:1–5; Acts 20:28; 1 Peter 5:1–3). Hebrews 13:17 tells us that shepherds are to watch over the sheep and that they will be called on to give account for the sheep. So in desperate and dangerous situations, the elders must get involved. They should recognize their responsibility, and the woman involved should be turning to them for the help that God says they are to give.

And under the guidance of the wife's spiritual church leaders, if proper biblical steps have been carefully taken and proved ineffective, it may become necessary to call the authorities or even to temporarily flee the situation. Scripture teaches us that God has ordained authorities for our protection, and we should use them when we must (Rom. 13:1–7). Moreover, if a person's life or the lives of the children are in danger, there is an appropriate time to temporarily, for the purpose of protection, get away from the situation.

But again, we must remember that whatever this woman does or is encouraged to do, she must do it not only for her own sake or the sake of the children, but also for the sake of her husband, who is seriously sinning against God as well as against her. The motive behind what she does must be not only self-protection, but also a concern that her husband might genuinely repent and receive God's forgiveness and help to become the man that God wants him to be. It is critical that as godly wives, our attitude in the midst of such circumstances—however dire they may be—always be one of love.

DISCUSSION
AND APPLICATION

1. What two reasons does this chapter suggest as to why some women fail to be submissive to their husbands?

2. Do you agree with this assessment?

3. Do you think there are other reasons why women fail to submit? What other reasons might there be?

4. What does it mean that some women fail to submit because of fear? Discuss how fear may be a hindrance. Give specific examples of situations or concerns that may encourage resistance to submission.

5. Discuss the solution to the fear hindrance.

6. What does it mean that some women fail to submit because of selfishness? Discuss how selfishness may be a hindrance. Give specific examples of situations or ways in which selfishness may encourage resistance to submission.

7. Discuss the situation in which some form of abuse takes place. What should the wife do if she is being abused by her husband? What biblical counsel would you give her? What are some of the biblically directed weapons she has at her disposal?

34

YES, IT DOES MEAN . . .

Now that we have considered some things that submission is not, let's look at what submission is. The Greek word *hupotasso*, translated "submit" or "be subject to," means "to arrange or place oneself in order under." It is a word that was also used to describe soldiers who served under the authority of a commanding officer and pillars that supported a building. These examples paint a picture of support and service for the purpose of accomplishing a greater goal. It is also a picture of order—everything having a proper place.

In speaking about the church, Paul said in 1 Corinthians 14:33 that "God is not a God of confusion but of peace . . ." All things, whether in the church or in the home, are to be done properly and in order. A home where no one was in charge would be a home in chaos. Just think what a business would be like if everyone were a boss and no one a worker, or what a church would be like if everyone were a pastor and no one a congregant. It is confusing when no one is in charge, and usually very little, if anything, gets accomplished.

For the sake of order, God has determined that husbands are the ones to be in charge. This means that the final responsibility for everything in the home belongs to the husband. Frankly, I'm glad that I do not have to answer to God for that. Our husbands have a huge responsibility before the Lord, and someday they will stand before Him and answer for it. Though there may be times when I think I want to be in charge for the sake of getting my own way, when I think about it clearly and rightly, I really do not want that responsibility.

A wife who is submissive to her husband is one who recognizes the need for functional order in the home and is willing to follow God's plan for attaining that order through the leadership of her husband. This is how we find true happiness and fulfillment in our marriages, and it is our only hope for being everything that God intended us to be.

It is very important for us to recognize—however pleasant or unhappy our current marriage circumstances—that God did not give us this command to make us miserable. That is not the kind of God we have. Matthew 11:30 says, "For My yoke is easy and My burden is light." It is only when we disobey and rebel against God's commands that we are miserable.

True happiness and freedom is found only in obedience. The Proverbs 31 woman was free to be all that she was gifted to be because she honored God and her husband in all she did. Scripture tells us, "She does [her husband] good and not evil all the days of her life" (31:12) and "She looks well to the ways of her household . . ." (31:27) because she is "a woman who fears the LORD . . ." (31:30). Some women want the freedom to do whatever they wish, but true freedom is doing what God wants us to do in the place that He has given us to do it.

ASPECTS OF BIBLICAL SUBMISSION

The most important aspect of submission is that it is, above all, a spiritual matter. It is a spiritual matter first because we are called to submit to our husbands "as to the Lord" (Eph. 5:22) and "as the church is subject to Christ" (5:24). When I first thought about the fact that my submission to my husband was to reflect the church's submission to Christ, I was really struck by it. What would the church look like if it submitted to Christ the way I do to my husband? I was humbled by this thought and realized, as we all must, that I have a long way to go before I attain what God really has for me.

If submission is essentially spiritual in nature, then this means that refusing to submit is an act of rebellion against God. We have been commanded—not asked—to submit. If we have confessed Jesus Christ as Lord of our lives, then whatever He commands we must do, regardless of our personal feelings about it. We must remind ourselves that submission depends on God, not our husbands.

Submission is also a spiritual matter because it can be done only in the power of the Holy Spirit. Ephesians 5:18 reminds us to "be filled with the Spirit." As with any of God's commands, we have no power within ourselves to obey. An unbelieving wife, no matter how pious she may seem, can never truly submit to her husband because she is not doing it as to the Lord. It is only when we turn our lives over to Christ and live daily by the power of His Spirit that we can do anything to please Him.

At the same time, submission as God intends means that the responsibility of obedience rests on us (by God's grace and with His help), not on our husbands. In other words, it is not up to our husbands to make us submit to them. Paul did not instruct husbands to force their wives to submit to them; he instructed wives to submit themselves.

This means that we must act on our will, not our feelings. We live in a very feeling-oriented society today that tells us such lies as "if it feels good, do it," and "do what you want to do, be what you want to be." It is not likely that Christ felt like going to the cross. Hebrews 12:2 tells us that Jesus "endured the cross, despising the shame . . ." Obeying God's command to submit should never depend on our feelings.

Another aspect of biblical submission is that it is continual and comprehensive. In other words, submission is a lifestyle, not an occasional event that depends on how we feel or how we are being treated at the time. A woman once said to me, "If my husband would love me the way Christ loves the church, then I would be submissive." As nice as that might sound, God has not given us that option. Yes, our husbands will someday have to answer for the way that they led us (see the earlier chapters on the husband's role and responsibilities to his wife), but we wives will also answer for the way that we submitted, regardless of how we were led.

Again, submission depends on God's character, not our husbands'. We submit because we have a great and powerful God who loves us, wants the best for us, and promises to protect us. We do not submit because our husbands are all-wise, well educated, highly talented, or spiritually advanced. In fact, 1 Peter 3:1 instructs wives to submit to their unsaved husbands so that they might win them to Christ.

A third aspect of biblical submission is that it is always relevant to our lives. It is not a cultural relic of a long-ago and much different time, as some might wish to believe. The headship of the man was established in the beginning of creation, according to 1 Corinthians 11:8–9: "For man does not originate from woman, but woman from man; for indeed man was not created for the woman's sake, but woman for the man's sake." It is true that in different cultures, submission is expressed in different ways. In some countries, it is proper for a submissive wife to wear a veil. Though it may be expressed differently from culture to culture, the principle remains the same.

Finally, it is important to remember that submission is a positive concept. Though many women view submission as something terribly negative, God never meant it to be so. Submission really means that the wife puts all her talents, resources, abilities, and energy at her husband's disposal. In a godly marriage relationship, the husband and wife function together as a team. Each one contributes his or her talents, skills, knowledge, and energy to the team in the role that he or she has been assigned to play.

My husband was a football player, and he often explains this idea in terms of a football team. When the players gather together in the huddle between plays, they don't stand around and argue with the quarterback, complain about the last call, or debate the next one. The quarterback is responsible for making the final decisions on the field, and when the game is over, the team either wins or loses together. No one operates alone.

In Genesis 2:18, God said that He made woman to be "a helper suitable" for man. Later in this book, we will discuss the wife's being her husband's helper in greater depth, but the main idea is that the submissive wife is to be on her husband's team—supporting, encouraging, and contributing in every way that God has gifted and commanded her to do.

DISCUSSION
AND APPLICATION

As you discuss these questions, please remember what was previously written in this book about the husband's responsibilities. When dealing with the husband, we focused on his responsibilities regardless of the kind of wife he had. In this section, we are focusing primarily on the wife's responsibilities and not making mention of the husband's. Now to the discussion questions:

1. What does the Greek word for *submission* really mean? In what ways was it used, and what do these examples of its usage indicate about its meaning and usage in Scripture?

2. What is the godly and good purpose that is fulfilled in the marriage by the wife's submission? Conversely, what often happens in any situation involving more than one person when no one has the leadership?

3. What biblical reasons are there for asserting that the wife who is willing to be submissive will be not only fulfilling, but also fulfilled?

4. What is meant by the statement that submission is primarily a spiritual matter?

5. What does it mean that submission is an act of the will, not of feelings?

6. What does it mean that submission depends on God's character, not a husband's character?

7. What does it mean that submission is a relevant matter?

8. What does it mean that submission is a positive concept, not a negative one?

9. What impact do the truths presented in this chapter have on you emotionally, intellectually, relationally, and behaviorally?

35

LET'S GET PRACTICAL

What does biblical submission look like in a very practical way? How do we wives demonstrate by our attitudes, words, and actions that we are obeying God's design for the marriage relationship? In this chapter, we will look at some of the ways that submission is demonstrated and consider the many ways in which we fail to submit in attitude, words, and actions.

Biblical submission begins with a right attitude. Everything else—all our words and actions—flows from the heart attitude, as Proverbs 4:23 tells us: "Watch over your heart with all diligence, for from it flow the springs of life." We have all heard the story of the little boy who was told to sit down. As he reluctantly obeyed, he declared, "I may be sitting on the outside, but I'm standing on the inside." If we are submitting only on the outside, while rebelling on the inside, we are not really submitting at all.

A wrong attitude manifests itself in many ways. When a husband makes a decision that his wife doesn't like or agree with because she is being selfish, she may pout or attempt to manipulate him through tears. Or she may simply ignore what her husband says. If she is tempted by fear, she may become anxious and worry about what he has done and how it might affect her. All of these things demonstrate an ungodly attitude toward submission.

What should the submissive wife's attitude be? As in all things, her attitude should be the same as that of Christ Jesus. Christ willingly submitted to His Father's will: "My food is to do the will of Him who sent Me and to accomplish His work" (John 4:34). In Psalm 40:8, David wrote, "I delight to do Your will, O my God; Your Law is within my heart." It should be the joy of our hearts to willingly submit to our husbands.

In a practical way, this means that the wife's attitude toward her husband will be respectful, appreciative, and undemanding. She will view herself as her husband's partner, not adversary. An adversary competes, always trying to use her gifts to come out on top. As her husband's partner and helper, however, the wife should instead be always thinking about ways to use her gifts to help him.

Submitting with the right attitude also means that there is no resistance to a final decision. As her husband's helper, the wife is responsible to give her input, thoughts, and opinions, but when her husband makes a decision, she is to support it joyfully and wholeheartedly, whether or not she agrees with it. If it really is not the right decision, God can be trusted to change the husband's mind, change the circumstances, or allow the husband to learn through the experience. And the wife can trust Him to change her mind if it is the right decision.

Many years ago, our family had the opportunity to move to California so that Wayne could be the chairman of the biblical counseling department at The Master's College. As we discussed the possibility, Wayne and I both agreed that this move was right for our ministry and family. The position that Wayne would be taking would provide an opportunity to influence many young men and women in the area of biblical counseling—a subject that he has much experience in, knowledge of, and passion for.

At the time, I was teaching fourth grade at a Christian school. In the initial parts of our discussion, I assumed that we would wait until the end of the next school year to leave, but Wayne said, "It would probably be better for us to move in January." Moving in January was not something that I had even considered, and so I was taken completely off guard by this development. I suggested to Wayne that if we left in January it would be difficult for me to leave school in the middle of the year. Wayne agreed and, since it was only June then, indicated that perhaps it would be better if I did not go back at all for the next school year.

I was both surprised and somewhat disappointed by this suggestion. I enjoyed teaching, so I shared with Wayne my reasons for wanting to wait a full year. He listened to and thought about what I said and weighed it against the reasons for our moving sooner. He explained that since he was replacing the man who had been to this point supervising the biblical counseling department, it would be important for him to be able to spend half a year shadowing the outgoing department head.

When he explained this to me, though I was disappointed at not being able to teach for one more year, I responded by saying, "If that's the wisest thing for us to do, then that's fine with me." By God's grace, I can honestly say that it *was* fine with me and that I went forward with a willing heart. I may not have initially wanted to go in January, but when Wayne explained his reasons for wanting to move at that time, it was clear to me that it was God's will as well for me to do that.

As it turned out, I was not disappointed by the hiatus in my teaching responsibilities. Fourth grade can be a bit wearing, and the Lord knew that I needed a break. I enjoyed having the time off before we left, and God was gracious in giving it to me without my ever asking for it or anticipating that I needed it. What a faithful and generous God we serve!

Biblical submission is practically demonstrated by our words as well. Proverbs 10:20 notes, "The tongue of the righteous is as choice silver . . . ," and Proverbs 31:26 says of the excellent wife: "She opens her mouth in wisdom, and the teaching of kindness is on her tongue." How we speak to and about our husbands is another important way in which we show our submission to them.

Ungodly words quickly give away the unsubmissive heart. Proverbs 27:15 says, "A constant dripping on a day of steady rain and a contentious woman are alike . . ." An unsubmissive wife will often correct, interrupt, or attempt to speak for her husband. She may be too outspoken when other people are around. She may complain to her friends or relatives about her husband. She may lie, nag, accuse, or threaten in order to get what she wants. She may remind her husband of his failings, mistakes, and weaknesses.

A truly submissive wife always speaks with grace: "Let your speech always be with grace, as though seasoned with salt . . ." (Col. 4:6a). She discusses things openly and lovingly. "Pleasant words are a honeycomb, sweet to the soul and healing to the bones" (Prov. 16:24). When she offers a suggestion or opinion that is different from her husband's, or makes a correction, she always does it in a way that makes her husband feel loved and respected by her. "The heart of the righteous ponders how to answer . . ." (Prov. 15:28).

When we were driving to a conference a few years back, Wayne said something to me about stopping for dinner when we got into town. My first thought was that it would be wiser to secure a motel room first and then look for dinner. At that point, I had a couple of options. I could have said something like, "Wayne, aren't we going to get a motel room first? That would be smarter." A response like that, however, would have been clearly adversarial—I'm trying to make my idea seem better than his. By God's grace, what I did say was, "If it's all right with you, I'd rather have us get a motel room first and then go for dinner?" The suggestion was the same, but the way in which it was said was respectful and helpful, not critical or dogmatic.

Finally, biblical submission is most clearly manifested in our actions. First Peter 3:1–2 tells us that unsaved husbands may be won over to Christ "without a word by the behavior of their wives, as they observe your chaste and respectful behavior." It is very true that our actions often speak louder than our words. We may say the "right things" to our husbands, but if our hearts are not right—we have an ungodly attitude—it will give itself away in our actions.

A wife who resists submission may show it by deliberately doing things that annoy her husband. Proverbs 21:19 describes this kind of wife when it says, "It is better to live in a desert land than with a contentious and vexing woman." A woman who is "vexing" is someone who is irritating, annoying, hard to understand, and always looking for an argument.

She may also neglect to discipline her children as she should. Proverbs 29:15 warns, "The rod and reproof give wisdom, but a child who gets his own way brings shame to his mother." A wife like this is shamed both by her child's lack of discipline and by her unwillingness to submit to her husband by fulfilling this responsibility.

An unsubmissive wife may attempt to usurp her husband's control of family affairs. She may refuse to stay within her budget. Proverbs 19:14 commends the financially prudent wife: "House and wealth are an inheritance from fathers, but a prudent wife is from the LORD." The unsubmissive wife may also make decisions without consulting her husband, or even directly defy his wishes, which the Bible specifically condemns: "For rebellion is as the sin of divination, and insubordination is as iniquity and idolatry" (1 Sam. 15:23).

She may have greater loyalty to other friends or family members than to her husband. Proverbs 31:11 says, "The heart of her husband trusts in her, and he will have no lack of gain." Some wives would rather call their mothers and tell them everything than spend time talking to their husbands. Others put more priority on getting together with girlfriends than making time to spend alone with their husbands. And some women will actually take sides with their children against their husbands in family disagreements. As a result, these women find it very difficult to submit to their husbands.

Scripture commands wives to submit to their husbands "as to the Lord" (Eph. 5:22). In a practical way, this means that our actions should mirror the kind of service of which our Lord is worthy. One way that we can do this is by making our homes a refuge for our husbands—a place of comfort, encouragement, and understanding—to which he looks forward to returning each night. For some husbands, this may mean having the house picked up when he gets home; for other husbands, it may just mean that supper is ready and waiting for him.

Being trustworthy and dependable is another way in which we show submission by our actions. Proverbs 31:11–12 says, "The heart of her husband trusts in her, and he will have no lack of gain. She does him good and not evil all the days of her life." Our husbands ought to be able to trust that when they are away, we are honoring their wishes and following through on their requests.

We also demonstrate submission by being patient and forgiving. Ephesians 4 calls all believers to "walk in a manner worthy of the calling with which you have been called, with all humility and gentleness, with patience, showing tolerance for one another in love . . ." (4:1–2). We show submission by meeting our husbands' needs—physical, emotional, and sexual. This means that we have to make an effort both to find out what our husbands' preferences and desires are and to fulfill them.

We can demonstrate submission by our actions in countless other ways, and many of them will be discussed in the next several chapters as we consider how to be our husbands' helpers as God intends. None of us is at the point—or ever will be—where we can say that we are obeying perfectly in all areas of life. Take some time to consider each of the three areas of submission—attitude, words, and actions—and do some honest evaluation. Ask for forgiveness and make plans to change. And may God give us wives the grace to daily do His will in this important area of the marriage relationship.

Application
and Discussion

Having read this chapter, spend some time as a married couple discussing or, if you're reading this as an individual, thinking through your answers to the following scenarios. If someone were to present these situations to you, how would you respond, and why would you respond that way? Seek to plug in the material that you have read in the previous chapters as you formulate your answers.

> After reading this chapter, some wives might respond, "What you say about the wife's role and responsibilities in the home sounds right, but my husband takes advantage of me and makes me wait on him hand and foot. Am I supposed to be his slave?"
>
> Or some may ask, "Can a woman be the kind of wife that the Bible says she should be and still develop her individuality? Can she pursue a career?"
>
> Or they might ask the question, "Is it legitimate for a woman to be involved in activities that take her out of the home and cause the rest of the family to fend for themselves in some areas that she would normally take care of?"

Or they might ask, "What exactly should I do and how specifically should I be a submissive wife? What difference should this make in my day-to-day activities?"

"HOW TO BE YOUR HUSBAND'S LOVER" INVENTORY[1]

How do you rate as your husband's lover? What is your LQ (love quotient) in reference to your husband? How are you doing at being the lover that God wants you to be (Eph. 5:25–33; Col. 3:18)? Are you loving your husband autobiographically (i.e., the way you want to be loved), or are you loving him in the way that he wants to be loved? The following list will help you to assess your LQ and, perhaps, reaffirm that you are doing a pretty good job in this area or help you to understand some ways in which you can improve. Carefully read and think about every statement. Having done this, (1) put an "X" next to the expression of something you are already doing, (2) put a check mark next to the things you are not doing or doing poorly and infrequently, (3) put a "+" (plus) mark in front of any of the expressions that you think your husband would appreciate most, and (4) put a "–" (minus) mark in front of any of the statements that you think your husband would not appreciate at all. To get the maximum benefit out of doing this exercise, after you have completed your inventory, work through the inventory with your husband and ask him for his perspective on each item. Then have him put a check mark in front of any of the ways of showing love that are especially meaningful to him.

___ I (never ___ , seldom ___ , sometimes ___ , often ___ , regularly/daily ___) use words of endearment with him such as: *I love you, honey, darling, dear, sweetheart.*

___ I (never ___ , seldom ___ , sometimes ___ , often ___ , regularly/daily ___) let him know how much I appreciate him.

___ When I know he'd like for me to demonstrate my affection for him physically, I (never ___ , seldom ___ , sometimes ___ , often ___ , regularly/daily __) do so by holding his hand __ , taking his arm __ , giving him a hug __ , giving him a kiss __ , putting my hand on his leg __ , sitting close to him __ .

____ I (never __ , seldom __ , sometimes __ , often __ , regularly/daily __) enthusiastically support and cooperate with him when he has made a decision.

____ I (never __ , seldom __ , sometimes __ , often __ , regularly/daily __) try to anticipate and fulfill his desires and wishes.

____ I (never __ , seldom __ , sometimes __ , often __ , regularly/daily __) try to fulfill his spoken requests.

____ I (never __ , seldom __ , sometimes __ , often __ , regularly/daily __) try to fulfill his unspoken desires and wishes.

____ I (never __ , seldom __ , sometimes __ , often __ , regularly/daily __) enthusiastically share his hobbies and recreational preferences.

____ I (never __ , seldom __ , sometimes __ , often __ , regularly/daily __) invite him to join me in my recreational preferences.

____ I (never __ , seldom __ , sometimes __ , often __ , regularly/daily __) attempt to make him aware that I admire and respect him and am thrilled to be his wife.

____ I (never __ , seldom __ , sometimes __ , often __ , regularly/daily __) enthusiastically cooperate with him in devotions and prayer.

____ I (never __ , seldom __ , sometimes __ , often __ , regularly/daily __) structure my time and use it wisely.

____ I am (never __ , seldom __ , sometimes __ , often __ , regularly/daily __) willing to work with him on projects.

____ I (never __ , seldom __ , sometimes __ , often __ , regularly/daily __) ask for his advice/counsel when I have problems or decisions to make.

____ I (never __ , seldom __ , sometimes __ , often __ , regularly/daily __) accept his counsel and follow through on it.

____ I am (never __ , seldom __ , sometimes __ , often __ , regularly/daily __) his best cheerleader and fan, enthusiastically expressing my appreciation, confidence, and respect for him as a person, for his accomplishments, and for his abilities.

___ When I sin or fail in any way, I (never __ , seldom __ , sometimes __ , often __ , regularly/daily __) don't excuse myself, blame someone else, or defend myself, but take full and personal responsibility for whatever I have done that is wrong.

___ When I sin against him, I am (never __ , seldom __ , sometimes __ , often __ , regularly/daily __) quick to ask for forgiveness.

___ When I sin against him, I (never __ , seldom __ , sometimes __ , often __ , regularly/daily __) try to change my sinful thoughts, attitudes, feelings, words, actions.

___ I (never __ , seldom __ , sometimes __ , often __ , regularly/daily __) share my thoughts and feelings with him.

___ I (never __ , seldom __ , sometimes __ , often __ , regularly/daily __) patiently listen to him when he wants to share his concerns with me.

___ I am (never __ , seldom __ , sometimes __ , often __ , regularly/daily __) willing to allow him to disagree with me without becoming upset about it.

___ I am (never __ , seldom __ , sometimes __ , often __ , regularly/daily __) willing to calmly and respectfully discuss his concerns even if they involve my having done something he doesn't like or wants me to change.

___ I (never __ , seldom __ , sometimes __ , often __ , regularly/daily __) put the best possible interpretation on something he says, does, or doesn't do.

___ I (never __ , seldom __ , sometimes __ , often __ , regularly/daily __) willingly listen to him without interruption.

___ I (never __ , seldom __ , sometimes __ , often __ , regularly/daily __) stop what I'm doing, thinking, or saying and give him my full attention when he wants to talk.

___ I (never __ , seldom __ , sometimes __ , often __ , regularly/daily __) wait until I've heard all that he has to say before I decide what he means by his remarks.

___ I (never __ , seldom __ , sometimes __ , often __ , regularly/daily __) wait until I've fully heard what he has said before I plan my response to it.

____ I (never __ , seldom __ , sometimes __ , often __ , regularly/daily __) let him know by my words, actions, and attitudes that I enjoy being with him.

____ I am (never __ , seldom __ , sometimes __ , often __ , regularly/daily __) a fun person to be around.

____ I (never __ , seldom __ , sometimes __ , often __ , regularly/daily __) take life seriously.

____ I (never __ , seldom __ , sometimes __ , often __ , regularly/daily __) focus mainly on the things in life, in our own relationship, and in our relationships with other people that are right, just, lovely, honorable, pure, excellent, and worthy of praise.

____ I (never __ , seldom __ , sometimes __ , often __ , regularly/daily __) seriously consider what will encourage him when he is discouraged.

____ When I sense that he is discouraged, I (never __ , seldom __ , sometimes __ , often __ , regularly/daily __) make it a matter of prayer.

____ When I sense that he is discouraged, I (never __ , seldom __ , sometimes __ , often __ , regularly/daily __) seek God's direction and help and then do what I think will encourage him.

____ I (never __ , seldom __ , sometimes __ , often __ , regularly/daily __) join with him in his Christian service (ministry) opportunities.

____ I (never __ , seldom __ , sometimes __ , often __ , regularly/daily __) empathize with him when he is experiencing difficulties and let him know that he can count on me.

____ When he is honored in any way or accomplishes some task, I (never __ , seldom __ , sometimes __ , often __ , regularly/daily __) enter into his joy and seek to let him know how pleased I am.

____ I (never __ , seldom __ , sometimes __ , often __ , regularly/daily __) want to have mutual friends and join with him in doing things with these friends.

____ I (never __ , seldom __ , sometimes __ , often __ , regularly/daily __) make an effort to understand the nature of his work.

____ I (never __ , seldom __ , sometimes __ , often __ , regularly/daily __) discuss spiritual truths __ and problems __ with him.

___ I am (never __, seldom __, sometimes __, often __, regularly/daily __) available to him when he desires sex relations.

___ I (never __, seldom __, sometimes __, often __, regularly/daily __) pamper him and make a fuss over him.

___ I (never __, seldom __, sometimes __, often __, regularly/daily __) refuse to nag.

___ I (never __, seldom __, sometimes __, often __, regularly/daily __) do not treat him like a child or an incompetent person.

___ I (never __, seldom __, sometimes __, often __, regularly/daily __) refrain from giving advice or telling him what to do when he already knows what needs to be done.

___ I (never __, seldom __, sometimes __, often __, regularly/daily __) take the initiative in seeking sex relations.

___ I (never __, seldom __, sometimes __, often __, regularly/daily __) think about what pleases him in our physical relations.

___ I am (never __, seldom __, sometimes __, often __, regularly/daily __) willing to do what pleases him in our sex relations.

___ I (never __, seldom __, sometimes __, often __, regularly/daily __) respond warmly and enthusiastically to his physical expressions of affection.

___ I am (never __, seldom __, sometimes __, often __, regularly/daily __) uninhibited when we are having physical relations.

___ I (never __, seldom __, sometimes __, often __, regularly/daily __) try to make sure that all problems between us are settled before we have sex relations.

___ I am (never __, seldom __, sometimes __, often __, regularly/daily __) willing to participate with him in doing new and different things (sexually and otherwise).

___ I (never __, seldom __, sometimes __, often __, regularly/daily __) seek to develop an interest in the things that interest him.

___ When we're apart, I (never __, seldom __, sometimes __, often __, regularly/daily __) really miss him and look forward to seeing him again.

___ I (never __ , seldom __ , sometimes __ , often __ , regularly/daily __) share with him what I'm reading or what is going on in my life.

___ I (never __ , seldom __ , sometimes __ , often __ , regularly/daily __) tell the children and others about his good qualities or accomplishments.

___ I (never __ , seldom __ , sometimes __ , often __ , regularly/daily __) refuse to complain or gossip to others about him.

___ When I have agreed to do something, I (never __ , seldom __ , sometimes __ , often __ , regularly/daily __) do it.

___ When I have agreed not to do something, I (never __ , seldom __ , sometimes __ , often __ , regularly/daily __) don't do it.

___ When I know that there is something he'd like me to do, I (never __ , seldom __ , sometimes __ , often __ , regularly/daily __) try to do it.

___ When I know that there is something he doesn't want me to do, I (never __ , seldom __ , sometimes __ , often __ , regularly/daily __) either don't do it or discuss it with him and seek to discern whether it is just a preference or more than that.

___ When he shares something with me and I know he wants me to keep it confidential, I (never __ , seldom __ , sometimes __ , often __ , regularly/daily __) keep it confidential unless to do so would violate God's will and he or someone else would be hurt or really hindered by my keeping it confidential.

___ When we have serious and continuing problems or conflicts that we can't personally resolve, I am (never __ , seldom __ , sometimes __ , often __ , regularly/daily __) willing to seek godly counsel to secure resolution.

___ I am (never __ , seldom __ , sometimes __ , often __ , regularly/daily __) more interested in his opinion than I am in anyone else's opinion.

___ I am (never __ , seldom __ , sometimes __ , often __ , regularly/daily __) willing to cover his faults (Prov. 10:12) and not allow them to influence my attitudes and actions toward him.

___ I (never __ , seldom __ , sometimes __ , often __ , regularly/daily __) get great joy out of seeing him growing in his walk with God.

_____ If I have a problem with him, I (never ___ , seldom ___ , sometimes ___ , often ___ , regularly/daily ___) pray about it and seriously consider what God would have me do before I do or don't do anything.

_____ If I think something in his life is seriously hindering him in his relationship with or service to God and effectiveness with others or at his work, I am (never ___ , seldom ___ , sometimes ___ , often ___ , regularly/daily ___) willing to do the hard thing and gently and carefully bring it to his attention (Prov. 27:6–7).

_____ I (never ___ , seldom ___ , sometimes ___ , often ___ , regularly/daily ___) pray for him throughout my day.

_____ I (never ___ , seldom ___ , sometimes ___ , often ___ , regularly/daily ___) attempt to help him to make important changes out of love for God and him.

_____ I am (never ___ , seldom ___ , sometimes ___ , often ___ , regularly/daily ___) ready to leave at the appointed time and punctual in keeping time commitments we have made.

_____ I am (never ___ , seldom ___ , sometimes ___ , often ___ , regularly/daily ___) lovingly honest with him and don't withhold the truth that may hinder our present or future relationship.

_____ I am (never ___ , seldom ___ , sometimes ___ , often ___ , regularly/daily ___) willing to dream with him and join with him in discussing future plans and aspirations.

_____ I (never ___ , seldom ___ , sometimes ___ , often ___ , regularly/daily ___) run errands gladly.

_____ I (never ___ , seldom ___ , sometimes ___ , often ___ , regularly/daily ___) cook creatively and keep his likes and dislikes in mind.

_____ I (never ___ , seldom ___ , sometimes ___ , often ___ , regularly/daily ___) do a good job of keeping the house neat and clean.

_____ I (never ___ , seldom ___ , sometimes ___ , often ___ , regularly/daily ___) handle my areas of finances responsibly.

_____ I (never ___ , seldom ___ , sometimes ___ , often ___ , regularly/daily ___) a good example to the children.

_____ I (never ___ , seldom ___ , sometimes ___ , often ___ , regularly/daily ___) make plans carefully, prayerfully, and biblically.

___ I am (never __ , seldom __ , sometimes __ , often __ , regularly/daily __) tender, gentle, polite, and courteous with him.

___ I (never __ , seldom __ , sometimes __ , often __ , regularly/daily __) yell or scream at him.

___ I (never __ , seldom __ , sometimes __ , often __ , regularly/daily __) refrain from being overbearing, pushy, or domineering.

___ I (never __ , seldom __ , sometimes __ , often __ , regularly/daily __) ask for his prayers and assistance in overcoming sinful habits.

___ I (never __ , seldom __ , sometimes __ , often __ , regularly/daily __) surprise him by planning date nights, mini-honeymoons, or some kind of getaway for the two of us to be together without interference.

___ I (never __ , seldom __ , sometimes __ , often __ , regularly/daily __) compliment him on his appearance or something he is wearing.

___ I (never __ , seldom __ , sometimes __ , often __ , regularly/daily __) write love notes, send a card, make a special call, remember birthdays and anniversaries.

___ I (never __ , seldom __ , sometimes __ , often __ , regularly/daily __) seek to be his helpmate in helping him to avoid provoking the children to wrath and to bring them up in the discipline and instruction of the Lord.

___ I have been and still am (never __ , seldom __ , sometimes __ , often __ , regularly/daily __) willing to discuss child-rearing issues and practices with him.

___ Unless his decisions violate the revealed will of God, I will (never __ , seldom __ , sometimes __ , often __ , regularly/daily __) support his decisions and act accordingly.

___ I (never __ , seldom __ , sometimes __ , often __ , regularly/daily __) protect and defend him (physically, emotionally, spiritually, socially) against all people, including family members, who would seek to hurt him.

___ I (never __ , seldom __ , sometimes __ , often __ , regularly/daily __) remember to keep him informed about items that will involve and affect him (such as meetings, people, finances, work responsibilities, the car, evening events, etc.).

___ I (never ___ , seldom ___ , sometimes ___ , often ___ , regularly/daily ___) maintain my own spiritual life through Bible study, prayer, regular church attendance, and fellowship with God's people.

___ I (never ___ , seldom ___ , sometimes ___ , often ___ , regularly/daily ___) make sure that I'm available and that we make time to truly communicate on a regular (usually daily) basis.

___ I (never ___ , seldom ___ , sometimes ___ , often ___ , regularly/daily ___) consider him to be my best earthly friend and seek to do those things that promote the continuance and development of our friendship.

___ I (never ___ , seldom ___ , sometimes ___ , often ___ , regularly/daily ___) yield to his desires and let him have his own way unless to do so would violate God's Word.

___ I (never ___ , seldom ___ , sometimes ___ , often ___ , regularly/daily ___) delight in being his helper and submitting myself to him (Gen. 2:18; Eph. 5:22–24; 1 Peter 3:1–6).

___ I (never ___ , seldom ___ , sometimes ___ , often ___ , regularly/daily ___) do not knowingly or defiantly do what I know would be contrary to his will unless what he desires is contrary to the revealed will of God.

___ I (never ___ , seldom ___ , sometimes ___ , often ___ , regularly/daily ___) know that being his helper and being in submission to him is part of God's will for me.

Add to the previous inventory any other biblically consistent ways in which you either do show love or think your husband would like you to show love.

_____

_____

_____

_____

_____

_____

_____

_____

Make a list of the ways that you will, with God's help, seek to be your husband's lover. Especially list the ways in which you can improve.

_____

_____

_____

_____

_____

_____

36

BE YOUR HUSBAND'S HELPER

Scripture tells us that after creating Adam, God determined him to be in need of greater companionship than the animals could provide. In Genesis 2:18, God said, "It is not good for the man to be alone; I will make him a helper suitable for him." When God created Eve, the first woman, it was for the express purpose of providing Adam with a helpmate. Every man and woman, husband and wife since then is a descendant of that first couple and thus an heir to God's purpose in creating them.

What, then, does it mean for a woman and wife today to be a "helper suitable" for her husband? When I got married, I had no idea what God meant for me to be my husband's helper. I figured that it would be nice for him to have someone to talk to, cook his meals, do the wash, clean the house, and that sort of thing. If anyone had asked, I would have said that I really did not think he needed much more than that. Needless to say, I have learned a great deal in the last forty-some years about the importance of this special role that God has given to me.

Learning how to be her husband's helper is important because it is God's intention for the wife, but there are other important reasons as well. First, it is important for her own heart in terms of her spiritual growth as a believer. I doubt that any married woman would be willing to say that she is the model of godliness, the perfect helper for her husband, and in need of no further instruction. We all have room for growth and areas of persistent weakness.

Second, it is important for us to learn and remind ourselves of God's teaching about marriage so that we can help, teach, and encourage others. In Titus 2:3–4, Paul instructed older women to "be reverent in their behavior, . . . teaching what is good, so that they may encourage the young women to love their husbands . . ." We ought to be willing and able to teach the younger women that God brings into our lives. Even single women can benefit from learning these things so that, if God someday gives them husbands, they can avoid some of the painful lessons that others of us have struggled through.

To be honest, these next few chapters are not going to reveal any great, new secrets about being a husband's helpmate. I have not discovered anything new in my forty-some years of marriage. The truths that I am going to share have been revealed in Scripture and known for a long time. So what is the point of reading further? I encourage you to continue on because I believe that we all need someone to stir us up from time to time.

When we lived in California, we often visited the orange groves that were very close to our home. We would pick fresh oranges, bring them home, and enjoy the wonderful, fresh-made orange juice. The leftover juice was put into the refrigerator, but when we would take it out the next day, we noticed that the good stuff had all settled to the bottom. If we simply poured off the top, what we would get to drink was little more than orange-flavored water. We quickly learned that each time we wanted to enjoy the orange juice, we had to shake it up.

In the same way, our hearts and minds often need to be stirred or even shaken up to bring the good things that we know about godliness to the top. The apostles often did this, writing to the churches the same things that they had been taught before, but needed to hear again: "This is now, beloved, the second letter I am writing to you in which I am stirring up your sincere mind by way of reminder, that you should remember the words spoken beforehand by the holy prophets and the commandment of the Lord and Savior spoken by your apostles" (2 Peter 3:1–2).

Being her husband's helper means that the wife will be his companion and friend. Proverbs 2:17 and Malachi 2:14 both refer to the wife and husband as being each other's companion. In other words, a woman's husband ought to be her best friend. I know that for some wives, their best friend is one of their children or a longtime girlfriend. Such a wife would much rather spend time with her best friend, who is usually the first person that the wife talks to when something happens.

For me, there is no one that I would rather spend time with than my husband, Wayne. When something significant happens to me, my first thought is to tell him about it as soon as possible. I am glad that we learned very early in our marriage to be each other's friend, but friendship is something that can be developed and improved at any time. In the next two chapters, we will consider some of the characteristics of friendship, especially friendship with our husbands.

APPLICATION AND DISCUSSION

1. What are your husband's five favorite foods (list his most favorite first)?

2. What are his five favorite kinds of meals (list his most favorite first)?

3. What are his five favorite desserts (list his most favorite first)?

4. What are his five favorite restaurants (list his most favorite first)?

5. What is his favorite color?

6. What are his five favorite hobbies (list his most favorite first)?

7. What are his five favorite recreational activities (list his most favorite first)?

8. What are his five favorite sources of reading (list his most favorite first)?

9. What gifts does he like?

37

Be Your Husband's Friend

In practical terms, a wife's being her husband's best friend means sharing everything with him, just as Jesus shared everything with His disciples: "I have called you friends, for all things that I have heard from My Father I have made known to you" (John 15:15). We ought to share our time by making time to spend alone with our husbands. Not everything can be shared over the dinner table with the children listening. We also need to share our ideas, fears, joys, goals, and dreams with our husbands. And it ought to be safe for the husband to share with his wife as well; in other words, she needs to make sure to listen to him with a trusting and encouraging attitude.

In the early years of our marriage, Wayne was a pastor. Sometimes, on Monday mornings, he would share with me his ideas about other types of ministries that he thought he might like to be involved in instead of the pastorate. Rather than listening and trying to be an encouragement to him, I would immediately panic. "How can we move to another place now? We can't take the kids out of school in the middle of the year! There's no way this could work out . . ."

After hearing this from me a few times, Wayne finally said, "I'm not going to do anything that would not be good for you and our children. I'm certainly not going to just pull up everything and move without any concern for what's best for our family. Our family is at the top of my list. Why don't you just trust me and let me dream and share with you?" Needless to say, I was greatly convicted by his words. He needed the freedom to share his thoughts with me without my jumping to conclusions and assuming that he was disregarding our needs.

That was a valuable lesson for me. Now, Wayne and I would have to live to a hundred and fifty to accomplish all the things that we dream about doing together, but we enjoy sitting down and sharing our ideas with each other. If a wife wants her husband to share with her, she must be careful to guard her reaction.

The wife should also consider whether or not she is really sharing with her husband on a deep level. In other words, how well does she really know her husband? We women like to complain about men's never sharing, but too often we are guilty of the same thing.

A FRIEND IS TRUSTWORTHY

A friend who shares and is shared with must be trustworthy. Proverbs 31:11–12 says of the excellent wife: "The heart of her husband trusts in her, and he will have no lack of gain. She does him good and not evil all the days of her life." As her husband's friend, the godly wife should also be his confidante. In other words, her husband should never wonder whether or not he should share something with his wife. He ought to know that whatever he shares will be safely kept.

Wayne and I experienced the California earthquake of 1994. Up until that time, I had never been in an earthquake before and had no idea what a frightening experience it could be. We were in a waterbed asleep when it hit, and for the forty-five seconds that the quake lasted, it felt as though we were being thrown around by a tidal wave. The TV in our bedroom flew over the bed and landed on the other side. Every cabinet door in the kitchen opened, and things fell all over the floor. It was probably the most frightening event we have ever experienced.

When we found out later that the quake had lasted for only forty-five seconds, I was quite surprised. I would have guessed it to be much longer because no one could have quoted as many Scripture verses as Wayne did in forty-five seconds. And for some time after the quake, we heard that many men struggled with significant fear. Husbands are supposed to protect their families, but in an earthquake, everything is completely out of their control.

It was very discouraging for me to hear some women make fun of their husbands' fears. We heard things such as: "Can you believe that he sleeps with his shoes on?" and "He won't get into bed. He just sleeps on the sofa by the door." Some people slept in their cars for a while afterward because they just could not face their fear of going back into the house. A friend never mocks or makes fun of serious struggles. We wives ought to be safe for our husbands to confide in, to share their fears and struggles with, without thinking that they might be made fun of.

A FRIEND SACRIFICES

A wife's being a friend and companion to her husband requires sacrifice as well. In John 15:13, Jesus said, "Greater love has no one than this, that one lay down his life for his friends." Jesus demonstrated His great love for us by giving His life. Though we will probably never be asked to make that kind of sacrifice for our husbands, we will have to sacrifice many lesser things. Sometimes those are the hardest things.

Most of us would be willing to sacrifice whatever was needed if our husbands' lives were in danger, but would the typical wife be willing to sacrifice a trip to the mall for an afternoon of football? Would she gladly give up a Saturday afternoon of reading and relaxing because he wants to go car-shopping instead?

Sacrificing for our husbands means that we will be interested in their interests. For me, that meant sports—especially football. My father had been a big basketball fan, so I didn't mind watching basketball, but I knew very little about football when I married Wayne. Wayne had been a football player in college and enjoyed watching games from time to time. At first, I would work in the kitchen while he watched in the family room. Then I began to sit beside him while he watched the game, but I kept the light on and knitted. Eventually, I realized that being interested in his interests meant that I needed to put the knitting down, turn out the light, and really watch the game.

We are such selfish people by nature. Spending a few hours each week watching a football game with my husband was not a major sacrifice—it was hardly a minor one—but for a while it was too much for my husband to ask of me. I am reminded of the words of the apostle Paul, "Having so fond an affection for you, we were well-pleased to impart to you not only the gospel of God but also our own lives, because you had become very dear to us" (1 Thess. 2:8).

Sacrificing also means finding out what kinds of things say "I love you" to our husbands. I knew an older couple who never learned this. When the husband was sick, he wanted only to be left alone. His wife, on the other hand, wanted constant attention when she was not feeling well: her pillow fluffed, her tea brought, and constantly being asked how she was doing. So when the husband got sick, the wife smothered him with unwanted attention, and when the wife got sick, the husband ignored her. They never learned how to love each other as the other wanted to be loved.

Why is this a sacrifice? When a wife loves as her husband wants to be loved, it often means doing things that do not come naturally. She may have to suppress her urge to baby him when he is sick. She may have to bite her tongue when he has had a long day and does not want to talk about it right away. She may have to learn to be a night owl when she would rather be an early bird, or an early bird when she would rather be a night owl. These types of sacrifices, though not very difficult, do require effort.

Sacrificing means learning to let things go as well. In our house, my husband and I have a deal: he controls the TV remote and I control the thermostat. Wayne prefers to have the house a little cooler in summer and a little warmer in winter, but I am too cheap to spend the extra money on the electric bill. He lets it go because I have agreed to let him control the TV remote.

I do not particularly enjoy watching ten seconds of fifty different programs during a two-minute commercial. I have a hard time remembering what we were watching in the first place when he finishes running through the channels. But if that makes him happy, is it really a big deal? I could sit there and be annoyed, but I choose not to be. After all, it really is just a little thing, and I have learned to let it go. Being her husband's friend means that the wife is willing to sacrifice for him.

APPLICATION AND DISCUSSION

1. What is your husband's favorite book of the Bible? Why?
2. What are his favorite Bible verses? Why?
3. What is his favorite song?
4. What makes him the most fulfilled or happiest as a man?
5. What makes him the most fulfilled or happiest as a husband?
6. What makes him the most fulfilled or happiest as a father?

38

MORE ON FRIENDSHIP

Service is another important aspect of a wife's being her husband's friend. After washing the disciples' feet, Jesus said, "For I gave you an example that you also should do as I did to you" (John 13:15). Later, Jesus said, "You are My friends if you do what I command you" (John 15:14). A friend is willing to serve, and the true test of a wife's willingness to be a servant comes when she is treated like one. When her husband asks her to do something that he could just as easily, or perhaps more easily, do himself, how does the Christian wife respond? She ought to serve joyfully no matter how small or large the request.

Even better than a wife's serving with a willing heart is making an effort to anticipate her husband's needs. Instead of being annoyed when he asks for the salt after she has finally gotten everything on the table and sat down, she can make an effort to remember to put it on the table for him. Instead of being annoyed when he asks for a glass of water as he is sitting beside her on the couch, she can think to ask him if he wants something to drink.

The last year I taught school, I had a classroom aide who had perfected this kind of service. I had twenty-four kindergartners, and about the time I would start to say, "Would you get the papers for . . . ," she would already have them in her hand, ready to pass out. She seemed to always know what we were going to do next and was ready to help me with it. We wives ought to be willing to serve our husbands in that way as well.

I know some husbands who are jealous of their children because their wives serve their kids more unselfishly than they do their husbands. Do we complain or make excuses when our husbands ask us to do something, but immediately jump up to help our kids when they ask for help? A relative of ours used to tell us that his wife made beautiful clothes for their daughter but could never seem to get around to sewing a button on a shirt for him. She was perfectly happy to serve her daughter, but not her husband. Being a friend means being willing to serve joyfully, unselfishly, and without being asked.

A Friend Is Sensitive

Sensitivity is an important part of a wife's being her husband's friend and companion. Proverbs 27:14 says, "He who blesses his friend with a loud voice early in the morning, it will be reckoned a curse to him." What could be wrong with telling someone how much we love and appreciate them? It is when we do it in a way or at a time that they are not able to appreciate it.

My daughter loves me and we are very close friends, but if I called her at five in the morning and said, "Hey, Beth! I just wanted to tell you how much I love you!" she would not appreciate it very much. She probably would not curse me, but she would definitely not be happy. I expect that her response would be something like a groan followed by a click. Calling her the first thing in the morning, except for an emergency, would not be being sensitive to her.

We need to be sensitive to our husbands as well. There are times when our husbands need encouragement, not advice. There are times when they need peace and quiet, not chatty company. There are better and worse times in the day to bring up problems that need to be addressed. For example, when a husband comes home from work, the first ten or fifteen minutes that he is in the house are probably not the best time for a wife to unload all the woes of her day.

We need to be sensitive to our husbands' sexual needs, spiritual needs, and emotional needs as well. And we ought to be very careful about what and when we comment or complain about things, if at all. My daughter once had a family stay with her, and she later shared with me how the wife was constantly complaining about her husband and what he was and was not able to provide for them. She saw how devastated this man was by his wife's insensitive complaints. Being a friend means being sensitive.

A FRIEND SUPPORTS

As her husband's friend and companion, the wife needs to be a support to him. Proverbs 17:17 says, "A friend loves at all times . . .," and Ecclesiastes 4:9–12 talks about two being better than one. Our husbands need our support all the time through daily demonstrations of respect and encouragement. My daughter-in-law once said: "I think my job as a wife is to make my husband look good." Our son Josh is blessed because he knows that wherever he goes, whatever happens, his wife is going to support him and do things to make him look good to others.

We can show our support for our husbands in many ways. We can do it by listening to our husbands respectfully, by praying for them, and by being with them as much as possible. Several years ago, Wayne and I were in South Africa at a conference where Wayne was preaching and teaching. The way the conference was set up, he was doing the same thing every week of the six weeks we were there, so by the fifth week I had heard him five times.

One day that week, a woman followed me to the ladies' room and said, "I bet you've heard this a lot of times, but I've been watching the way you listen." She was encouraged by the way that I paid attention and listened to my husband. Not that I find it difficult because Wayne never preaches anything exactly the same way twice, but my listening attentively showed others at the conference that I supported my husband's ministry. The experience also made me realize that although I might not be aware of it, others could be watching me at any given time.

Our husbands especially need our support in difficult times. We had a pastor friend who made a very poor judgment call (nothing immoral, just a really poor choice) for which he needed to apologize to his congregation. As he was preparing to do this, someone asked his wife, "Aren't you going to stand beside your husband when he talks to the church?" She replied, "No, I'm so embarrassed. I'm so ashamed of him." She may have been ashamed of what he did, but not standing beside him at that difficult time demonstrated to her husband and everyone else that she did not support him.

A husband needs to know that his wife supports him even when he does wrong. That does not mean, of course, that she must agree with what he did or that she is just ignoring what he did. But a friend loves at all times. If the wife is going to be her husband's friend, then she needs to listen to him when he is hurting, support and encourage him when he makes mistakes, enter into his problems without being critical, and be understanding of his weaknesses.

A FRIEND MAKES TIME

Being a friend to her husband means that the wife will schedule time to be with him. This means time alone—not with the children, friends, or relatives. As any mother knows, finding that time can be very difficult. But if she cannot find a way to leave her children (with appropriate care) for a day or even just an evening, then she has a problem—and so do the children.

Although Wayne and I never did it when our own children were young (and I'm sorry we never thought of it), some women trade babysitting for an evening so that they can go out with their husbands. Wayne and I tried to get away once every year for several days so that we could spend time alone together. It was wonderful to catch our breath, get some perspective, get caught up with each other, and enjoy each other's company in a way that we could not at home. Such time away will never just happen, of course; it takes planning and scheduling.

When Wayne was in his first pastorate, Monday was his day off. We lived only about an hour and a half from both sets of parents, so we often went to one of their houses on Mondays to get away and relax for a bit. When we went to Wayne's parents' house, my mother-in-law was always doing the laundry when we arrived because in her house, the wash was done on Monday—always.

So every Monday morning when we walked into her kitchen, she would say to me, "Well, Carol, I guess you already have your wash done."

And every Monday I would smile and answer, "No, I'll do it tomorrow." I must have been a great disappointment to her because in her mind, Monday was wash day. But if I had insisted on staying home until the wash was done, we probably would have never ended up leaving at all. Wayne would have started doing something while I worked, then I would have gotten involved in something else, and the day would have quickly vanished. It was important for Wayne to have that time off, however, so I needed to be his friend by being flexible with my schedule and making time for his needs.

When Wayne made hospital calls, we all went along. The children learned to nap in the car, and I learned to put aside what I was doing and finish it later. Most things really are not as important as we tend to think they are at the moment. The dishwasher can be turned off, the knitting put aside, the homework saved for later, and the phone calls made another time. A wife's spending time with her husband is more important than any of these other little things. Her friendship with her husband is worth the sacrifice in her schedule.

APPLICATION
AND DISCUSSION

1. What makes your husband saddest as a man?

2. What makes him saddest as a husband?

3. What makes him saddest as a father?

4. What is his greatest fear?

5. What are his other fears?

6. What does he look forward to the most?

7. How much sleep does he need?

8. What things (personal, home, etc.) need mending, attending to, or taken better care of?

9. With what chores and responsibilities does he like your help?

39

BE YOUR HUSBAND'S COLABORER

Being her husband's helper also means that the wife is his colaborer. The word *helper* used in Genesis 2:18 conveys the idea of woman working alongside man. In the New Testament, Priscilla and Aquila were a good example of this principle. The Scripture says that this couple worked as tent-makers and also that when Apollos was in need of some instruction, "they took him aside and explained to him the way of God more accurately" (Acts 18:26). Though Priscilla may not have been as involved in tent-making and teaching as her husband was, they were together in all they did.

IN THE HOME

As her husband's helper, the wife has a responsibility to be his colaborer in the home. That means that she willingly does all that is required to make the home comfortable, inviting, and satisfying for him. If he likes to have dinner on the table when he gets home from work, she ensures that it is ready on time. If he likes to come home to a house that is neat and in order, she ensures that things are picked up before he arrives. Every husband has different preferences, of course, so the wife needs to find out what pleases her husband most.

Wayne did not like to come home to a messy house. I had no argument with that, but it took a little while for me to realize that our definitions of a mess were quite different. As far as I was concerned, the children could have every toy they owned out on the floor, but it was not a mess until they walked away. I was perfectly happy with that amount of disorder as long as they were actively playing with their toys. Wayne, on the other hand, wanted to come home to a house that was cleaned up. If all the toys were out, the house was a mess regardless of whether the children were playing with them.

In order to please Wayne and be his helper in the home, I had to learn that at five o'clock all the toys got picked up and put away so that when Wayne got home, the house was neat. And really, it was not a big deal because the toys would have to be picked up sometime anyway. If he arrived home early, I told him he was on his own, but since it made Wayne happy to come home to a house that was in order, I was happy to do my part to make sure that it was done for him.

A wife's being her husband's colaborer in the home includes training and disciplining the children. Proverbs 1:8 says, "Hear, my son, your father's instruction and do not forsake your mother's teaching . . ." Mothers have a responsibility to teach their children and often have the most opportunity as well. We are more likely to spend much time with them when they are small and, when they are older, to be the first to see them when they get home from school.

Wayne used to tell me how he envied the fact that I was there when the children got home from school. On occasion, Wayne would get home before they did and would eagerly await their arrival. Unfortunately, his eagerness was usually rewarded with: "Where's Mom?" When he asked about their day, they would give him little more than "It was fine," because they were so programmed to tell me everything.

We wives should help our husbands to make plans—both for the present and for the future—for our families. Planning ahead is very important in terms of training our children. It helps us to be proactive, anticipating and being prepared for each new stage of life, rather than being reactive, making decisions as we go along. Wayne and I often spent time alone together for the specific purpose of making plans for our family. We would talk about what we were going to do differently, what new challenges we were going to face, and how we would address those challenges.

The wife needs to be her husband's colaborer in the home in terms of the family finances as well. It is critical that as wives, we operate responsibly within the limits of the family budget and according to our husbands' wishes. And we ought to be very careful that we do not ever complain about a lack of money because that is very demeaning to our husbands. God has given them the ability and means to provide certain resources for their families. When a wife complains about her husband's provision for her, she is really complaining about God's provision for her.

Some types of complaining are fairly obvious: "I wish we could afford a vacation like the Smiths had" or "I wish we had enough money to get another car" and comments like that. But we also need to watch that we do not regularly say things such as this to our children: "I know you want that new toy, but we can't afford it." The wife may not mean to put her husband down by saying things like that, but when it is done on a regular basis, the children are being taught to think that their father cannot adequately provide for them.

I avoided this problem by keeping a small notebook in my purse. If the children asked for something ridiculous that cost a great deal of money, I had no problem saying, "We can't afford that," but when they asked for something small, I simply replied, "I'll put in on my list." And then I would take out that little notebook and write the item down.

If a certain item came up a number of times, it often became a birthday or Christmas present. But regardless of whether a child asked for it once and then promptly forgot about it, or asked for it several times and eventually got it as a gift, all the children always knew their requests were heard and considered. It allowed me to show them that I cared about their interests while at the same time helping me to avoid always saying, "We can't afford it."

Finally, being her husband's colaborer in the home means that the godly wife will labor with him spiritually for the family. As wives and mothers, we ought to encourage family devotions by making them easy for our husbands to hold. In our house, we always had devotions after dinner. I am quite sure that if I had insisted on having the table cleared, the dishes washed and put away, and the kitchen in order before devotions started, it would have been so late that we would have rarely, if ever, had them.

We should be regularly praying for and with our husbands. I believe that husbands and wives ought to spend time together in prayer for their children and for the needs and concerns of their families. In addition, we should be praying for our husbands and the special needs and concerns that they have shared with us about their work or other personal issues. Laboring for them in prayer is a wonderful and highly effective way for us to be an encouragement and blessing to our husbands.

In His Workplace

A wife should also be her husband's colaborer in his workplace. Obviously, this does not mean that she follows him to work each day, but rather that she has a continual interest in what he is doing, in the people he works with, and in his struggles and successes in his job. This interest should go far beyond simply asking how his day went when he walks in the door. It means that the wife must find practical ways to be involved in what he does.

For many years, Wayne taught courses at The Master's College in California. One year, he had a whole class full of girls, about half of whom were on the volleyball team. So my husband went to quite a few volleyball games that year, and I always went with him. If there was a function at the college—a dinner or other campus event—we always attended it together. That was one way that I was able to participate and take an interest in his work during that time.

We should always encourage our husbands to share the events of the day with us so that we can pray for them. When I was teaching school, Wayne knew the name of every child in my classroom because we discussed them together. He knew the ones whom I struggled with and the ones who were exceptional, and he prayed for them with me. Whatever a husband's occupation may be, there are many ways in which his wife can be involved in a helpful, supportive way.

1. What are your husband's skills?

2. What are his spiritual gifts?

3. What are his weaknesses?

4. What caresses does he enjoy the most?

5. What caresses does he enjoy the least?

6. What actions of yours provide him with the greatest sexual pleasure?

7. What other things stimulate him sexually?

8. At what times does he need assurance of your love the most?

9. How can that love be shown?

40

BE YOUR HUSBAND'S COMMENDER

Jesus once said, "A prophet is not without honor except in his home-town and in his own household" (Matt. 13:57). This should *never* be true for a husband. Part of a wife's job as her husband's helper is being his personal cheerleader. She ought to make every effort to see that her husband is respected by his children and respected and encouraged by herself. And she should make it a point to be his public-relations agent to the world, commending him to others as well.

COMMENDING HIM TO OTHERS

A woman once came to me and said, "I just don't understand why my mother doesn't like my husband. She used to, when we first got married, but now she doesn't anymore." As I investigated further, I found that this woman's mother thought so poorly of her husband because she was always complaining about him to her mother. Mothers often instinctively believe and take the side of their children. Though this is not necessarily the right thing for them to do, we should do our best to avoid putting them in a position in which it is easy for them to do so by complaining to them.

I know some people who are happier when their spouses are away than when they are home—and are not afraid of sharing that fact with others. After forty-some years of marriage, I think my husband is great, and I make a point of telling people so because I believe it is part of my job as his wife. Other people—especially ones that know the wife better—are going to form their opinion of her husband, to some extent, based on what she says about him. Though no husband is perfect (or wife, for that matter), we need to make sure that others are hearing about the good things.

We should also be careful that we do not use public occasions to make remarks that we would not make in private. Sometimes it is tempting to make critical comments "in fun" that are really not "in fun" at all. Usually those things that we say seemingly half in fun are really wholly in earnest. Really, we are just thinking that it might be safe to say something in front of other people that we have wanted to say in private but were afraid of how it would be received. There are appropriate ways and times for a wife to make constructive criticisms to her husband, but it should never be done in public.

COMMENDING HIM TO HIS CHILDREN

The Christian wife needs to be her husband's cheerleader to their children. Since wives are usually the primary caretakers of the children, what a mother says to the children and how she treats her husband in front of them will play a major role in building or destroying their respect for him. Wayne never knew the effort it was for me to get the children excited for his arrival at the end of the day, but I know he really appreciated seeing their smiling faces yell, "Daddy's home!" as he walked in the door.

When the children are older, they need to see their mother being an example in terms of respecting their father's opinion and obeying his wishes and instructions. She should never contradict him in front of the children or tell them to do something different after he has gone. That kind of disregard for him will quickly undermine their respect for him and his authority over them in the home.

A wife ought to be very careful about disagreeing with her husband in front of their children. If it is a minor issue of preference and can be resolved quickly and graciously, then the children can certainly benefit from seeing a difference of opinion resolved properly. I believe that major issues, however, should be discussed in private, especially if a disagreement is something that could take awhile to work through. On the whole, children should see that their mother fully supports their father both when he is present and when he is not.

SHOWING APPRECIATION

Being her husband's cheerleader means that the wife will show him appreciation for who he is and what he does. She can do this in many ways. She can make special days, such as holidays and family birthdays, really special for him. She can take time to stop what she is doing and really listen to him when he has something to share with her. Those types of things show him that he is important to her and worth her time and energy.

Thank him for both the big and little things that he does to help out. Wayne always helped me get the children ready for bed, and for years he sometimes put their pajama bottoms on backwards. When he did that, I could have said, "Oh, Wayne! I can't believe you put their pajamas on backwards again!" But he probably would not have helped me for very long if that had been my reaction. Instead, I thanked him for his help. And none of our children grew up with crooked feet or any other ill effects from wearing backwards pajamas.

I know a woman who told me that she had finally figured out why her husband had stopped helping her fill the dishwasher. Every time he loaded the dishes, she would come back and rearrange them when he was finished. I know how tempting it is, when there is room for one or two more dishes, to rearrange things, but how important is it in the long run? If what a wife is doing is a discouragement to her husband and makes him feel unappreciated, she is not being his helper.

Here is a poem from an unknown source that is a good reminder to me of the importance of appreciation:

If with pleasure you are viewing any work a man is doing,
If you like him or you love him, tell him now.
Don't withhold your approbation till the parson makes oration
As he lies with snowy lilies o'er his brow.
For no matter how you shout it, he won't really care about it,
He won't know how many teardrops you have shed.
If you think some praise is due him, now's the time to slip it to
   him,
For he cannot read his tombstone when he's dead.

MAKING THE HOME A REFUGE

A wife needs to be her husband's cheerleader by making his home a refuge from the world, a place where he longs to be and where he knows that she wants him to be. He ought to be able to look forward to a cheerful welcome when he gets home from work, not wonder what kind of mood she might be in and what problems are going to greet him at the door.

One of the greatest compliments that Wayne ever paid me was one that he never knew about. A man who had been away with him at a men's retreat later told me, "I just couldn't believe your husband. He was so eager to get home!" I know many men who are glad to get away from their homes, so I was happy to know that Wayne looked forward to returning to his.

The wife can also be her husband's cheerleader in the home by desiring him and taking the initiative in expressing her desire for him. One of my sons came home one day to find rose petals and candles on the steps leading upstairs to the bedroom. What a way to make a husband feel desired! We need to let our husbands know how much we enjoy their company physically and sexually.

APPLICATION
AND DISCUSSION

1. What do you do that makes it uncomfortable or difficult for your husband to discuss certain things with you? What can you do that will make it easier to discuss and work on these areas or problems?

2. What concerns does he have that you do not seem interested in?

3. What things do you do that irritate him?

4. What desires does he have that the two of you haven't discussed?

5. What does he enjoy doing with you, with the most enjoyable first?

6. What things can you do to show your appreciation of him?

7. What varying desires (spiritual, physical, intellectual, social, appreciation, recreational, protection, etc.) would he like for you to meet? How?

8. In what ways would he like for you to protect him (physically, spiritually, socially)? How?

9. In what ways would he like for you to sacrifice for him? How?

10. As he thinks of you, what things does he think are first in your life? What does he think should be your priority? What other priorities would he like for you to have, and in what order?

41

BE YOUR HUSBAND'S CHALLENGER, COUNSELOR, AND CROWN

A wife ought to be her husband's helper by being his challenger. Hebrews 10:24 exhorts us to "consider how to stimulate one another to love and good deeds." Wives should be looking for ways in which they can help, motivate, and encourage their husbands toward godliness.

One way that we can do this is by sharing with them what we are learning in our personal devotions. The truths that are challenging and encouraging us could also serve to challenge and encourage our husbands. Another way would be for the wife to learn or read about something that her husband is interested in. We had a friend who was taking a college course, and as he was preparing for class one night, he was not able to locate his book for the class. After searching for a while, he finally asked his wife if she had seen it and was delighted when she replied that it was in the bedroom because she had been reading it. He was encouraged by his wife's interest in what he was learning.

The wife should also serve as her husband's counselor. She is probably one of the first people that he will come to with difficulties or decisions that he is struggling with. He needs her intelligent, wise, and thoughtful input. Proverbs 31:26 says of the excellent wife, "She opens her mouth in wisdom, and the teaching of kindness is on her tongue." In any situation, the wife may be able to bring a different perspective to the question and think of things that her husband has not.

As we discussed earlier, a wife's simply saying "yes" to everything her husband says is not being submissive, nor is it helpful. But at the same time, the wife must remember that though she is to be his counselor, she is never to be his commander. She must always respect her husband's leadership and let him know that whatever final decisions he makes, she will respect and follow them.

Our youngest son, Josh, has a hard time spending money. He is content to have a few dollars in his pocket—enough to pay for something small—but he hates to spend money on something big. Not long ago, he and his wife were looking to buy a house and found what looked to be the perfect place. It was very inexpensive, required no money down, was in decent shape for the price, had a large living room for Bible studies and church meetings, and was within easy walking distance of his office at church.

When he asked Wayne and me for our input, we said that it sounded great. His wife, Marda, was very excited about the house also, so they went ahead and put in a bid for a little less than the asking price. The realtor called them back a short time later and gave them the counteroffer—a few thousand higher—from the owners. Again, Wayne and I said we thought it was still a good deal, and Marda was in favor of accepting their offer as well.

So Josh prayed and thought about it, but finally decided that he had to say no. He told his wife, "Marda, I just can't do it. It's happening too fast; we don't have to be out of our place yet, so let's just wait." As much as Marda really wanted that house and was ready to go ahead with the sale, she was able to step back and say to Josh, "That's fine. I would love to have it, but if you've decided that this isn't right, then we shouldn't do it." In her heart, I know she was disappointed, but she remained Josh's helper in the truest sense by giving her input and then following his leadership.

Though not every situation, of course, will work out exactly how we were hoping it might, this story does have a happy ending. The realtor talked the owners into accepting the first offer, and Josh and Marda were able to buy the house for the amount that Josh wanted to spend. They definitely enjoyed the time that the Lord gave them in that house, and as his parents, Wayne and I were so delighted that they got it. But I will always remember what a tremendous example Marda was in the way that she sincerely and lovingly followed Josh's leadership in the whole situation.

YOUR HUSBAND'S CROWN

Proverbs 12:4 says, "An excellent wife is the crown of her husband ..." As a Christian wife works toward becoming more and more of the "helper suitable" that God intended her to be, she will indeed be a valuable treasure to her husband. Her husband will be proud and thankful to have her as his wife because of the way that she submits to him and helps him.

From the very beginning, God knew that it was not good for man to be alone. It was His design and plan for woman to complete man in the marriage relationship. If men and women were exactly the same, the marriage relationship would be unnecessary. Our husbands could never complete the picture of the relationship between Christ and the church without the wives that God has given them.

Proverbs 29:18 challenges: "happy is he who keeps the law." It is not enough to know what to do; we must do what we know. As God's gift of a helper to man, the wife needs to rededicate herself to the purpose of being a suitable helper for her husband. She ought to carefully consider and evaluate how she is doing as his companion and friend, his colaborer, his cheerleader, his challenger, and his counselor so that she can truly be his crown.

Our heavenly Father has given us a high calling as wives. On our own, we can never adequately fulfill our responsibilities to our husbands and to our Lord. Only by the help of the Holy Spirit at work within us can we conquer the selfishness, fears, and rebellion in our hearts—the sin that keeps us from living as God has called us to live. We need to confess our failures and ask for God's help in putting His holy and perfect plan into practice. He will be faithful to help us love our husbands and be the helpers that we were created to be.

APPLICATION
AND DISCUSSION

1. What implied or unspoken desires and wishes of your husband would he like for you to fulfill? How?

2. What concerns and interests of his would he like for you to support—perhaps even more than you are doing right now? And in what ways would he want you to provide that support?

3. How much time does he think the two of you should spend together each day?

4. What motivating factors would be helpful for you to use in enabling family members to use their skills and develop their abilities? How could you improve as a motivator?

5. What can you do that provides the greatest comfort and encouragement for him when he is hurt, fearful, anxious, or worried?

6. What personal habits do you have that he would like changed?

7. In what ways does he see you demonstrating to him that he is a very important person who is as important as or more important than you are?

Summarize how you were impacted as you went through the exercises of these last few chapters (what you felt, how you were responding emotionally and relationally, how you were challenged, how you will change):

_____

_____

_____

_____

_____

_____

_____

_____

_____

Summarize what you learned about your mate that you didn't know before or ways in which your understanding of your mate was corrected or enlarged:

_____

_____

_____

_____

_____

_____

_____

Appendix

Biblically Sound Resources for Marriage and Family Enrichment and/or Counseling*

Author	Name of Book/Tape/Pamphlet	Publisher
Adams, Jay	*Biblical Forgiveness* (8 audiotapes)	Timeless Texts
	Christian Living in the Home	Zondervan
	From Forgiven to Forgiving	Timeless Texts
	Marriage, Divorce and Remarriage	Zondervan
	Marriage, Divorce, and Remarriage (8 audio tapes)	Timeless Texts
	Solving Marriage Problems	Zondervan
	What to Do When Your Marriage Goes Sour	P&R
Bunyan, John	*The Pilgrim's Progress* (revised by Cheryl Ford)	Tyndale
	Little Pilgrim's Progress (adapted for children)	Moody

Author	Name of Book/Tape/Pamphlet	Publisher
Clarkson, Margaret	*Growing Up*	Eerdmans
	Susie's Babies	Eerdmans
Decker, Barbara	*Proverbs for Parenting*	Lynn's Bookshelf
Duty, Guy	*Divorce and Remarriage*	Bethany
Elliot, Elisabeth	*Let Me Be a Woman*	Tyndale
Forster, Pam	*For Instruction in Righteousness*	Doorposts
	Plants Grown Up	Doorposts
Gallagher, Steve	*Sexual Idolatry*	Pure Life Ministries
Getz, Gene	*The Measure of a Family*	Regal
	The Measure of a Man	Regal
	The Measure of a Woman	Regal
Glickman, Craig	*A Song for Lovers*	InterVarsity
Harper, Michael	*Equal and Different*	Hodder/Stoughton
Jenkins, Jerry	*Loving Your Marriage Enough to Protect It*	Wolgemuth/Hyatt
Kennedy, James	*Your Prodigal Child*	Nelson
Knight, George	*Role Relationship of Men and Women*	P&R
Kotesky, Roland	*Understanding Adolescents*	Victor
Leuzarder, John	*The Gospel for Children*	Calvary Press
MacArthur, John	*Different by Design*	Victor
	Series on Marriage and Family (Audiotape series)	Grace to You
Mack, Wayne	*A Christian Growth and Discipleship Manual*	Focus Publications**
	A Fight to the Death	P&R**

Author	Name of Book/Tape/Pamphlet	Publisher
	Anger and Stress Management God's Way	Calvary Press**
	Christian Family Seminar—The Family Life	
	(10 audiotapes)	Hensley**
	Christian Life Issues, Part 1 (15 videotapes)	Strengthening Ministries International (Smi)**
	Christian Life Issues, Part 2 (15 videotapes)	Smi**
	Conflict Resolution Counseling (3 videotapes)	Smi**
	Defining and Developing Love	
	(2 videotapes or 2 audiotapes)	Smi**
	Down, but Not Out	P&R
	Effective Family Communication (4 videotapes)	Smi**
	God's Plan for Rearing Children (5 audiotapes)	Smi**
	God's Solutions to Life's Problems	Hensley
	Homework Manual for Biblical Living,	
	Volume 1 (Personal and Interpersonal Issues)	P&R**
	Homework Manual for Biblical Living,	
	Volume 2 (Marriage and Family Issues)	P&R**
	How to Do Premarital Counseling (2 audiotapes)	Smi**
	Humility: A Forgotten Virtue	P&R**
	Introduction to Biblical Counseling	
	(with John MacArthur)	Word**
	Leadership God's Style (2 videotapes)	Smi**
	Life in the Father's House	P&R**
	Marriage and Family Counseling Course	
	(18 audiotapes and syllabus)	Smi**
	Marriage and Family Counseling Course	
	(13 videotapes and syllabus)	Smi**
	Marriage and Family Topics	
	(14 videotapes and syllabus)	Smi**
	Parenting God's Way (8 audiotapes)	Smi**
	Parenting God's Way (4 videotapes)	Smi**
	Post Divorce Counseling (2 videotapes)	Smi**
	Preparing for Marriage God's Way	Hensley**
	Preparing for Marriage God's Way	
	(13 audiotapes)	Smi**

Author	Name of Book/Tape/Pamphlet	Publisher
	Preparing for Marriage God's Way (course syllabus/outline for student)	Smi**
	Preparing for Marriage God's Way (teaching material)	Smi**
	Preparing for Marriage God's Way (manual for teacher/counselor)	Smi**
	Reaching the Ear of God	P&R**
	Real Love or Reel Love (3 audiotapes)	Smi**
	Rebuilding a Marriage After Adultery	Smi**
	Solving Life's Problems God's Way (48 audiotapes)	Smi**
	Staying Pure in an Impure World (2 videotapes)	Smi**
	Strengthening Your Family (6 audiotapes)	Smi**
	Strengthening Your Marriage	P&R**
	Strengthening Your Marriage (27 audiotapes)	Smi**
	Study Guide for The Pilgrim's Progress	Smi**
	The Fear Factor	Hensley**
	The Role of Women in The Church	Smi**
	Sweethearts for a Lifetime	P&R**
	To Be or Not to Be a Church Member	Calvary Press**
	True Success and How to Attain It	Calvary Press**
	Twin Pillars of the Christian Life	Grace & Truth**
	Understanding and Counseling Adolescents	Smi**
	Understanding Pain and Suffering Biblically (1 videotape)	Smi**
	You Can Resolve Interpersonal Conflicts	Smi**
	Your Family God's Way	P&R**
Miller, John, Barbara Juliani	*Come Back, Barbara*	Zondervan
Murray, John	*Divorce*	P&R
Peace, Martha	*The Excellent Wife*	Focus
Piper, John, Wayne Grudem	*Recovering Biblical Manhood and Womanhood*	Crossway
Priolo, Lou	*The Complete Husband*	Calvary Press
	The Heart of Anger	Calvary Press

Author	Name of Book/Tape/Pamphlet	Publisher
Ray, Bruce	*Withhold Not Correction*	P&R
Schaeffer, Edith	*What Is a Family?*	Revell
Schooland, Marian	*Leading Little Ones to God*	Eerdmans
Tripp, Paul	*War of Words*	P&R
Tripp, Tedd	*Shepherding a Child's Heart*	Shepherd Press
Voorwinde, Steven	*Wisdom for Today's Issues*	P&R
Wheat, Ed & Gay	*Intended for Pleasure*	Revell
	Love Life	Zondervan

RESOURCES FOR PARENTING*

Author	Name of Book/Tape/Pamphlet	Publisher
Adams, Jay	*Biblical Forgiveness* (8 audiotapes)	Timeless Texts
	Christian Living in the Home	Zondervan
Bunyan, John	*Little Pilgrim's Progress* (adapted for children)	Moody
Clarkson, Margaret	*Growing Up*	Eerdmans
	Susie's Babies	Eerdmans
Cromarti, James	*A Year of Devotions for Children*	Evangelical Press
	Other Devotional Books	Evangelical Press
Decker, Barbara	*Proverbs for Parenting*	Lynn's Bookshelf
Forster, Pam	*For Instruction in Righteousness*	Doorposts
	Plants Grown Up	Doorposts
Getz, Gene	*The Measure of a Family*	Regal
Kennedy, James	*Your Prodigal Child*	Nelson

Author	Name of Book/Tape/Pamphlet	Publisher
Leuzarder, John	*The Gospel for Children*	Calvary Press
MacArthur, John	Tape Series on Marriage and Family	Grace to You
Mack, Wayne	*Christian Family Seminar—The Family Life* (10 audiotapes)	Hensley**
	Conflict Resolution Counseling (3 videotapes)	Smi**
	Effective Family Communication (4 videotapes)	Smi**
	God's Plan for Rearing Children (5 audiotapes)	Smi**
	Homework Manual for Biblical Living, Volume 1 (Personal and Interpersonal Issues)	P&R**
	Homework Manual for Biblical Living, Volume 2 (Marriage and Family Issues)	P&R**
	Life in the Father's House	P&R**
	Marriage and Family Counseling Course (18 audiotapes and syllabus)	Smi**
	Marriage and Family Counseling Course (13 videotapes and syllabus)	Smi**
	Parenting God's Way (8 audiotapes)	Smi**
	Parenting God's Way (4 videotapes)	Smi**
	Post Divorce Counseling (2 videotapes)	Smi**
	Real Love or Reel Love (3 audiotapes)	Smi**
	Strengthening Your Family (6 audiotapes)	Smi**
	Strengthening Your Marriage	P&R**
	Strengthening Your Marriage (27 tapes)	Smi**
	Study Guide for the Pilgrim's Progress	Smi**
	Understanding and Counseling Adolescents	Smi**
	You Can Resolve Interpersonal Conflicts	Smi**
	Your Family God's Way	P&R**
Miller, John, Barbara Juliani	*Come Back, Barbara*	P&R
Priolo, Lou	*How to Help Angry Kids*	Calvary Press
	Losing That Loving Feeling	Calvary Press
	Teach Them Diligently	Calvary Press
Ray, Bruce	*Withhold Not Correction*	P&R

Author	Name of Book/Tape/Pamphlet	Publisher
Schaeffer, Edith	*What Is a Family?*	Revell
Schooland, Marian	*Leading Little Ones to God*	Eerdmans
Tripp, Paul David	*Age of Opportunity*	P&R
Tripp, Tedd	*Shepherding a Child's Heart* (Ted Tripp has many other resources for parenting that may be purchased from Shepherd's Press)	Shepherd's Press

*These lists are not exhaustive. I'm sure that other biblically sound marriage and family resources are available. The resources on this list just happen to be the ones that I have personally found most helpful and useful to me in my own marriage and family life and in my ministry to others.

**All Mack resources may be ordered through the www.mackministries.org Web site under the Books and Tapes section. All other materials not listed with ** may be secured through your local Christian bookstore or through another distributor.

Notes

Chapter 1: Committing to God's Purposes for Marriage

1. R. C. Sproul, *The Intimate Marriage* (Phillipsburg, NJ: P&R, 2003), 149–50, emphasis added.

Chapter 3: Don't Forget about the Children

1. Wayne A. Mack, *Strengthening Your Marriage*, 2nd ed. (Phillipsburg, NJ: P&R, 1999); Tedd Tripp, *Shepherding a Child's Heart*, 2nd ed. (Wapwallopen, PA: Shepherd Press, 1995).

Chapter 5: An Overlooked Aspect of God's Blueprint

1. Wayne Mack, *To Be or Not to Be a Church Member* (Amityville: Calvary Press, 2005).

2. Barbara B. Hart, "A Christian Home," *The Celebration Hymnal* (Waco, TX, 1998), no. 451.

Chapter 7: More about Oneness

1. J. R. Miller, *The Home Beautiful* (Grand Rapids: Zondervan, 1912), 10–13.

2. Adapted from Wayne Mack, *A Homework Manual for Biblical Living*, vol. 1 (Phillipsburg, NJ: P&R, 1979), 164–65.

3. Wayne Mack, *Strengthening Your Marriage* (Phillipsburg, NJ: P&R, 1999).

4. Wayne Mack, *Your Family God's Way* (Phillipsburg, NJ: P&R, 1991).

Chapter 9: Be a Bargain

1. Jhumpa Lahir, *The Namesake* (New York: Mariner Books, 2004).

2. Adapted from Wayne Mack, *A Christian Growth and Discipleship Manual* (Bemidji: Focus Publishing, 2005).

Chapter 10: Your Spouse, a Priority

1. Jay Adams, *Solving Marriage Problems* (Grand Rapids: Zondervan, 1986).

Chapter 14: Other Types of Leaving

1. *Preparing for Marriage God's Way* (Tulsa: Hensley Publishing, 1995).

Chapter 15: Purity Is Essential

1. Adapted from Wayne Mack, *A Christian Growth and Discipleship Manual* (Focus Publishing, 2005).

Chapter 16: Every Marriage Needs Some Hedges

1. Jerry Jenkins, *Loving Your Marriage Enough to Protect It* (Wolgemuth & Hyatt: Brentwood,TN), 1989, adaptation of hedges listed on pages 78–130.

2. Adapted from Wayne Mack, *A Christian Growth and Discipleship Manual* (Focus Publishing, 2005).

Chapter 17: More about Hedges

1. Alistair Begg, *Lasting Love* (Moody Press: Chicago, 1997), 16.

Chapter 18: Good Marriages Require Some Perspiration

1. John Piper and Wayne Grudem, *Recovering Biblical Manhood and Womanhood* (Wheaton: Crossway, 1991) 283–92).

2. Anne Moir and David Jessel, *Brain Sex: The Real Difference Between Men and Women* (New York: Dell, 1991), 5.

3. Deborah Tannen, *You Just Don't Understand: Women and Men in Conversation* (New York: Ballantine, 1991), 16–17.

4. Tom Eisenman, *Temptations Men Face* (Downers Grove: InterVarsity Press, 1980), 95.

5. J. R. Miller, *The Home Beautiful* (Grand Rapids: Zondervan, 1912), 6–8. I would add that in addition to wise and loving patience, a marriage also requires a lot of work.

6. Wayne A. Mack and Joshua Mack, *A Fight to the Death* (Phillipsburg, NJ: P&R, 2006).

Chapter 19: Till Death Us Do Part

1. R. C. Sproul, *The Intimate Marriage* (Phillipsburg, NJ: P&R, 2003), 159–61.

2. Harold Myra, *Love Notes to Jeanette* (Wheaton, IL: Victor Books, 1979).

Chapter 21: Overcoming Obstacles to Christ's Preeminence

1. Adapted from Wayne Mack, *A Homework Manual for Biblical Living*, vol. 2 (Phillipsburg, NJ: P&R, 1980).

Chapter 22: Husbanding Involves Being a Real Lover

1. J. R. Miller, *The Home Beautiful* (Grand Rapids: Zondervan, 1912), 15–17.

Chapter 26: Loving Involves Cherishing and Nourishing

1. Adapted from Wayne Mack, *A Homework Manual for Biblical Living*, vol. 2 (Phillipsburg, NJ: P&R, 1980).

Chapter 27: Loving Involves Following History's Greatest Example of Love

1. John MacArthur, *Ephesians*, The MacArthur New Testament Commentary (Chicago: Moody Press, 1986), 298.

2. Ibid., 297.

Chapter 28: Husbanding Involves Leadership

1. Adapted from Wayne Mack, *Preparing for Marriage God's Way* (Tulsa: Hensley Publishing, 1995).

Chapter 35: Let's Get Practical

1. Adapted from Wayne Mack, *A Homework Manual for Biblical Living*, vol. 2 (Phillipsburg, NJ: P&R, 1980).

INDEX OF SCRIPTURE

1 Timothy

1:15—123
2:15—30, 221
3:2—75
3:4—75
3:6–7—75
3:15—36–37
4:14–15—34
5:1–2—33
5:1–10—92
5:4—204
5:8—176

2 Timothy

1:5—35
1:5–6—34
1:5–7—37
1:7—35
1:16—34
2:15—36
2:22—105
2:24–25—33
3:14–17—37
3:15–17—35, 212–13
3:16–17—74
4:5—34
4:11—34

Titus

1:5–9—195
1:6–8—34
2:3–4—252
2:4—75

Philemon

3–5—34
4–18—37
21—33

Hebrews

3:13—25
8:10–12—16

10:24—274
10:24–25—36–37, 52
12:2—232
13:1–2—37
13:1–3—93
13:4—98, 117
13:7—37
13:17—37, 220, 228
13:24—37

James

1:13–14—109
1:19—34
1:19–20—37
3:13–18—34
3:16–18—37
4:1–2—123
5:12—33
5:16—24–25, 34

1 Peter

1:14–15—109
1:22—93
2:2—36
2:13—220
3:1—22, 26, 233
3:1–2—99, 238
3:1–6—223, 227, 249
3:2—26
3:4–5—35
3:5—224
3:7—22, 26, 174–75, 201, 204
3:8—25, 93
4:8–9—24, 93
4:10—34, 221
5:1–3—228
5:5–6—93

2 Peter

3:1–2—253

STRENGTHENING
MINISTRIES
INTERNATIONAL

Strengthening Ministries International exists to provide training and resources to strengthen you and your church. We as individuals and as a ministry exist to glorify God by doing what Paul and his associates did in Acts 14:21–22. Luke tells us that Paul and his associates went about preaching the gospel, making disciples, strengthening the souls of those disciples, and encouraging them to continue in the faith.

Like Paul, we are dedicated to using whatever gifts and abilities, whatever training and experience, whatever resources and opportunities we have to strengthen individual Christians and churches in their commitment to Christ and in their ministries for Christ.

And like Paul, we are attempting to strengthen the church and individual Christians in a variety of ways. Fulfilling our ministry involves conducting seminars and conferences all over the United States and in many foreign countries. It includes writing and distributing books and booklets and developing and distributing audiotapes and videotapes on numerous biblical/theological/Christian life/counseling subjects.

Fulfilling our purpose for existence, as described in Acts 14:21–22, also includes developing and sustaining a Web site:

www.mackministries.org or audubonpress.com.

On these sites you will find fuller descriptions of the various aspects of our ministry, as well as instructions about how to order materials.
Strengthening Ministries International
Mailing Address: P.O. Box 249, Center Valley, Pennsylvania 18034
E-mail: strengtheningmin@aol.com
Web site: www.mackministries.org

Wayne A. Mack (M.Div., Philadelphia Theological Seminary; D.Min., Westminster Theological Seminary) serves Christ and His church as professor of biblical counseling for eight months out of the year at Grace School of Ministry in Pretoria, South Africa, where he also conducts conferences and seminars. For the remaining four months of the year, he teaches at The Expositor's Seminary in Little Rock, Arkansas.

Dr. Mack is adjunct professor of biblical counseling at The Master's College and director of Strengthening Ministries International. He is an executive board member of F.I.R.E. (Fellowship of Independent Reformed Evangelicals) and a charter member and executive board member of the National Association of Nouthetic Counselors. Wayne is also a member of the board of directors of the missionary agency Publicaciones Faro de Gracia.

He is the author of a number of books, including *A Fight to the Death*; *Humility*; *Reaching the Ear of God*; *Strengthening Your Marriage*; *Down, but Not Out*; and *Your Family, God's Way*. He and his wife, Carol, have four children and thirteen grandchildren.

Carol Mack, a graduate of Wheaton College, has spoken and participated in many marriage and family seminars and retreats for women. She has been a pastor's wife for many years and a spiritual mentor to wives of men in seminary or the pastorate. Prior to and after her child-rearing years, she served for years as a teacher, mainly in Christian schools.

Her ministry of counseling women and children has been greatly blessed of the Lord, with many women seeking her out for direction and assistance on problematic issues. She frequently joins with her husband in counseling married couples.

Mrs. Mack now serves with her husband as a missionary in South Africa, filling many of the same roles she did in the States.

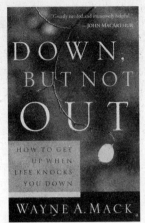
"This book is greatly needed and immensely helpful. There is a supernatural way to overpower trouble, to live in contentment with a deep down peace and an unassailable joy. Every believer can enjoy triumph in trouble. In fact, that is what God wants for us. Wayne Mack shows us how."

—JOHN MACARTHUR

"*Down, but Not Out* is written with the theological integrity and biblical practicality that you have come to expect from one of the world's foremost Christian counselors. This is a book that worriers (and those who want to help them) have been waiting for."

— LOU PRIOLO
DIRECTOR OF COUNSELING AT EASTWOOD PRESBYTERIAN CHURCH,
MONTGOMERY, ALA., AND AUTHOR

"If you are a Christian looking for practical answers from Scripture when the circumstances of life have hammered you into the ground, you must read this book. If you love the Bible, this will be a breath of fresh air."

—JOHN D. STREET
PROFESSOR, MASTER'S COLLEGE AND SEMINARY

"What a timely message for a troubled age. Wayne Mack writes with the wisdom of a seasoned counselor and the knowledge of a biblical scholar. This book will be a blessing to people in trouble and those trying to help them."

—STEVE VIARS
PASTOR, FAITH BAPTIST CHURCH, LAFAYETTE, IND.

"*Down, but Not Out* will be an encouragement to those who are 'down' to look 'up' to find answers in God and his sufficient Word. I was struck with its relevance to the contemporary 'downs' my counselees face everyday."

—RONALD A. ALLCHIN SR.
EXECUTIVE DIRECTOR OF THE BIBLICAL COUNSELING CENTER, ARLINGTON, ILL.

Also in the
STRENGTH FOR LIFE
series

Price: $10.99
To order, visit
www.prpbooks.com
or call 1(800) 631-0094

"It's always with confidence and joy that I recommend Wayne Mack's books. He's so thorough and so thoroughly biblical that, when you read them, you know you've just spent valuable time with our Lord and his powerful Word."

—ELYSE FITZPATRICK
AUTHOR AND COUNSELOR

"Sometimes a book reads you while you are reading it. This is that kind of book. It has eyes!"

—JIM ELLIFF
PRESIDENT OF CHRISTIAN COMMUNICATORS WORLDWIDE

"Wayne and Joshua Mack do an excellent job of diagnosing the cancer of pride and providing inspired biblical treatment. With the scalpel of Scripture they carefully do surgery on the reader's soul. Drawing wisdom from biblical examples and great preachers of the past, they offer practical instruction for extracting pride and replacing it with its counterpart—humility."

—JACK HUGHES
SENIOR PASTOR, CALVARY BIBLE CHURCH,
ADJUNCT PROFESSOR OF HOMILETICS AT THE MASTER'S SEMINARY

"Every Christian should read this book, especially those in the ministry or preparing for ministry. It will help you deal with the painful problem of pride and point you to the loveliness of Christ, where you will meet humility in all of its glory."

—JOHN SALE
PASTOR/TEACHER, VALLEY CENTER COMMUNITY CHURCH